Discourses on Ageing

Discourses on Ageing

Sumita Saha
Somrita Sengupta
Trishna Chaudhuri
Nilanjana Goswami

RAWAT PUBLICATIONS
Jaipur • New Delhi • Bangalore • Guwahati • Kolkata

ISBN 978-81-316-1281-1

Published by
Prem Rawat for **Rawat Publications**
Satyam Apts., Sector 3, Jawahar Nagar, Jaipur 302 004 (India)
Phone: 0141 265 1748 / 265 7006
E-mail: info@rawatbooks.com
Website: www.rawatbooks.com

New Delhi Office
4858/24, Ansari Road, Daryaganj, New Delhi 110 002
Phone: 011-23263290

Also at *Bangalore, Guwahati* and *Kolkata*

Typeset by Rawat Computers, Jaipur
Printed at bound in India

Contents

Foreword

This book would enlighten the students pursuing Sociology about the prevailing conditions of elderly. It is based on several case studies and hence it would be of great help for students to learn theories and get acquainted with several sociological terms with the help of real-life examples.

The present book is a product of an ethnographic research on elderly plight in 'Beleghata' slum of Kolkata. The book depicts the reality of elderly populace in lower income households who live in slum areas. The present world is already characterized by rising elderly issues of loneliness, degrading health and many other issues. Various researches are addressing elderly issues and therefore exploring the situation of the senile population, with reference to class and environment, which will itself bring an interesting reflection within the elderly discourses.

The book also provides a generalized understanding of elderly discourses and theories, which will be helpful for the beginners. They will get a vivid picture of elderly issues of the country as well as the outside world along with various theoretical dimensions. In brief, the book raises various questions on elderly constructions as well as strives to bring new dynamics on elderly discourse.

Dr Ruby Sain

Professor, Jadavpur University

Director, Centre for Religious Studies, Jadavpur University,

Kolkata

Preface

The present book has delved into the world of elderly. It is specifically a reflection of the detailed research done in Beleghata slum area (a slum in proximity to Beleghata area of Kolkata, India). In fact, the book is a product of an intensive fieldwork based research which inherently is a reaction to the increasing intolerance towards the elderly population and their consequent marginalization. Despite governmental measures towards the rising deplorable conditions of the aged people, the elderly population faces social exclusion both from their own family who believe that they should become 'inactive entities' as well as from the society for whom, their importance gradually diminishes. The book provides in-depth theoretical insights with examples from various problems of the elderly population involving micro-level narratives and case studies. The book attempts to relate the theories with narratives, henceforth the readers will get a visualized picture of the elderly scenario and the understanding of their own reality.

The book starts with a vivid detail of the concept of gerontology and various theoretical understandings related to the term. It covers an in-depth understanding of the world situation as well as Indian elderly scenario. The book deals with various issues of elderly population which includes elderly depression, their social status and their position in family, their understanding of leisure, their economic position, their health concern and the role of religion in their life.

The book starts with an introduction of old age situation, wherein the description of the elderly crisis is well elaborated. Later on, the core concept of gerontology is enlightened in a detailed manner. Various citations and references are used so that vast theoretical insights could be given to the readers. The main purpose of the book is to bring before the readers the elderly situation of the country as well as to provide them with theoretical information, as a result of which the readers can easily relate the field reality with the theoretical insights; hence the reading will be an interesting experience. Here old age is also analysed from the perspective of the body, viz., the effect of old age on physical attributes as well as pursuits of the person. Various narratives and references are used to give a wider understanding of the issue. Elderly situation of the country and across the world is also thoroughly discussed.

The next chapter of the book deals with old age and depression. It is quite evident that mental illness is gradually increasing in the modern society wherein old-age population is not left out. Loneliness and lack of interaction have made this population vulnerable to depression. At the same time, their physical weakness, lethargy and often disability also act as a conductor to depression as well as other mental illness. The second chapter of the book covers this issue and at the same time highlights the aspect of depression from subaltern perspective.

The book also covers the status of the elderly in their family as well as society. It is well known that Indian society and some other Asian societies are based on the value of gerontocracy. However, the scenario has changed where the forces of modernity as well as westernization is responsible for change of values, wherein our society which is predominated by nuclear family, the status of the elderly is reduced to a mere liability.

The book has also covered an in-depth detail on economic vulnerability of the elderly population. Series of information on Indian government's policy on safeguarding elderly population is also mentioned along with various suggestions to improve it. Health is the most important issue for the elderly, who are often anxious about it. Physical illness as well as disabilities of the elderly often makes them dependent on others, whereupon they are often treated as an unwanted liability. They are often ignored and their health issues often go intentionally unnoticed. The above mentioned issue is shown with various field notes which clearly showcases elderly vulnerabilities. Religious orientation is also seen to be a characteristic feature of the aged. Often, we visualize an old person as someone who recites various religious hymns of God, who are often termed as 'spiritual'. Hence, there is a need to analyse the religious orientation of the elderly population. Religion often plays an optimistic role in the life of the elderly population. Religion appears to provide health advantages by reducing the adversities of stress and by becoming the protective layer for the elderly population. Henceforth, there is a need to deal on the relation of religion with that of the elderly population.

In concluding chapter, the book intends to explore the theme of elderly social constructions. The book aims to discuss on the discourses of elderly social constructions which inherently had been acting as a strait-jacket prescribing the do's and don'ts for the above-sixty population.

In the above mentioned paragraphs, a brief description of the book is given where the interaction of the elderly with various denominations have been described. However, the rationale behind writing this book is to focus on the increasing vulnerability of the elderly population in the modern society, which is gradually turning into an intolerant entity towards the aged population or let us say 'the Dependant Souls' and it is rampant in the society irrespective of class, caste, religion as well as gender. However, this book was an attempt to shed light on the elderly population of the lower class strata and to penetrate into the geronto-logical arena.

In brief, the book is well written in simple yet lucid fashion backed up with case studies and narratives which is obviously going to make the whole reading process an interesting one with visualized understanding of the elderly situation of the country as well the world. Finally, the book has also added glossary and rich references which will be an enriching experience for the readers for further researches as well as understanding.

Glossary

Ageism: Discrimination against particular age group, particularly old age.

Clinical Depression: This kind of depression is serious and happens when symptoms last for more than normal period and disturbs the normal functioning of an individual.

Depression: A mood disorder that causes a continuous feeling of gloominess, sense of worthlessness and hopelessness, affect a person's sleep and everything that is related to a person's daily life starting from his level of appetite to interest and participation in the various activities. Concentration gets disturbed and activities which previously interested them no longer attract them and they do not enjoy doing it any longer because of depression during later life. It does not stop here as it extends all the way to affect the overall functioning of the person and affects his morbidity and eventually his chances of survival as well.

Devaluation: Devaluation means the consideration that aged people are not important. They are treated indifferently, with no compassion, with their knowledge and experience considered out-dated and least needed. They are being sometimes rejected openly by people and are forced to go through a negative environment where people would treat them with pessimism.

Distress-Deterrent Model: It is such a model which does not depend on stress. Although it does not depend on any stress factor, but according to such a factor religion is advantageous for all those who follow such a model.

Endogenous Depression: It is such a state of mind when an individual person is down in the dumps without any specific cause that may turn out to become more strong and serious as they age.

Exclusion: When value of elderly is so less and they would be so insignificant that they would not be greeted to take part in social activities of any sort, it is called exclusion.

Geriatrics: The study of diseases affecting the elderly.

Gerontology: The study on old age process is called gerontology.

Health: Complete well-being in all spheres of life right from physical, mental to social and not just the disappearance of diseases or weaknesses in a person who is healthy or fit. When a person is sound socially, physically and mentally only then he or she is healthy.

Involutional Depression: This kind of depression is related to problems related to lifespan related issues. It occurs when during middle years there is a biological deterioration. This biological decline might be reactive when one steps in old age.

Moderator Model: Religion helps in reducing stress at times of reducing stress only when the stressful factor has become very acute.

Negative Religious Coping: (a) less secure bonding with God (b) a weak view about the world (c) a religious fight to search for ultimate meaning in life.

Old Age: There is no fixed definition of old age. Meaning of old age varies from one society to the other. Engagement in activities and one's participation in social roles is accompanied with various changes as old age advances. Regenerative abilities decline and one becomes more susceptible to diseases and can be more easily prone to sickness than any other adult. One thing has to be kept in mind is that age as such does not really tell much about a person and stands just a trait of a person. It just says the number of years a person lived. The process of ageing is a social and not biological where the major life events stand as a marker of age.

Positive Religious Coping: (a) a sense of holiness (b) secure bonding with God (c) faith that meaning is to be found in life (d) sense of spiritual association with others.

Prevention Model: According to this model, such religious practices encourage adoption of such practices that prevent individuals from falling prey to such behaviours that are stress-inducing, like smoking, unsafe sex, divorce, getting addicted to alcohol, etc. and instead adopt practices that are stress-reducing.

Reactive Depression: This depression occurs when there is a mild depression because of a loss or when a range of loss gets accumulated and piles up and adds up to increase depression.

Religion: Definition of religion is varied. It is thought to be an experience which is distinct from everyday experience, where interaction takes place with God and supernatural being. It can be defined as belief in existence of God, or in practicing of religious rituals which includes attending church or temple and other religious institutions and observations related to one's own religious faith, etc. Religion according to some can be defined as a private and individual practice. For sociologists, however, it is a system of institutionalized platform of values, symbols, beliefs, practices which a certain group of people feel, respond and react and interpret to sacred aspects and then provide answers to questions.

Rheumatoid Arthritis: It is a chronic progressive disease. It causes inflammation in the joints as a result of which deformation happens and immobility is often its consequence.

Role Loss and Role Ambiguity: People when young are occupied with several roles and while managing these multiple roles they often face role conflict.

However, being always within the environment of role performances they do not realize what it is to be like to live a life where there will not be any role to play. When a person ages, slowly he loses the roles he once used to do and end up in a time where there isn't any specific thing to do. There is no recognized activity in which they can take part. This is role loss and role ambiguity.

Stereotyping: Harsh reality of the life of the elderly who are forced to be attached with negative tagging by people on the basis of their age. Old people are often regarded unwell, senile, worthless, lonely, impotent and stuck in acute economic deprivation. They are therefore often associated with terms like 'touchy', 'cranky' and many such negative tagging.

Suppressor Model: With increase in stress, amount of religious practice also increases so that stress can be eased or at least be reduced.

Youthful Self-image: Old image is often believed by the elderly to be an invitation to negative stereotypical comments by other people. Therefore, to evade such negativity aged people often reject the old image and try to look more youthful in order to create an enduring sense of self. This kind of an image at times is seen with criticism by both the young and old generation themselves where the old who wanted to refute the old imagery is mocked and ridiculed for their actions, eventually leading to a strenuous relationship.

1

Gerontological Concepts and Understanding

Ageing is a lifelong process which starts with our birth and continues until death. Physical and mental development occurs with an individual's growth however with the increase in age, human beings face 'ageing crisis' which can be well comprehended by the physical and mental disconformities faced by the aged population. Ageing is, therefore, a global problem. It is a well-known fact that population growth, lower mortality rates as well as drastic progress in the medical field have brought in new challenges for the world which can often be summed as 'Greying Population'. Hence, understanding various facets of elderly realms became important resulting in the evolution of gerontology as a scientific discipline, to explore ageing as a phenomenon.

In simple words, gerontology is known as the study of the elderly populace. The Oxford Mini Reference Dictionary defined gerontology as the study of ageing. The new Websters Dictionary of English Language (1994) edition, defines gerontology as a study of the phenomenon of old age. The *Encyclopedia on Ageing* (2001) defined gerontology as the scientific study of ageing and older population. The term gerontology is derived from a Greek word, 'Geron' which means old man and 'Logia' which meant study. Thus the etymological meaning of gerontology is the study of old. It was at the beginning of the 20th century that Elie Metchnikoff coined the term 'gerontology'. He was a Russian Zoologist, who is best known for his work on immunology. In 1909, Ignatz L. Nascher coined the term Geriatrics, from two Greek words 'geronto', meaning old man and 'iatrike', meaning surgery, medicine or the treatment of the old man'. Geriatrics, then, refers to the medical treatment of the old person and gerontology refers to the study of older persons and the ageing process (Cox and Newton, 1993). Later on, Tibbits (1960) in her quest on various social aspects of ageing have coined the term 'social gerontology', referring to the fact that aspects of gerontology have a major component of social factors and forces. Included in these social forces are roles and status of the old, how society views the old and the degree to which normative aspects of ageing determine the behaviour of older persons (Cox and Newton, 1993).

Gerontology evolved as a scientific study of ageing which explores the elderly realm from sociological, psychological as well as the biological viewpoint (Brossoie, 1997). This study aims to understand the factors associated with elderly as well as to find out the problems associated with the rising trend of the elderly population. It is regarded to be an interdisciplinary subject since the gerontological inquiry is not limited to the idea of physical and social facets of ageing, but it also deals with public policies related to ageing (Wilmoth and Ferero, 2007).

The fountain of gerontological discovery

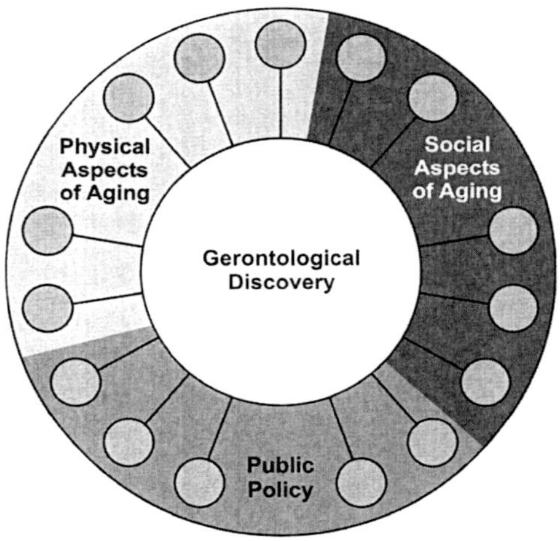

Courtesy: Wilmoth and Ferero, 2007.

The above diagram clearly states that gerontological inquiry not only deals with the physical mechanism of elderly and its consequence on body and mind. It also analyses the society's overview as well as response to ageing. Finally, gerontological inquiry is not complete without including the legal overview and infrastructure to confront ageing (Wilmoth and Ferero, 2007).

While describing the concept of gerontology, Onyenemezu and Olumati (2013) highlighted that gerontology encompasses the following aspects:

1. It Studies the physical, mental and social changes in people (adults) as they age.
2. It analyses the ageing process itself (biogerontology).
3. It explores the edge of normal ageing and age-related diseases (geroscience).

4. It studies the effects of our ageing population on our society; including the fiscal effects of pensions, entitlements, life and health insurance and retirement planning.
5. It is also applicable to policies and programmes; including a macro-scopic perspective, i.e. (running a nursing home).

In this regard, it can be remarked that the need to study ageing as a concept was indeed a later development and is still in its budding stage. At the same time, the concept of ageing is too big to fit into the banner of a singular subject. Hence, it needs both a multidisciplinary as well as an interdisciplinary approach to the research question.

Branches of Gerontology

Previously, it is already mentioned that gerontology adopts a multidisciplinary approach. In this regard, the subject matter of gerontology can be classified into various branches which are highlighted below.

Biogerontology

One of the branches of gerontology is biogerontology. It attempts to explore the biological aspects of ageing. This branch of gerontology is concerned with the biological process of ageing. Ageing became an important point of discussion for the biologists with increasing lifespan. In this regard Gems (2011) has opined that biogerontology is still in the process of development.

Medical Gerontology

This branch of gerontology studies the biological causes and effects of ageing, medical and biogerontology are considered by many scientists to be the most critical frontier in ageing research (Gracia, 2010).

Social Gerontology

This is a multidisciplinary sub-field of gerontology that specializes in studying and working with older adults. Social gerontologists are responsible for educating, researching and advancing the broader causes of ageing in older adults by giving informative presentations, publishing books and articles that concern the ageing population, producing relevant films and television programmes and producing new graduates in colleges and universities.

Tibbits (1960) coined the term 'social gerontology', referring to the fact that aspects of gerontology have a major component of social factors and forces. Included in these social forces are the roles and status of the elderly, how society views the old, the degree to which normative aspects of ageing determine the behaviour of older persons. While the subject of ageing is of interest to some scientific disciplines, the focus of this book will be on sociology's contribution to the field of social gerontology.

Biomedical Gerontology

This is also known as experimental gerontology or life extension. Life extension is a sub-discipline of biogerontology that endeavours to slow, prevent and even reverse ageing in both humans and animals by curing age-related diseases and showing the underlying processes of ageing. Some biogerontologists are at the intermediate position, emphasizing the studying of the ageing process as a means of mitigating ageing-associated diseases. They claim that maximum life cannot be altered.

Defining Ageing

Ageing, in simple terms, refers to the physical and mental deterioration, as an organism develops. Rose (1991) in his seminal book on the evolution of ageing defines ageing as 'a persistent decline in the age-specific fitness components of an organism due to internal physiological degeneration'. Ageing has now become an urgent matter of discussion, owing to the increasing rate of 'Population Ageing' throughout the world. In this regard, Sanderson and Scherbov (2007) have opined that the concept of ageing has become a complicated issue since average life expectancy has increased dramatically.

Ageing entails a broader perspective and can be interpreted in various ways. First, it can be analysed chronologically by an individual's survival since his/her birth. Ageing can also be classified in a biological manner, which centres explicitly on an individual's physical characteristics as he or she climbs the age hierarchy. In simple words, biological ageing focuses on a physiological aspect of the individual as he/she moves ahead. The third dimension of ageing focuses on the psychological aspects of ageing. It analyses an individual's psychological changes, as well as mental functioning as an individual approaches sixty and beyond. The last dimension of ageing stresses on its social implications. Social ageing focuses on changes in a person's roles and relationships, both within their networks of relatives and friends and informal organizations such as the workplace and houses of worship.

Theoretical Underpinnings

Ageing or the discipline of gerontology is a multidisciplinary phenomenon. As a result of this, various disciplines have initiated theories according to their own (subject) perspective. In this part of the chapter, we will be focusing on psycho-social theories of ageing.

Activity Theory

Activity is regarded as one of the parameters of leading a healthy life. In fact, to keep oneself healthy, individual needs to live an active life which involves engaging in various forms of activities. In the case of the elderly, leading an active lifestyle results in enhancing their quality of life. Activity theory is based on this idea, wherein staying active, will allow the elderly to live a good life. It is a well-known fact that living an active life with physical movement as well as stress-free attitude brings betterment to the quality of life being led by an individual. It is applicable irrespective of any age and these parameters bring healthy ageing. As a result, confronting the challenge of elderly fear can be easily overcome.

Havighurst and Albrecht were the first, who have proposed this theory in their book *Older People* in 1953. The theory, which they proposed was based on an empirical survey done on the participation rate of the elderly into various socially appropriate activities. Activity theory was labelled as 'implicit' theory of ageing (Havighurst, 1961) because it naturally guided most medical and social work practice in the post-World War II era – and still does, to some extent, since it so well reflects American values of productivity and the desire to remain youthful (Bengtson and Kuypers, 1971). This theory sees a positive relationship between activity and ageing.

Activity theorists believed that an individual should try to live happy, engrossed in various forms of tasks which will keep him lively. In this regard, DeLiema and Bengtson (2015) stated that elderly people might involve in various forms of activities which include interaction with family and friends, participation in organizations and more solitary recreational activities like reading, watching television and doing household chores. Hence, it can be stated that activities should not be restricted to work and other responsibilities. Activity theorist stressed the participatory role of elderly people in those activities which keep them healthy as well as stress-free. The basic tenet of the activity theory of ageing is that the individual should try to live healthy and active throughout his/her life until and unless his/her satisfaction is compromised (DeLiema and Bengtson, 2015). Activity theorists thus believed that staying active, helps people to live with youthful vigour and at the same time, individual never thinks of withdrawing from mainstream society or various activities.

Disengagement Theory

In contrast to the activity theory, disengagement theory comes up with new assumptions which stressed on the universality of withdrawal in every culture. Lueckenotte (2000) has stated that the disengagement theory viewed ageing as a developmental task in and of itself, with its own norms and appropriate patterns of behaviour. This theory believes in the presumption that an individual should relinquish all his responsibilities, activities as well as meaningful roles as he/she approaches the greying years. It states that it is advantageous to both society and the individual to contribute to a procedure of withdrawal from significant roles and responsibilities as that person enters the later years of life. This theory was first proposed by Elaine Cumming, Lois Dean, David Newell and Isabel McCaffrey in 1960. Later on, Elaine Cumming and William E. Henry published an article in the year of 1961 named 'Growing Old: The Process of Disengagement', where the theory was discussed in detail, based on an empirical evidence obtained from Havighurst's Kansas City Study of Adult Life, an interdisciplinary community-based investigation to examine health, employment, leisure and civic participation activities of older adults (Knapp, 2009).

Cumming and Henry believed that disengagement is a universal affair as it is influenced by the culture of various parts of the world. They believed that disengagement is a law of nature which can be initiated by the individual and society. In Growing Old (1961), Cumming and Henry described disengagement as, 'An inevitable mutual withdrawal or disengagement, resulting in decreased interaction between the ageing person and others in the social systems he belongs to' (Cumming and Henry, 1961).

In this regard, DeLiema and Bengtson (2015) have opined that 'This was the first formal attempt to explain normal or 'successful' late life development from the perspective that combined psychodynamics with social systems analysis in response to the functional theoretical underpinnings of Durkheim and Talcott Parsons. This theory can often be seen from functionalist orientation. Structural functionalism expresses the nature of social order and the relationship between the various parts (structures) of society and their contribution to the equilibrium of the society by examining the functionality of each to determine how it contributes to the stability of society as a whole. The structural-functionalist has been exclusively concerned about the maintenance of order in the society which in other way is dependent on the balanced relation between institutions as well as a collective whole. It is evident that with age individual needs to transfer/handover the duties to his/her successor or the younger ones. In this way, the social relations will be at equilibrium. Hence, disengagement theorists propose that elderly people should lessen their intervention in various processes of life. In this way, theorists believe that the problem of elderly can be overcome from a macro lens. Disengagement theory stresses that an individual's age increases, there is a steady but foreseeable constraints in 'social life space', evidenced by declining number of social partners and frequency of social interactions. At the same time, there is withdrawal from social institutions (transition from work to retirement). Disengagement, therefore, is functional for both the social system and for the individual. It prepares society for the loss of the individual through the disengagements of retirement and then death; it prepares the individual for death through progressive disengagement from society (role loss). Thus, through this process of mutual withdrawal, there is no disruption to the social equilibrium (Cumming and Henry, 1961; Achenbaum and Bengtson, 1994).

Disengagement theory believed that withdrawal is a universal affair. However, this theory has been criticized by various social scientists. In this regard, Knapp (2009) has stated that the disengagement theory has been examined by behavioural scientists, who believed that the fundamental presupposition of this theory is flawed and empirical evidence can not back it.

Continuity Theory

Continuity theory dismisses the assumption of both activity theory as well as disengagement theory. Havighurst et al. (1963) stressed that continuity theory criticizes both the theories by stating that being active, trying to maintain a sense of being middle-aged, or willingly withdrawing from society does not necessarily bring happiness. The continuity theory believes that the elderly make specific choices to maintain consistency in the internal (personality structure, beliefs) and external structures (relationships), by remaining active and involved throughout their older years. The continuity theory proposes that a person will live in the same way as he/she was 'continuing' to live.

Lynch et al. (2015) has opined that there is a long history of continuity theory. However, G.L. Maddox (1968) is regarded to be the most immediate precursor of the modern theory of continuity. Maddox had criticized as well as questioned the validity of the propositions of disengagement theory. Maddox stressed that older people tend to maintain a continuity of their lifestyle if they are satisfied with it. Hence, Maddox examined the relationship between social activity and life satisfaction and proved through empirical study that elderly population tends to maintain a consistency of social engagement throughout their life.

Robert Atchley was among the first to name and research continuity theory and to formally apply it exclusively to ageing adults. Atchley opines that continuity theory was a general skeleton and was developed as an umbrella approach to systematizing a range of theories that attempt to clarify different facets of adult development and ageing (Lynch et al., 2015).

Continuity theory believes that human thought and human behaviour is in a state of continuous evolution. Human beings tend to adapt to the changes, which is regarded to be one of the positive signs of successful ageing. According to this theory, the latter part of life is a continuation of the earlier part and therefore an integral component of the entire life cycle.

Atchley (1989) in his study has often stated that individual tends to adapt to the changes occurring in the society as well as culture throughout the world. Individual's adaptive capacity is often a consequence of his experiences of his lifetime. Hence, elderly population adapts to the environment or habitus as a continuity of their early years.

Age Stratification Theory

Age stratification theory overtly takes account of how time, group as well culture plays a role in affecting the ageing process as well as bringing in new challenges. This theory is one of the recent theories which developed in 1970s. This theory concentrates on understanding the relationship between ageing and socio-structural forces. Martinez and Lightfoot (1995) have stated that Riley, Foner and Johnson are the precursors of this theory.

In this regard, Riley (1985) identifies the five major concepts of this theory: (a) Each progresses through society in groups of cohorts that are collectively ageing-socially, biologically and psychologically, (b) New cohorts are continually being born and each of them experiences his/her unique sense of history, (c) Society itself can be divided into various strata according to the parameters of age and roles, (d) Not only are people and roles within every stratum continuously changing, but so is society at large and (e) The interaction between individual ageing people and the entire society is not stagnant but remains dynamic (Lueckenotte, 2000).

In brief, age stratification theory is the first to suggest that members of society might be stratified by age, as they are segregated with race, class and gender. In case of age stratification, theorists have claimed that age serves as a basis of social control, different age groups will have different access to social resources such as political and economic power. Within societies, behavioural age norms, dictate what members of age cohorts may reasonably do.

Social Exchange Theory

Social exchange theory explains the concept of ageing by exchange principles. James Dowd is regarded to be one of the proponents of this theory. He extended the basic social exchange theory to address the circumstances of older people He argued that as people age, the ratio of rewards to costs associated with social interactions might shift based on social status, e.g. being an elder and personal resources, e.g. money, power, the ability to work or provide care to others. In his exchange theory of ageing, Dowd highlighted the perceived loss of status and power that he assumed is associated with ageing (Dowd, 1975). He argued that because resources, e.g. health, income, loss of work or community roles decline with age; older people are more likely to be in a different or imbalanced kind of social exchanges. These imbalanced relationships can result in a power disadvantage, wherein the older person is required to depend or rely on others to meet their basic needs.

Dowd (1975) has opined that social relations are based on the idea of exchange between individuals, which are determined by power relations. In case of ageing, it is quite evident that individual's power declines with age. Thus he/she is unable to enter into a 'balanced exchange relations' with other members of the society. Hence, elderly populations go through the phase of disengagement, or they try to retreat themselves from various social, participatory events. Often, due to their age, they are often ignored or are unable to completely involve in exchange relations. Hence, Dowd (1975) states that 'An imbalanced exchange ratio consequently results in which the aged are forced to exchange compliance – the most costly of all generalized reinforces – for their continued sustenance'.

Modernization Theory

From the nomenclature itself, it is quite apparent that this theory tries to relate the concept of modernization or the consequences of modernization on the elderly population. Donald Cowgill and Lowell D. Holmes were regarded to be the precursors of this theory. In their book *Aging and Modernisation* (1972), they have first tried to relate the issue of ageing with modernization. According to this theory, the forces of modernity have brought a series of changes within the society. As a result of this, it has also affected the individuals including the elderly population. Modernization theory believed that the agents of modernity have both positive and negative effects on the elderly population. Drastic progress in the field of technology, medicines and public health has resulted in bringing higher longevity rate as well as improvement of the health of people. At the same time agents of modernization are also backed up with negative consequences. These include greater dependency, greying of the economy, loss of income, prestige (in case of elderly) and scarcity of labour capital. Thus the negative consequences of modernization are leading to degradation of status in the case of elderly population. Cowgill and Holmes (1972) suggest that modernization trend results in the decline of prestige and power of the elderly. The primary cause of this includes the parallel forces of industrialization and modernization. This theory presumes that an inverse relation exists between modernization trends and status of elderly in the society.

One of the significant consequence of modernity includes changes in the value structure of the individual as well as the increasing trend of individualism. One of the primary reasons behind this is the increasing trend of nuclear families which are replacing the extended and joint family structure. Hence, in an individualistic social structure, caring for an elderly person is seen as a voluntary often unwanted commitment that may be ignored without fear of social censure. In brief, the central theme of this theory is the gradual decline of elderly importance in the society followed by the rising trend of modernity, wherein an individual's importance is based on his/her utility to the society.

The Subculture of Ageing Theory

This theory was proposed by Arnold Rose, who stated that older people interact with each other more than with younger adults both because they share similar interests and concerns and because they have been excluded from other social circles. According to this theory, the elderly population will connect with their contemporaries in a better way than that with the other members of the society. It is quite evident that age plays a dominant role in influencing tastes and inclinations. For Example, a man of 20 to 30 years will always opt for adventure trip while people belonging to the grey population will mostly opt for hassle-free trip or pilgrimage. Hence, this theory suggests that older people will be comfortable in the company of people with similar tastes and mindset. Hence, they try to create a sub-group of people in their age group. In this process, they may often try to disengage themselves from other members and affairs of the society. Rose (1965) has opined that the elderly population thereupon create a sub-culture, wherein the access is restricted to them only. This unique sub-culture within society acts as a shield from the intolerable attitude of the society. At the same time, an elderly population often try to protect their self-respect and status with this unique subculture which for them is a canopy of protection as well as a means to disengage them from the whole of society.

Lange and Grossman (2010) have stated that there is a scarcity of research work to support or refute Rose's work. They opined that there is a rising trend of elderly population and thus there is an urgency to look into the matter of elderly needs as well as a transformation of society's response towards the greying population.

Person-Environment Fit Theory

This theory, proposed by Lawton (1982) explores the individual's primary strategies to overcome the environmental challenges as posited. Person-environment theory analyses the interaction between human beings and the environment in which they survive. Habitus may act as a support system, but at the same time, it may often posit challenges, which individual has to overcome. This theory mainly aims to focus the interaction between an older individual with his/her habitus. Madigan (2006) has stated that individuals have specific personal aptitudes that help them mould or adjust themselves throughout their life. The aptitudes which law had mentioned includes personality forte, level of motor skills, individual biological health and cognitive and sensory-perceptual capacities. All these skills help a person to interact with the environment in which one lives.

This theory states that with age, competencies wane to a certain extent, which posits a challenge for the elderly population to adjust within their habitus. Health problems or psychomotor disability often act as a significant setback for the elderly population to 'fit' into their environment. This theory stresses that environmental challenges increase with age and the elderly often feel a threat to survive because of their involuntary incompetency.

Recent Concerns

Although as a formal discipline, gerontology is a recently evolved subject, the concern for the elderly is not a new one. In other chapters we have dealt with various issues of elderly including abuse, policies, literacy, dependency, herein we will be dealing with current studies and researches on elderly.

Ageism

Old age is often viewed as a social problem throughout the world. The elderly population is often treated as an unwanted liability in the society. Families and other institutions treat and make the elderly people believe they are unwanted. Various studies showed the pathetic status of the elderly population in the society.

Ageism refers to the regular practice of discrimination or maltreatment or stereotyping individual because of his/her old age. It is a process whereby society's youth often treat the elderly people as different entities and often isolate themselves from the older people. Robert Butler coined the term 'Ageism'. In his words,

> (a) process of systematic stereotyping or discrimination against people because they are old, just as racism and sexism accomplish with skin colour and gender. Ageism allows the younger generations to see older people as different as themselves; thus they subtly cease to identify with their elders as human beings. (Butler, 1975)

Butler has compared the process of ageism with that of racism as well as sexism. In this regard, Butler (1980) has opined that there are three interrelated aspects to the problem of ageism. It includes the following:

1. Prejudicial attitude towards the aged or the older people or ageing process, which also involves the attitudes of the elderly too.
2. Discriminatory attitude towards the elderly population, including in employment policies as well as in various another social role.
3. Institutional practices and policies which intentionally undermine the personal dignity of the elderly population.

Macnicol (2006) in this regard has stated that ageism is deeply embedded within the mind, within the patterns of thinking as well as within unspoken assumptions, stereotypes and popular imagery. It is often termed as 'Implicit' ageism. Ageism describes the subjective experience implied in the popular notion of the generation gap. Butler (1995) believed that cultural attitudes of the society often pamper these kind of beliefs. He cited that mandatory retirement policy is one of the dominant factors to isolate them from mainstream culture as well as roles and responsibilities.

Elderly and Mass Media

Media is a powerful agent of today's era. Access and reach of media is quite an invincible reality. Media has an impact on people to a quite considerable extent. Thus, media is an important agent of change of the society. Since media has a wider reach, it may act as an essential medium to transform society's mindset toward the elderly. However, it is often seen that the elderly are not portrayed in 'good' way I by media agent. Often aged people are portrayed as weak, feeble, inactive, dependent entities. The Aging Watch reports that the elderly population is often projected as helpless victims. Hence, incompetency of elderly population is often highlighted which in other way nurtures a negative attitude among the members of the society and thus enunciate 'ageism'.

Vasil and Wass (2006) have opined that the negative portrayal of the elderly population is often a matter of concern. Media acts as a powerful socialization agent. Thus, negative stereotyping often results in the creation of a rift between the elderly and youth populations of the society. Vasil and Wass (2006) did an empirical study concerning this issue and had concluded that representation of the elderly population is inadequate and detrimental in the mass media platform. At the same time, elderly people are often marginalized which inherently encourages ageism and later on increases isolation and disintegration.

Mass media is the instrument of the society. In fact, media representation is related to society's understanding of individuals. The characters depicted by media channels are a representation of the society as a whole. Thus media representation of the elderly is always seen to be negative, 'victims', vulnerable as well as weak and dependent. Media's influence over its consumers/viewers is terrifying, as the gap between generation continues. Also, there is no willingness among the younger and the middle aged to accommodate the greying population within the mainstream society and its various roles.

Elderly and Companionship

It is a well-known fact that man is a social animal. It can also be stated that a man cannot live alone. In fact, the issue of companionship is hidden in this popular quote of Aristotle. A human being needs company or dependency to survive. Individual's urge for companionship increases to a greater extent when he/she is vulnerable. Vulnerability increases if a person is weak either physically or emotionally. Hence, aged population faces the need for companionship.

The present-day society is mostly characterized by dual earning nuclear household. Hence, the elderly population stays alone within the four walls, often with no one to interact. The institution of marriage was established with the sole aim of providing dependency to each other, however, with age followed by death of the partners, it is widely seen that the percentage of married elderly persons decreases. In other words, it can also be stated that with age an elderly person may become a widow or widower, a divorcee as well as they may stay unmarried throughout their life. However, various studies have indicated that there is a positive relationship between marital status and elderly well-being. In this regard, Robards et al. (2012) have stressed that the quality of life of the elderly is found to be better if they live a married life, in comparison to single individuals. Herein it can be aptly remarked that elderly individual need companionship as well as emotional dependency.

Hogan (2013) has stated in her article that relationships or love can happen at any age. At the same time relationships affect an individual's physical and mental well-being positively. It is often seen that the elderly population is facing loneliness which often leads to severe depression as well as death. Now, relationships act as a major way of easing loneliness. Aged people need company for interaction as well as for dependency, which may help them in living a good life.

Elderly and Intimacy

The Oxford Dictionary states the meaning of intimacy as some form of closeness or friendship. Kaplan (2005) has defined intimacy as a close feeling shared between two people, based on an acquaintance of and familiarity with the other person. It includes emotional, social (based on shared experiences) and physical intimacy (e.g. touching, cuddling, sexual intercourse). Hence, intimacy can be both physical as well as mental. The urge for intimacy increases with age after that physical intimacy gets subsumed by emotional intimacy with increasing age. However, the collective understanding of the concept of intimacy is restricted to sexual intimacy. When we talk of intimacy among the elderly, it is often seen that the society views it in a negative, derogatory manner. Now a question arises whether intimacy is a taboo for the elderly? In this regard Bienko (2015) had stated that often society likes to view an asexual portrayal of elderly people. However, Bienko (2015) had also asserted that the society's opinion on elderly intimacy is also changing and now, intimacy is seen to be less 'sinful'.

King (2013) has opined that intimacy is important for the elderly. By interviewing various cases, he stated that for elderly population intimacy is an escape route from loneliness as well as conducive to the elderly's mental well-being. The concept of intimacy has a wider meaning after that, elderly relate themselves with emotional intimacy as well as physical closeness which is beyond the idea of sexual intimacy at a particular time. King's article highlights an interview which is given below:

Andrée, a 74-year-old retired journalist from London, UK, is a case in point. Sex and intimacy are crucial to her – especially the intimacy aspect. 'By intimacy I mean the loving friendship and support my lover and I have for each other, this includes kissing, cuddling and just being next to each other, even without any sexual activity', she told the Times. 'Our friendship and non-sexual intimacy is the most important thing to us both', she added.

From the above extract, the meaning and importance of intimacy for the elderly can be easily comprehended. In brief, intimacy is not only related to the elderly's well-being, but it often acts as a support system and source of confidence to confront the challenges of ageing.

Conclusion

Gerontology is a recently evolved discipline which will gradually have strong roots. One of the major reasons behind this is the increasing trend of elderly population which the world is facing. Hence, there is an urgent need to develop geriatric infrastructure as well as compassion within the society to confront the issue of the elderly. Elderly concerns are evolving day by day and therefore it becomes important for the society to accommodate them in the mainstream society and reduce exclusion. It is necessary that elderly population and their experience cum expertise be utilized properly to restrict greying of the world economy.

2

Elderly

A World Scenario

The present world is currently confronting the multifaceted challenges which the rapidly increasing elderly population is incorporating. At the same time, these challenges are predicted to increase in brisk scale in following days to come. Average life expectancy is escalating day by day, owing to the recent progression in the medical field. Hence, the average statistics of the elderly population is also growing. According to the UN Report (2015), the growth rate of the elderly population will be over 56 per cent from 2015–2030. Indeed with such inferences, it is quite clear that the world has to make themselves prepared to deal with elderly concerns which include not only the development of infrastructure facilities but at the same time, there is an urgent need to develop a compassionate mindset towards the aged population.

Any person who has attained the age of 60 years or more is generally regarded to be old. However, the aforesaid comprises exclusively to the physical facet of the definition of elderly, but the issue of old age is a broader concept and therefore there is a need to look into the issue through various aspects. Defining old age is a difficult task. 'Being old' is commonly correlated with some forms of physical disability, frail and occasionally mental illness. However, this may not be the scenario, since nowadays people are more conscious about their health and therefore tend to be healthy, despite being old (Freitas et al., 2010). Hence, old age should be comprehended in a holistic fashion, where it should not be restricted to physical facet but should also include social and cultural facet too.

The elderly issue is becoming a matter of prior concern. The world is increasingly greying in more days to come. The frontier of age and ageing is changing day by day, wherein in 1990 one in every 20 individual was found to be old, however by 2030, it will be one in every five which is quite an issue of concern. Advancement in the medical and scientific field has brought in a series of developments. One of them is the rising global 'Ageing Tide'. Ageing issue thus contributes to a major field of concern for not only the respective administrative bodies but also policy framers, gerontologist as well as social scientists. There are various reasons for this concern; one of the main issues involves the availability of health infrastructure for the elderly population of the world. Here the question which comes is, 'Are we prepared for the rising elderly scenario?

In this chapter, we will be dealing with the present global elderly scenario and emerging concerns.

Elderly Map

Coping with the newly emergent ageing society is one of the major gerontological concerns in the present day. Advancement in science and technology has also brought in massive advancement in the medical field. As a result of this, the world is witnessing a low mortality rate and higher longevity, making ageing society a stark reality, a truth which can neither be ignored nor escaped.

Concern for the alarming rise in elderly population became major point of discussion in Lund Declaration of 2009. The United Nations has predicted that by 2050, one-third of the population in developed countries and one-tenth of the population in developing countries will comprise of the elderly population (United Nations, 2009). Indeed, it will be a challenging issue which needs to be addressed skilfully since ageing in other terms also means higher dependency ration and low manpower, viz.

Figure 2.1

Number of persons aged 60 years or over by development group from 1980 to 2050 (United Nations, 2017)

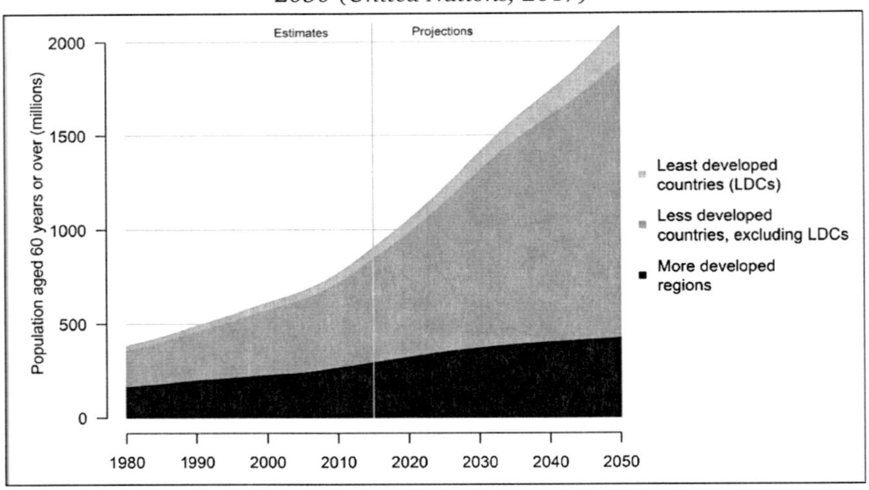

Source: World Population Prospects: the 2017 Revision.

low proportion of the workforce. At the same time, it will also create a negative impact on the health care infrastructure of various countries. According to data from World Population Prospects: the 2015 Revision (United Nations, 2015), the number of elderly persons has increased in proportion, in the majority of countries and regions and that growth is probably to accelerate in the coming decades.

The graphical highlights showcase the rising trend of the elderly population in the world. In this regard United Nations, in the year 2015 reports 'Globally, the number of people aged 80 years or over, the "oldest-old" persons, is growing even faster than the number of older persons overall. Projections indicate that in 2050 the oldest-old will number 434 million, has more than tripled in number since 2015, when there were 125 million people over age 80'. Population ageing has brought in major changes in population pyramid of various countries too. Herein, it is seen that the dependency ratio is increasing day by day. Thus the percentage of the youth population is running parallel to the elderly population. Hence, this may bring serious issues in the country's economic securities.

Global Elderly Concerns and Issues

With recent trends of population ageing, it is quite evident that elderly issues and concerns will result in its omnipresence. The 2015 UN report stated that the elderly population throughout the world is 901 million. Hence, elderly concerns are consequently increasing.

Life Support Issues

The present-day society is characterized by an increasing elderly population on the one hand and the consequent rise of nuclear families and households, on the other hand. This vicious cycle of the ever-increasing elderly population followed by elderly nuclear households acts as an important concern. The elderly population needs caregivers and compassionate people around them with whom they can spend some time as well as those who can take care of them. Unfortunately, there is a global crisis of caregivers as well as life support systems.

It is quite evident that there has been a structural change within the family structures, as a result of demographic, sociocultural and economic transitions. The demographic changes specifically bring an impact on the age-old traditional extended family structures resulting in the evolution of nuclear family structures. Nuclear family structures are a consequence of rapid industrialization, migration, urbanization and inclination for betterment. As a result of this, members of households/family leave their native place and opt to move out with their spouses. Hence, the reality depicts two separate households, one consisting of the present generation and the other consisting of the elderly household. Changes in the value structures and urge for privacy and acute individualism results in a decline of extended families too. Hence, the present reality includes elderly people taking care of themselves. In this regard, United Nations, 2013 report on ageing stated that most of the elderly population in industrialized countries live alone and the proportion is highest among the oldest age groups.

The keystone of every society is family. As a social institution, its influence can be felt in everyday lives. It is a place where a person finds and expects support, comfort and security. Elderly are most happy with family life, especially with their children (Laidmäe et al, 2012). Research in many cultural settings shows that older people prefer to be in their own homes and communities (WHO, 2015). Hence, it is quite evident that for the elderly population, a family which may comprise of their wives, sons or daughters or relatives is essential for their well-being and can be addressed as their life support system. However, the prevalence of extended families as well as joint families is gradually diminishing day by day and now most of these families are getting fragmented into smaller nuclear units of families comprising of spouses and their children. Nevertheless, the existence of extended families are still here but today's world comprises of dual-earning households, women of the household are also involved in formal labour markets, which results in a gradual decline of 'traditional' family caregivers (PACITA, 2014). Since both the husband and wife work and remain out of the house, it brings lonesomeness among the elderly who stay with their sons and daughters. At the same time, they are often treated scornfully and are often acknowledged as an unwanted liability.

Thus, lack of life support systems often act as a major elderly crisis in the global arena which often results in various other consequences.

Economic Issues

Another major concern for the greying population includes economic crisis to meet their needs. The present scenario proves that the elderly population is staying alone with their spouses and thereupon are solely responsible for fulfilling their needs both economically as well as socially. In other words, it can also be stated that they are reliant on their lifelong savings. However, as age unfolds, expenditures often increase due to health and other issues. During this phase, it becomes challenging for the elderly population to survive. In this regard, Bloom et al. (2010) in their study have mentioned that the older population is financially vulnerable, both in developed and developing countries.

The testimony mentioned below depicts a case study of an elderly person interpreting their economic crisis. From this perspective, it can be easily concluded that financial vulnerability may lead to social life isolation, at some point of time. According to the Organization for Economic Cooperation and Development (OECD), on an average, '13.5

> *Personal Testimony by Maryse Martin*
>
> I am 67 years old and have been retired since the age of 60. I have been a widow for 14 years. My life has changed. My total monthly income amounts to 600 euros. I live near the city centre and a housing allowance covers my rent. My resources do not allow me to do what I want, but thanks to the volunteers, like me, of the Association 'petits frères des Pauvres' I can partake in many activities such as swimming and painting. I receive convivial meals on the weekend and holiday, all for free or for a small fee. Living in the city provides me with access to free transportation (bus, metro, tramway and regional train) because I do not pay tax on my income. Nevertheless, my social life is limited because of inadequate financial resources.
>
> *Source:* http://www.age-platform.eu/images/stories/EN/olderpeoplealsosufferbcofthecrisis-en.pdf

per cent of over 65s in OECD countries live in income poverty, defined as an income below half the national median. Poverty rates are higher for older people than for the population as a whole, which averages 10.6 per cent'. The statistical figures depict the degree financial vulnerability of the elderly population which is gradually increasing with the coming years. Herein, it can also be stated that there are essential hidden differences when one looks at the sub-groups of older people comprising of older women, elderly single persons as well as elderly in the rural and urban belt (Report of Age Platform, Europe, November 2012)

Financial crisis faced by the elderly results in decline of lifestyle quality. Access to better health care systems as well as formal caregivers often incurs significant expenditure which the elderly population often try to avoid for the financial crisis. Finally, changes in the family structure are bringing in a significant shift in living arrangements. Thus with the increasing development of nuclear family as well as migration from native places, a case too familiar in developing countries, often results in elderly nuclear families, wherein their sons and daughters often forgo their responsibility toward their parents including financial assistance.

Health Crisis

Health crisis is another critical concern for the elderly population. In this regard, the World Health Organization (WHO, 2015) asks a simple question – 'Will population ageing be accompanied by a longer period of good health, a sustained sense of well-being and extended periods of social engagement and productivity, or will it be associated with more illness, disability and dependency? How will ageing affect health care and social costs? Are these futures inevitable, or can we act to establish a physical and social infrastructure that might foster better health and well-being in older age?'

Elderly is not only recognized as the facets of experience and maturity but is also characterized by physical and mental problems.

Although, rapid advancements in science and technology have been successful in bringing a cure to various deadly diseases, yet we find various other new types of both communicable and non-communicable diseases are gradually evolving which may sometime result in death or result in degradation of good health quality. WHO (2012) declares that there has been a steep rise of non-communicable diseases throughout the world. These chronic non-communicable diseases reflect a significant shift in lifestyle and dietary patterns. Diseases like cancer, heart diseases, diabetes or renal failure may sometimes have deadly consequences among the elderly. At the same time, it may often result in degrading the quality of life for individuals although it may not bring death. WHO (2012) has stated that reducing severe disability from disease and health conditions is one key to hold down health and social costs.

Herein, another major thing which the elderly are gradually burdened with is the enormous medical expenditure. The rapid advancement in the medical field has both a positive and negative impact. On the one side, various deadly diseases can be cured. On the other side, access to good medical facility also incurs major expenditure, which the elderly population is often unable to bear. In this situation, they may often ignore their health problems and try to compromise with the situation. At the same time, it is often seen that the elderly population's family members often ignore their health conditions, as it is believed to be too reasonable. Sometimes the elderly population is inhibited to inform their family members as the crisis is often ignored or the aged person is insulted. Hence, health has become a significant issue throughout the world, where huge expenditure, the evolution of new diseases, as well as degrading lifestyle patterns, acts as essential challenges to confront.

Elderly and Crime

The elderly population is often acknowledged as the most vulnerable population, who are easy victims of various forms of crime. They are often harassed, injured as well as killed for various interests. Herein the perpetrators included not only criminals comprising of thieves, robbers, but it may also include their family members. In this regard, James (1992) opined that crimes against the elderly could be classified into two forms. The first form includes predictable crimes such as robbery, theft, fraud, rape and homicide. The second encompasses the more concealed phenomena of neglect and abuse which includes any physical or psychological ill-treatment inflicted on an older person in either the home or an aged-person's institution.

In the first form, the elderly are often targeted for their helplessness. This helplessness is often related to their health factors, which tends to degrade day by day. At the same time, changes in living arrangement, as a result of which most of the elderly stay alone and are helpless. Due to these reasons, the elderly population is regarded to be 'Easy Targets' for various criminals who often attack and injure them for vested interests. At the same time, it is also seen that gender plays an important role in the occurrence of crime against the elderly. Older women are the best targets for the perpetrators as well. When the elderly are victimized, they suffer greater physical, mental injury and financial losses which are indeed life-threatening. Physical injury often results in their death or physical discomfort. Mental injury often acts as a trauma in their life which often enunciates mental illness in some cases. The economic loss is a serious issue when this type of crime occurs, the elderly are often snatched of their lifelong savings, which was their exclusive survival means.

In this regard, *The Guardian* reported on 7 November 2007, that 50,000 elderly throughout the UK are victims of crime. At the same time, it is often seen that there has been an under-reporting of crimes against older people, due to fear, embarrassment and a lack of access to trusted people to whom they can report their worries.

The second form of elderly crime comprises elderly abuse or neglect which mostly occurs within the domestic settings, i.e. houses and here the perpetrators include the family members. On the other side elderly abuse also occurs in institutional settings, which includes old-age homes In the next chapter, we have described the types and forms of abuse, herein we would focus on other details.

Elderly population throughout the world faces various forms of abuse which includes physical, mental, financial as well as sexual abuse. The STAGE project in their findings on elderly abuse has stated that the prevalence of elderly abuse varies from country to another, with figures ranging from 2.2 per cent in Ireland to 13.4 per cent in Italy. The American Psychological Association (2012) has reported in their article on elderly that there is no single pattern of elderly abuse, which 'is a continuation of long-standing patterns of violence and physical, emotional, or financial abuse within the family. More commonly, elder abuse is related to changes in living situations and relationships brought about either by the older person's growing frailty and dependence on others for companionship and for meeting basic needs or by a family member's increased reliance on an older relative for shelter and financial support'.

One of the significant reason behind elderly abuse included dependant on the aged population on their family members or caregivers, who later on exploit them in various ways. The elderly are often subjected to various forms of abuse when the perpetrator's needs to get unfulfilled. Mental abuse and financial is the most common form of abuse; an elderly has to face in their lifetime. It is a well-known fact that his/her productive capacity often judges an individual's value in the family and this parameter, the elderly serve to be poor performers. Thus they are often mocked or psychologically harassed. At the same time, the perpetrators often want to exploit the aged financially, thus turning the elderly individual's life into a nightmare.

> James is a financially secure 85-year old man who has been healthy and active until the last year. He has finally agreed to allow his oldest son, Tom, to help him manage his daily affairs. Tom now believes his father 'owes him' more of his money than his brother and two sisters are entitled to. He convinces his father into giving him power of attorney for his bank accounts 'as a convenience' and then writes himself large checks that he tells himself are for 'expenses'. Soon Tom has come up with excuses to transfer a significant portion of his father's investment holdings into his name. James has no energy to oversee his finances and is entirely trusting that his son has his best interests at heart.
>
> *Source:* American Psychological Association, 2012.

From the above extract, it is quite clear about the perpetrator's perception of aged people and their resources and assets. Hence, it can be aptly remarked that caregivers often dominate the elderly people, where the latter often live with fear and helplessness.

Elderly and Access to Technology

It is quite evident that ageing is a global phenomenon and every nation has to prepare itself to face the rising trend of elderly population which in itself will bring some issues to consider and take action. This particular subject will concentrate on the importance of technological accessibility for the elderly and its benefits.

Sixsmith and Sixsmith (2008) have opined that there is a sharp increase of elderly population throughout the world which nearly comprises of 10 per cent of the total population of the world, which is predicted to rise to 20 per cent within 2050. This clearly shows the rising trend of elderly population and the need to intervene into the problem of elderly which not only included the development of health care infrastructure, but it also involves the need to make them self-sufficient to some extent. In this background, information and communication technologies (ICTs) are viewed as having a considerable prospective (Sixsmith and Sixsmith, 2008).

Technological development is a boon for the whole of humanity. It is a well-known fact that technology makes jobs and tasks easier and less complicated. For the elderly population, it will also be a blessing in disguise, especially for those elderly population who lack life care support and those who are compelled to look after themselves. However, it is seen that most of the elderly population is not well acquainted with technological use and find it 'complicated'. The following graphical presentation gives a statistical description of ICT usage by age and year.

Figure 2.2

Internet use by age and year

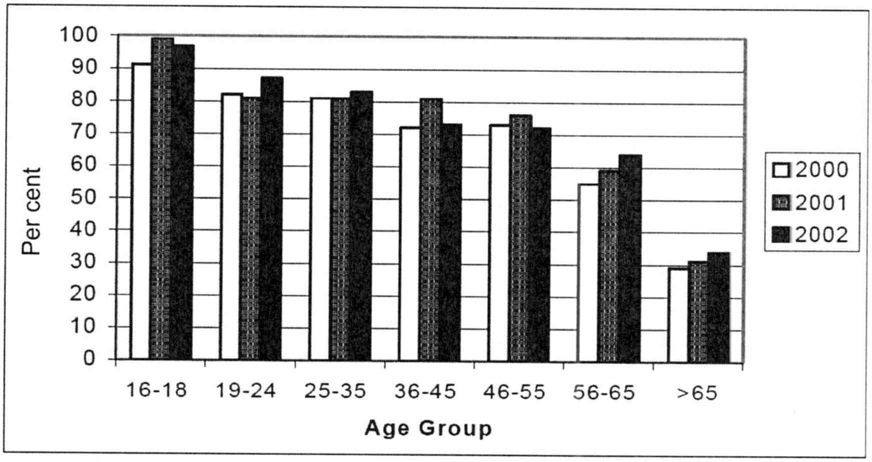

Source: The UCLA Internet Report – 'Surveying the Digital Future'.
UCLA Center for Communication Policy, January 2003 (Courtesy: Czaja, 2005).

The above shown graphical representation clearly shows that lowest per cent of people above 65 use internet facilities. However, at the same time, it is quite evident that elderly people may access technology if needed or made aware of its advantage. In this regard, Czaja (2005) opined that there is a myth that elderly population, are believed to be resistant to any form of technology and its utility, but this stereotype can be challenged by available data as given above. Hence, the elderly population may be late adopters of technological gadgets, but they will use it if they are convinced enough.

In this regard a study by Brophy et al. (2015) has provided an interesting observation on the use of various technological mediums by the elderly and level of difficulty, they face, which has been interestingly codified in scale. Following graphical representation highlights their study.

The following Figure 2.2 clearly describes the difficulties and resistance faced by the elderly population regarding their access to various technological gadgets. In this regard, it can be aptly remarked, that the elderly population may resist change, but they need to be aware of its advantages in their daily life.

It can also be stated here that ICT is itself projected as 'Youthful', where most of the companies who produce and market technological gadgets tend to target the youth and the middle-aged population, almost ignoring the elderly population, which in other way is increasing in size and importance within the society. In brief, it can be concluded that the

Figure 2.3

Level of difficulty to give up technologies already used by older people

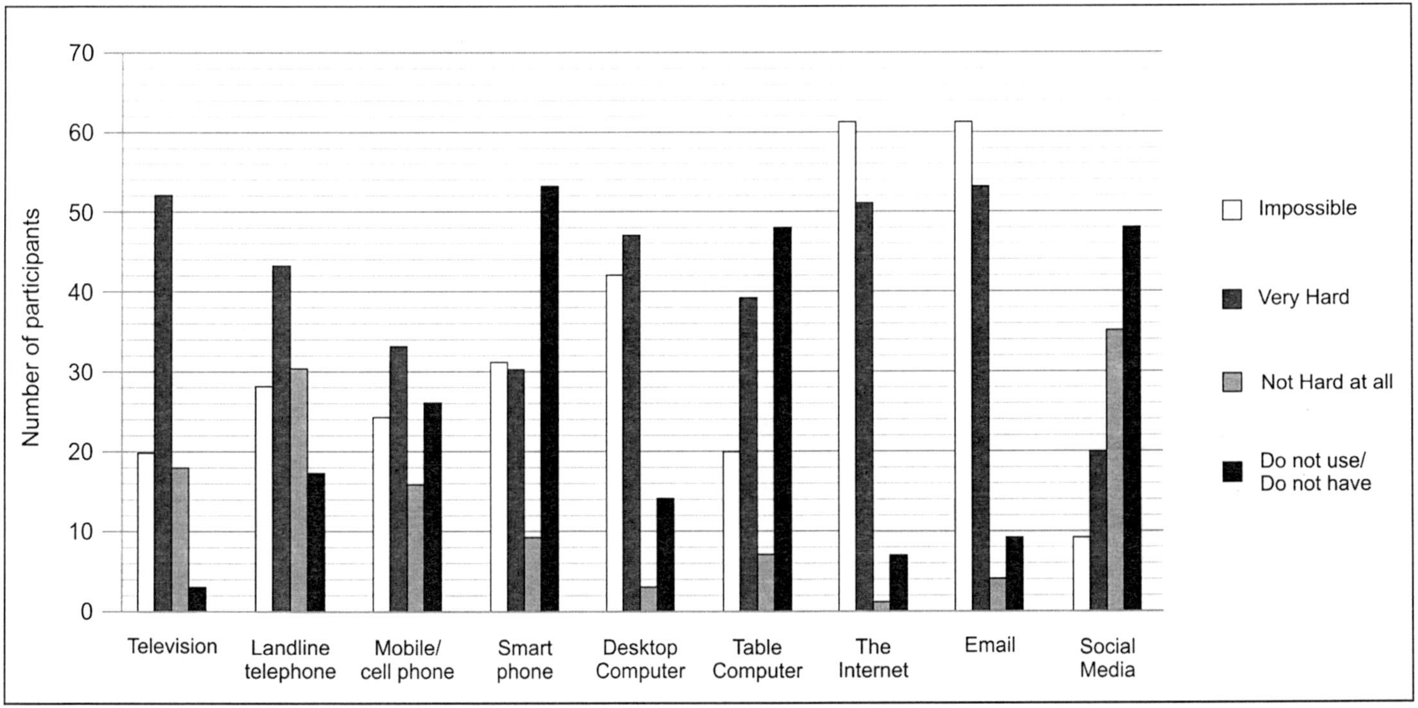

Source: Brophy et al., 2015.

elderly population should get the platform to access ICTs. There is a need for state-level intervention in this issue since technology can make their life more comfortable as well as independent. At the same time, electronic gadgets should be designed or customized as per elderly needs. An example can be cited of big keys mobile phones which helps the elderly population to access it despite weak vision.

Conclusion

The world population is ageing day by day and every country shares rising trend of elderly growth. With this demographic transition, a series of new concerns are emerging which need global intervention. The rise of the elderly population is bringing new challenges of degrading labour capital as well as greying of world economics. At the same time, there is an urgency to accommodate the elderly population into the mainstream roles and functions of the social institution, which inherently will bring in social integration and equilibrium.

> 'Population ageing is a triumph of development', Dr Babatunde Osotimehin, Executive Director of the United Nations Population Fund told IPS. The elderly can make a social and economic contribution to society, he said 'Harnessing these contributions will be very important'. (Osotimehin, 2014)

The above quote suggests models for elderly assimilation and provision of importance and self-sufficiency to the elderly. In this regard, Japan Model of elderly care can be looked upon as a matter of reference. The country has excelled itself in elderly care where micro-level intervention to elderly concerns is prevalent. Here long-term medical care and support is provided to the aged population.

In brief elderly population needs compassion, support and the company which world has to provide to face this challenge efficiently.

3

Old Age in India

One of the major challenges which India faces includes the higher growth rate of population, as a result of which the country confronts the alarming rise of the elderly populace. It is predicted by various demographic experts that the dependency population is increasing day by day and therefore the country's population pyramid has transformed from conical pyramid to somewhat barrel-shaped structure, which signifies that the elderly population of the country outnumbers country's adult as well as child population. The present-day scenario witnesses a major rise in the elderly population in contrast to the decline of fertility rates; hence fall in the population percentage of children. By such facts, it is clear that the issue of elderly needs a serious discussion.

Demographic Profile

India is a 'Greying Nation', as per the parameters of the UN, which has defined a country as 'Ageing' or 'Greying Nation' where the proportion of people over 60 reach 7 per cent of the total population. According to Census 2011, India's total population is 1210.9 million, out of which near about 8.6 per cent of the population comprised of aged people. It proves aforesaid that India exhibits a rapid increase in the elderly population, owing to the drastic advancements in the medical arena. Recent data published by Ministry of Statistics and Programme Implementation, Analysis (2016) shows that the share and size of the elderly population is increasing day by day, wherein in 1961 India's elderly population comprised of 5.6 per cent which has increased to 8.6 per cent in 2011. This rapid rise in the elderly population is also followed by a declining trend in the fertility and mortality rates of the country, followed by an increase in the average life expectancy rate, which is a significant factor behind the rise of the elderly population in India (Udhayakumar and Ponnuswamy, 2012).

Another important feature of the demographic scenario in the case of the elderly population is that there is an eventual rise in both male and female elderly population. In the year 2011, the elderly female population was as high as 9 per cent in comparison to the elderly male counterparts which was marginally lower with 8.2 per cent. At the age of 60 years, the average Indian life expectancy is predicted as 78 years (16.9 for males and 19.0 for females) and that at age 70 was less than 12 years (Ministry of Statistics and Programme Implementation, Government of India, 2016). It is clear that in India, the rate of population rise is higher among the aged females. Hence, a significant question arises on the issue of the vulnerability of these populations, who are often subjected to various forms of abuse.

Table 3.1

Percentage share of elderly population (aged 60 years and above) in total population in India

Years	*Male*	*Female*	*Total*	*Rural*	*Urban*
1961	5.5	5.8	5.6	5.8	4.7
1971	5.9	6.0	6.0	6.2	5.0
1981	6.4	6.6	6.5	6.8	5.4
1991	6.7	6.8	6.8	7.1	5.7
2001	7.1	7.8	7.5	7.7	6.7
2011	8.2	9.0	8.6	8.8	8.1

Source: Census of India for 1961–2011.

The demographic picture brings a need for the development of infrastructural facility of the country concerning the aged. Population ageing has profound social, economic and political implications for a country. The increasing number of older persons put a strain on health care and social care systems in the country. Old age comes with a lot of ailment and diseases. In case of large number of elderly persons in the population, the country needs more and more health and medical services, facilities and resources. Government spending on health care is increased with the increase in average age of the population (Ministry of Statistics and Programme Implementation, Government of India, 2016). Hence, the elderly situation in India needs serious consideration.

Elderly and Dependency Status

We often address the elderly with various names which include old, Senior citizens, Aged. Now a question may arise who are known to be elderly? Elderly refers to that group of the population which is above 60 and have retired from their full-time jobs. Hence, in simple terms, retired men and women may often be referred to as elderly. From what is said above, it is clear that the population above 60 is bound to take permanent leave from their job, for legal obligations, even if they are 'active' enough to continue with it. Herein, owing to the recent trend of increase in the elderly population, a question may arise on the reliability of the retirement age since it is gradually increasing the country's dependent population. The elderly dependency population has increased from 10.9 per cent in 1961 to 14.2 per cent in 2011 for India as a whole. For females and males, the value of the ratio was 14.9 per cent and 13.6 per cent in 2011 (Ministry of Statistics and Programme Implementation, Analysis, 2016). Differences across the formal and informal sector in both retirement patterns and access to old-age social security is extreme in India; a small percentage of the workforce employed in the formal sector in India, have formal wage employment, retire between 55 and 65 years and are entitled to some form of financial support, post-retirement. Informal sector employees who constitute around 94 per cent of the total labour force, by contrast, lack access to any form of social security such as pension support and also expect to work until relatively late in their lives (Reddy, 2012). Hence, it is seen that pension schemes are available to those people who were formally employed. However, the percentage of employment in the non-formal sector is quite high and since it never provides job security and retirement benefits, it creates a burden for the elderly people who thereupon face many hurdles to survive in their later age, when the cost of living increases gradually.

The elderly population is therefore addressed as the dependent population. This means that this population is economically as well as physically (to some extent) dependent on their sons or daughters. This dependency makes them vulnerable since their physical and mental well-being depends on their children's whims to a certain extent. However, it is also seen that due to survival instincts, some of the elderly are compelled to opt for employment opportunities. They often choose various odd jobs which are hazardous for their physical well-being. It is also found that they are often exploited in this regard. In contrast to most of the developed countries, in India, workers employed in the formal and informal sector face significantly different retirement systems.

Elderly and Vulnerability

The Census 2011 data revealed that there is an increase in the life expectancy of the population. India is currently known as 'Ageing India' at the beginning of the 21st century. Thus the 21st century is the century of old (Liebig and Rajan, 2003). With the increase in life expectancy of the average Indian population, comes up a new issue of the rising elderly population. The changing scenario of the country has brought new challenges for the elderly population. One such challenge is the increasing vulnerability of the elderly population. The elderly population in India is unevenly distributed both in rural as well as urban areas where their population is higher in rural areas than in the urban areas. In most of the rural areas, it is found that there is an increasing trend of migration of the younger population to urban areas in search of jobs and various other reasons (Sarkar, 2016). As a result of this, elderly parents are left behind who had to support themselves for their own survival needs. It is found that they often try to opt for various odd jobs in search of a living which often affect their health. It is also seen that in the country the traditional joint family structure is disintegrating, with which the value system of the society is transforming. As a result of this, respect for the elderly has degraded where people are often judged by their utility. The emergence of the nuclear family has resulted in bringing emotional, financial as well as physical insecurity among the elderly population (Mane, 2016).

The elderly population is often seen as 'Easy Targets' by criminals who often victimize them for various illegal activities. Safety concerns are a major reason for the vulnerability of the elderly. We are aware of some news on the elderly attack which indeed raises a question of the social security system of the country.

> BHUBANESWAR: When 73-year-old eye surgeon Prafulla Chandra Mishra and his 67-year-old wife Sushma, a pathologist, were brutally hacked to death in their house for loot in Sailashree Vihar area here last November, there was much hue and cry over safety of senior citizens in the capital city. (*Times of India*, 2016)
>
> Two senior citizens fall prey to crimes like murder, dacoity and robbery every three days in Karnataka, a statistic that shatters the benign elder-friendly image the state otherwise showcases. Even more alarming is the fact that Bengaluru, that once flaunted the tag of Pensioners' Paradise, tops the state in crimes against the elderly, underlining the fact that the city is anything but safe for its seniors. (*India Times*, 2016)

The above highlights clearly show the vulnerability of the elderly as well as the loopholes in the social security system of the country. With the dominance of 'Two member household', it is seen that most of the elderly depend on domestic help for their various needs and are often subjected to various forms of abuse as a result of their helplessness (Rajan, 2006).

Old age is characterized by immense knowledge and experience on the one hand as well as physical and mental illness on the other hand. The elderly of the country suffer from some diseases which may be communicable as well as non-communicable. According to Government of India statistics, cardiovascular disorders account for one-third of elderly mortality. Respiratory disorders account for 10 per cent mortality while infections including tuberculosis account for another 10 per cent. Neoplasm accounts for 6 per cent and accidents, poisoning and violence constitute less than 4 per cent of elderly mortality with more or less similar rates for nutritional, metabolic, gastrointestinal and genitourinary infections (Guha, 1994). *The Indian Express*, 2016 reports that India may have

60 million cases of osteoarthritis in India where the most will affect the elderly. From those that is said above, it is quite clear that there is a dire need of geriatric health infrastructure in the country where the access to health care system should reach all, irrespective of class, caste and gender. However, the health care system is costly for the country as a result of which the elderly are often left untreated. In India, health insurance coverage is mainly limited to hospitalization. The concept of geriatric care has remained a neglected area of medicine in the country. Despite an ageing population, geriatric care is relatively new in many developing countries like India with many practicing physicians having little knowledge of the clinical and functional implications of ageing (Ingle and Nath, 2008).

In brief, it can be aptly remarked that the elderly population is increasing in number, but the quality of life is falling as a result of the emergence of nuclear household, change in value systems, migration of younger population, loneliness, lack of social security system and finally inaccessibility to proper health care system and compassion.

Elderly Health in India

Health is a major issue for every individual and with age, it becomes a concern. With the increase in the average life expectancy of Indian, there is significant doubt about the physical and mental well-being of these individuals. With increase in individual's age, the health issue is a typical affair. The UN report, 2008 suggests that the physical and mental well-being indicators of the elderly in India shows a significant level of poor health of the elderly. The analysis on self-rated health shows about 55 per cent of the elderly rate their health as poor or fair on a five-point scale. Thus, the self-rated health appears to be lower in comparison with that of the elderly population in developed countries. Self-rated health also has a close connection with the mental and physical health of the elderly. In India, communicable and non-communicable diseases affect the elderly where the former is a direct effect of declining immunity and low nutritional diet. With these diseases, low vision and hearing impairment, as well as osteoarthritis, are major health issues which often act as a barrier to living freely and independently (Ingle and Nath, 2008).

Physiological Problems

Physiological problems refer to the problems related to physical decline of health conditions of an individual. Age results in a physiological decline of the normal body functioning resulting in poor mobility, visual and hearing impairment to some extent as well as liver issues including indigestion, loss of memory as well as inability to control certain bodily functions (Kaur et al., 2014).

Age is always a matter of anxiety for every individual. It is often imagined with uncertainty and fear. One of the main reasons behind this stress is related to physiological uncertainty. Owing to the present environmental situation, lifestyle patterns as well higher life expectancy trend, there are a series of health problems which individuals face. In this regard, it can be aptly remarked that one of the dangerous effect of late modernity or Ulrich Beck's 'Risk Society' is increasing new risks such as health, lifestyle or economic risks (Reifova and Fiserova, 2012).

In India, health is always an issue of concern among the elderly population. The major reasons behind this include ignorance towards health, low-quality nutritional diet as well as religious actions. Before going through this detail, it is important to understand the composition of the elderly population in the country. Elderly in India constitute 8.2 per cent of the population (Census, 2011), which is inherently increasing day by day. The elderly population can, therefore, be classified into rural and urban elderly, married and unmarried elderly, widow and widower. Elderly can also be described into various phases. The older adult population can be divided into three life-stage subgroups: the young-old (approximately 65–74), the middle-old (ages 75–84) and the old-old (over age 85) (Little, 2014). This classification provides a picture of the elderly scenario of the country which has a direct relationship with that of health issues. For the first classification of rural and urban elderly, it can be aptly remarked that the rural elderly population is less aware and less conscious about their health and nutrition. As a result of this, they are affected by numerous physiological problems which often get unnoticed as well as untreated. On the other hand for the urban elderly, the situation is a bit different where in urban areas, pollution, as well as food and lifestyle patterns, may have a derogating effect on the physiological condition of the elderly population.

Marital status can be used to classify the elderly population in the country. In research by Perkins et al. (2016), it was concluded that marital status and health of the individual is causally related. Marriage may offer economic, social and psychological benefits, which may promote good health. These mechanisms may include access to sufficient economic resources, social control of behaviour by one's spouse, or a sense of social support within the marital relationship (Perkins et al., 2016). Marital status and marital well-being affect physical and mental health outcomes of the elderly in India. Coming to the second aspect of the marital status includes widowhood which is inherently a gendered and cultural experience. Widowhood is itself a painful experience after that it is more excruciating for the women elderly population in general. As a woman becomes a widow, she has to follow many restrictions which include her food habits, her lifestyle patterns to name a few. As a result of this, nutritional deficiency is a standard affair along with their vulnerability. In India, a country with strict gender norms and traditional kinship systems, widowhood is considered to be a dreaded phase of life among some groups, particularly for women. Traditionally, in India the woman's central role was to care for her husband. Upon losing her husband, the primary purpose of life was lost. As she belonged to her husband's family, in-laws frequently viewed widowed women as a burden. In the past, a traditional Hindu custom (which is the dominant religion in India) called for widows to commit suicide upon the death of their husband and although the practice is illegal now. More recently, the 'city of widows' in India has been highlighted, which is a holy site that is home to thousands of widowed women who live in dire circumstances and beg for money. In general, widowhood for women in India is a very tenuous period of life, highlighted by significant poverty, lack of social support, lack of ability to remarry and a higher risk of mortality. Widowhood for elderly women in India may be a highly stigmatizing and potentially public experience as, according to traditional customs, they may shave their heads, wear only and every day white clothing, eat only two or fewer meals per day and not be permitted to attend social gatherings or to re-marry (Perkins et al., 2016). As a consequence physiological problems backed up with mental illness becomes a common affair. It is quite evident that immunity power is destroyed with low nutritional quality.

Elderly in the world can also be classified into three phases (as mentioned above) comprising of young, middle and older elderly which is directly related to physiological problems which increase with an increase in age. As a result, the older elderly population is facing, the higher amount of physiological problems than the population classified into other two phases. The elderly constitute a vulnerable section. Frailty and fatigue create physical limitations and social withdrawal. Common locomotors, visual, hearing and psychomotor deficits may compound problems (*The Hindu*, 2014).

Mental Illness

Mental illness refers to a series of mental problems/disorders that affect an individual's mood, thinking and behavioural pursuits. They are generally characterized by some combination of abnormal thoughts, emotions, behaviour and relationships with others. Examples are schizophrenia, depression, intellectual disabilities (WHO, 1984). Mental and behavioural disorders constitute 12 per cent of the global burden of diseases (WHO, 2001). Hence, the issue of mental disorder is a matter of concern irrespective of age. However, the elderly population is prone to mental illness.

Age is regarded to be one of the essential determinants of mental illness. With age, it is found that individuals not only deal with physiological problems, but they have to prepare themselves for the challenges of the society, which affect their mental well-being (Grover and Malhotra 2015). There is a gradual transition of value structure of the society. As a result of this, old age or the elderly is often regarded as a burden and they are often excluded by their family and society as a whole. We have observed the elderly in our daily life. If we observe them minutely, we may find them with certain mental disorders, which involves partial memory loss or specific behavioural disorders. It is found that the elderly also involve the ageing of the brain, cerebral pathology along with physical ageing. As a result of this, mental and behavioural disorders tend to increase with an increase in age.

Elderly in India face a large number of psychological, social and physical health problems. As age advances, there is increased morbidity and functional loss. Also, the presence of a variety of depressive factors and occurrence of varying life events, impacts one's psychological status, making them more prone to depression (Jariwala et al., 2010). Depression is believed to be the most common form of mental disorder among the elderly. In a medical sense, depression refers to a kind of mood disorder which affects an individual's lifestyle patterns as well as his/her thinking process. If left untreated, it can have severe effects on the physical and social activities of the elderly, wherein the individual may face a loss of interest in daily life activities (Blanchard et al., 1994).

In various community studies conducted, it was reported that elderly in India face some psycho-social problems. In a study done on elderly in Mysore, it was concluded that mental illness is quite common among the elderly, with a significantly higher rate among the elderly who have crossed 75 years age (Boralingaiah et al., 2012). In another study in Surat city, it was reported that prevalence of elderly is moderately high, where it was also mentioned that depression is higher among the elderly people who are more aged (Jariwala et al., 2010). Studies have revealed that the prevalence rates for depression in community samples of elderly in India vary from 6 per cent to 50 per cent. Hence, there is a significant prevalence of mental illness among the elderly in India.

Some reasons can be cited for mental illness among the elderly. Loneliness is a significant reason behind psycho-social problems among the elderly. It has already been mentioned that there is a sharp rise of nuclear families where elderly husband and wife live alone with their various problems, for which they have to depend on outside help. It is quite apparent that helplessness grew among them which often results in various mental illnesses.

The rampant process of urbanization has also brought in the rise of individualism wherein interaction in physical space is degrading day by day. As a result of this, most of the people are restricted to their homes, where television is their only resort to boredom. Hence, lack of interaction, lack of coordination and increasing individualism which results in creating depression is directly related to helplessness.

In conclusion, it can be stated that elderly in India provides evidence of physiological problems as well as psychosocial problems which increase with the increase in age.

Elderly Abuse

Elderly abuse is a common term in the present day society. Debates about how to define elderly abuse and which types of behaviour to include in the definition significantly inhibited progress during the early period of research on this topic (Lachs, 2015). Elderly abuse is an inclusive term which includes physical, sexual, mental and neglect facets of abuse. The term elderly abuse appeared for the first time in the year of 1970s (Wolfe, 2003). After a series of discussion five forms of abuse were classified in elderly abuse. This includes physical abuse, psychological abuse, sexual abuse, financial abuse as well as neglect (Lachs, 2015).

Physical abuse refers to the form of abuse where acts are carried out with an intention to cause physical pain or assault. Sexual abuse describes a non-consensual sexual act which may or may not cause physical injury. Mental or psychological abuse refers to that abuse which may often termed as emotional torture. It may often involve verbal abuse or emotional pain or injury. Financial abuse refers to the form of abuse where the elderly are financially exploited, or their property and money are misappropriated. Neglect wherein if an elderly person's needs are continually neglected, or they are often ostracized mentally.

Types of Abuse

Abuse in any form has a terrible consequence on the individual as well as the society as a whole. In the case of the elderly, the situation is genuinely gloomy. Due to their physical incompatibilities in most of the cases, they are helpless and often treated as unwanted liabilities. In fact, this approach of the family members, as well as the society towards the elderly, is one of the specific reason behind the elderly abuse.

Physical abuse refers to that type of abuse where physical pain or injury is inflicted on the elderly population. It often includes assault, battering, caning. There are various indicators of physical abuse, this may include fractures, sprains, burns from cigarettes, hot water, internal injuries, bruises, hair loss. All these indicators exhibit the helplessness and vulnerability of the elderly population. Physical abuse among the elderly is gradually turning into the common issue as well as it is increasing in every country (WHO, 2016). In India physical abuse is a common phenomenon, often we hear various instances of physical pain meted to the aged people. According to the HelpAge India Report (2012), cases of physical abuse are gradually increasing in the country along with verbal abuse and neglect. Physical injury to the elderly is often caused by the perpetrator's lack of patience to deal with the elderly which increases tenfold if the elderly are physically or mentally disabled (Govil and Gupta, 2016). At the same time, the perpetrator's greed for property and assets often acts as a cause of physical exploitation of the elderly.

Sexual abuse is often meted out to the elderly which is often classified under the broader notion of physical abuse. Sexual abuse is an unwanted sexual activity where the victim is sexually exploited often followed by physical and mental injury. It may often include sexual encounter without the consent of the victim. Elderly are often sexually abused. The HelpAge India, 2014 reports that 3.01 per cent of the elderly in India is subjected to sexual exploitation. Although this form of abuse has a low percentage in the country, it still exists and the elderly population is easy targets because of their helplessness.

Verbal or psychological abuse is one of the most common forms of abuse. It is the most commonly reported abuse faced by the elderly from lower socio-economic strata (HelpAge India, 2012). Herein the perpetrators often provide emotional pain or stress on elderly victims. It often involves the infliction of anguish, pain, or distress through verbal or non-verbal acts. The elderly population is subjected to degradation of mental well-being. Often, various mental illnesses are a consequence of this form of abuse. It is the systematic perpetration of malicious and explicit non-physical acts against an elder. Examples include harassment, scolding, insults, denigration and stalking. Perpetrators of psychological abuse against older adults often take advantage of elders' vulnerability in ways that control or humiliate. Verbal abuse is such a common reality that often the perpetrators do not realize their mistake.

Neglect is another form of abuse where the caregiver does not provide the elderly person with basic necessities. Neglect is regarded to be a classification of abuse, since it may often be an intentional act, the caregiver intentionally hurt the helpless elderly person by not providing him with essential amenities. Examples of intentional neglect as a form of abuse can be cited, when an older person is abandoned, not provided with adequate food, clothing, shelter, medical attention or dental care. Neglect may be the improper use of medication, poor hygiene or personal care or the refusal to allow other people to provide adequate care. Neglect is a growing form of abuse since with the change in social values structure goes through a rapid transformation. As a result of this, elderly people are often acknowledged as an unwanted liability and often kept in isolation or treated as a burden. As a result of this neglect the consequent phenomenon which may first start as a non-intentional affair may gradually turn into an intentional affair.

Financial abuse is another form of elderly abuse. It spans a broad spectrum of conduct which includes the following cases when other people whom the individual trusts misappropriate an individual's savings, valuables or property. It may often involve forced changes of will or power of attorney in favour of the perpetrator. In this form of abuse, it is often seen that the elderly individual's signature is often forged to confiscate his/her assets. It is quite evident that most of the people save for their future, in other words, it can be stated that they save for their grey times when they are unable to earn. Health is a significant concern for the elderly and it is this sector where most of the elderly are compelled to spend. In India, provision of better medical facilities incurs huge amount of money. Hence, savings or financial security becomes essential. Elderly are the easiest targets for financial abuse. One of the obvious reasons behind this involves the dependency of the elderly population on others, for their various needs. Financial exploitation of the elderly population, go beyond physical injuries or scars, resulting in devastating effects, where the elderly are snatched of their lifelong savings and assets which were necessary for their survival in this period.

Perpetrators of Abuse

Abuse is a common term and the elderly are often subjected to various forms of abuse, as mentioned earlier. Usually, abuse in any form occurs within the four walls. In most of the cases, family members including their sons, daughter-in-laws, daughter, son-in-law or often other family members are involved. Beyond the family, caregivers who are supposed to take care of the elderly, abuse them. Abuse in any form is mostly targeted to those elderly who are physically or mentally disabled and often needs the help and care of their family member. Elderly who are physically and mentally disabled face the problem of helplessness and isolation. Verbal abuse or psychological abuse is the most common form of abuse followed by mental abuse wherein their present state is often mocked. With respect to perpetrator statistics, it has been stated that, nationally, the daughter-in-law is reported by 61 per cent as the main perpetrator of abuse and very closely followed by son, i.e. 59 per cent. Among these, 7 per cent elderly abused people reported daughter as the abuser, 6 per cent reported son-in-law, 3 per cent reported relative as the abuser and 3 per cent reported caregiver/servants (Govil and Gupta, 2016). In the present day urban society, we see that most of the families comprise of dual-earning households where both the husband and wife work, with their elderly parents at the mercy of caregivers and help. Often, it is seen that these caregivers play the role of perpetrator often resorting to various forms of abuse.

Reasons for Abuse

Abuse in any form is dangerous and often leads to death in case of elderly. There are various reasons of abuse meted out to the elderly. According to the recent statistics, India displays a gradual rise of the elderly population along with the increase of elderly abuse rates (HelpAge India, 2014). Some reasons can be cited for abuse against the elderly.

One of the significant reasons involves the gradual transformation of value patterns followed by changes in individual's perception towards the elderly. The consumerist society of today's century estimates an individual's utility and as a result elderly population is often ignored or maltreated (Soneja, 2001).

Lack of adjustment often plays an essential reason behind the elderly abuse. It is often seen that the new generation which includes sons, daughters, son-in-law and daughter-in-law, as well as grandchildren, cannot adjust with the elderly and often this leads to intolerance followed by elder abuse within the domestic setting which is supposed to be the abode of security for the aged.

Physical disability, as well as mental impairment, is quite a common issue for the elderly population. It is often observed that the helpless elderly population are often abused by their family members and their caregivers who are hired to serve them with care and patience. Herein, it is important to mention that the elderly are often believed to be the unwanted liability, wherein their physical or mental disability is often believed to bring economic burden. Thus elderly population faces abuse, which, in maximum cases, involves neglect and verbal abuse.

Elderly abuse is often a consequence of property and inheritance disputes. According to the HelpAge India Report, near about 35 per cent of the elderly face abuse because of property disputes. It was also observed that this type of abuse happens mostly in urban areas among the rich and to an extent the middle classes but much less in rural areas. Herein, it can be remarked that rural areas often try to preserve traditional value structure which includes respect for the elderly population. In fact, these areas are characterized by community living and collective conscience to some extent, hence the value of gerontocracy is dominant.

There are various reasons for elderly abuse, as mentioned earlier. However, the dominant context in which abuse against elderly can be seen includes the mindset of individuals who are gradually turning individualistic as well as mechanical where greed, profit as well as intolerance works out. Hence, elderly abuse is becoming dominant day by day and unfortunately, they are often not reported which in other sense encouraged the perpetrator to opt for severe acts of abuse.

Laws and Programmes for Elderly

As mentioned earlier, senior citizens in the country are subjected to abuse and are considered as easy targets. Thus they are often believed to be the vulnerable population who are at risk even in their domestic spheres, which includes their family. At the same time due to their dependency on various things they are often exploited which results in bringing devastating effects on the elderly population. In this regard, the legal, political infrastructure of the country has introduced various policies and programmes to safeguard the elderly populace's interest.

Legal Rights

Elderly security and vulnerability have been a matter of concern since age-old times henceforth, legal provisions were made as well as implemented for safeguarding them. The first legal provision in this regard is:

Hindu Adoption and Maintenance Act, 1956

According to this Act, children and heirs of the elderly are to provide for their dependent elderly parents' maintenance, which includes their food, clothing as well as shelter. The act suggested that it is the children's dutiful obligation to serve their parent who is helpless, dependent or mentally infirm.

Maintenance and Welfare of Parents and Senior Citizens Act, 2007

In the year of 2007, the Government of India launched the Maintenance and Welfare of Parents and Senior Citizens Act, 2007. It was enacted in December 2007. According to this act, children and heirs of the elderly are legally obligated to provide maintenance to senior citizens, which mean that they are responsible for providing food, clothing, shelter, medical attendance as well as treatment to the aged parents. At the same time, Senior citizens who are unable to maintain themselves shall have the right to apply to a maintenance tribunal seeking a monthly allowance from their children or heirs. In this regard, it is essential to know that children who have been adopted are also liable to look after their parents and even providing them with a monthly allowance. The Act has also directed that relatives who are in possession of the wealth of the particular elderly, are also obliged to take care of them.

The Act has also directed the state government to establish old-age homes in places which are accessible and to look after its infrastructural facilities and overall quality. Herein the State Government should also look into the medical facilities as well as entertainment of the inmates. The states governments are further directed to ensure their partially or fully funded treatment at government hospitals.

This Act had also mentioned that the State machinery must make the elderly aware of the benefits which this act provides. In this regard, media can be used as a significant tool. Herein, it can be aptly remarked that most of the elderly population are not aware of policies of the government which may be an essential benchmark to improve their position as well secure them from various forms of exploitation. The act had also stated that those children/heirs/relatives are not fulfilling their legal obligations to maintaining the elderly, can be punished and can be sentenced to imprisonment.

In this context, the Indian government adopted various policies and programmes as a mode to safeguard senior citizens of the country. The Government of India announced the National Policy on Older Persons in the year 1999. It was a step in the right direction in pursuance of the UN General Assembly Resolution to observe 1999 as International Year of Older Persons and in keeping with the assurances to older persons contained in the Constitution. The policy has following provisions:

1. Setting up a pension fund for ensuring security for those persons who have been serving in the unorganized sector.
2. Construction of old-age homes and day care centres for all 34 districts.
3. Establishing resource centres and re-employment bureaus for people above 60 years.
4. Concessional rail/airfares for travel within and between cities, i.e. 30 per cent discount in train and 50 per cent in Indian Airlines.
5. Enacting legislation for ensuring necessary geriatric care in all the public hospitals.

Economic Securities

Economic independence is of primary importance for the elderly. Access to a better health facility as well as their well-being depends on economic securities. The Government of India has launched a series of programmes in this regard:

Indira Gandhi National Old Age Pension Scheme (IGNOAPS)

Indira Gandhi National Old Age Pension Scheme (IGNOAPS) is a part of the greater programme of Government of India named National Social Assistance Programme (NSAP) which was launched on 15 August 1995. The latter was introduced to ensure a minimum national standard for social assistance in addition to the benefits that states are currently providing or might provide in future. It comprises of Indira Gandhi National Old Age Pension Scheme (IGNOAPS), Indira Gandhi National Widow Pension Scheme (IGNWPS), Indira Gandhi National Disability Pension Scheme (IGNDPS), National Family Benefit Scheme (NFBS) and Annapurna.

IGNOAPS was introduced with the objective of economic assistance to needy elderly people. It is an old age non-contributory pension scheme which covers Indian Citizens who are 60 years and above and who are below the poverty line. According to this scheme, all the beneficiaries will get ₹ 200 per month from the central government and the state government will also assist as desired. The number of beneficiaries is increasing day by day. In 2012–13, the number of beneficiaries reported under NOAPS/IGNOAPS was 2,27,12,043 in 2012–13. It increased by 13,27,639 as compared to 2011–12. In percentage terms, the growth was 6.21 per cent during the period. The number of beneficiaries reported under NOAPS/IGNOAPS was 2,23,31,089 in 2013–14. It decreased by –3,80,954 as compared to 2012–13 (Government of India, 2013–14).

National Pension System

Retirement plan ensures that people live with pride and without compromising on their standard of living during advancing years. Pension scheme gives an opportunity to invest and accumulate savings and get lump sum amount as regular income through annuity plan on retirement. National Pension System aims at the provision of financial security and stability to people, during old age when people do not have a regular source of income.

The Government of India established the Pension Fund Regulatory and Development Authority (PFRDA) on 23 August 2003. PFRDA is authorized by the Ministry of Finance, Department of Financial Services. It is an autonomous body set up by the Government of India to develop and regulate the pension market in India. PFRDA promotes old-age income security by establishing, developing and regulating pension funds and protects the interests of subscribers to schemes of pension funds and related matters.

The National Pension System (NPS) was launched on 1 January 2004 with the objective of providing retirement income to all the citizens. NPS aims to institute pension reforms and to inculcate the habit of saving for retirement amongst the citizens. It focuses on extending old-age security coverage to all citizens. The Government of India adopted National Pension System (NPS) based on defined contributions in respect of all new entrants to Central Government services, excepting the Armed Forces, with effect from 1 January 2004. Most of the State Governments have since notified a similar pension system for their new entrants.

It is a flexible and simple and regulated scheme. It offers a range of investment options to the subscriber and personal fund manager. The subscriber can switch from one to the other option subject to general regulatory norms. The subscriber can open an account with NPS which provides a unique Permanent Retirement Account Number (PRAN). It provides seamless portability across jobs and locations. The scheme is structured into two Tier I: permanent non-withdrawal account and Tier II: Voluntary withdrawal account for using funds and when needed. At the time of exit from NPS, the subscribers may use the pension wealth to purchase a life annuity from a PFRDA empanelled life insurance company apart from withdrawing a part of the accumulated pension weather as lump-sum.

Atal Pension Yojana Scheme

The Indian government is concentrating on old age issues. As a result of this, it has introduced this scheme as a part of a universal social security scheme in pension and insurance policies. In 2015–16, the government introduced the Atal Pension Yojana (APY) for people working in unorganized sector. According to this scheme, the government will provide a definite amount of pension based on the beneficiaries' contribution for a particular period. This scheme is liable for every citizen of the country who voluntarily joins the Nation Pension System, which is administered by the

Pension Fund Regulatory and Development Authority (PFRDA). Under the APY, the subscribers would receive the fixed minimum pension of ₹ 1,000 per month, ₹ 2,000 per month, ₹ 3,000 per month, ₹ 4,000 per month, ₹ 5,000 per month, at the age of 60 years, depending on their contributions, which itself would be based on the age of joining the APY. The minimum age of joining APY is 18 years and the maximum age is 40 years. Therefore, the minimum period of contribution by any subscriber under APY would be 20 years or more. The government would guarantee the benefit of a fixed minimum pension. The APY is viable from 1 June 2015.

This scheme is open for all Indian citizens who are bank account holder and have exceeded 18 years of age. Individuals are liable to get a fixed amount of pension ranging from ₹ 1,000 to ₹ 5,000 depending on their contribution between 18 and 40 years of age. This scheme aims to provide economic securities to that Indian citizen who is in unorganized sector and does not enjoy retirement benefits. As a result, this scheme will focus on providing economic security to all individuals of unorganized sector.

Health Securities

For every elderly, health is a major concern. Physical and mental well-being is important for survival and needs attention. It is this sector which involves much expenditure, in the case of the elderly. As a result of this, the Government of India has introduced a series of policies in this regard.

Rashtriya Swasthya Bima Yojana

The Government of India introduced this scheme with the sole aim of providing social security and health care assurance for all. This scheme was introduced and implemented on 1 April 2008. Ministry of Labour and Employment has launched RSBY, Government of India to provide health insurance coverage for Below Poverty Line (BPL) families, but later on, it has extended its beneficiary classification to include individuals from an unorganized sector.

RSBY has two-fold objectives:

1. To provide financial protection against disastrous health costs.
2. To improve access to quality health care for below poverty line households of pocket expenditure for hospitalization and other vulnerable groups in the unorganized sector.

RSBY provides insurance coverage to its beneficiaries. Under the scheme the beneficiaries are eligible for health care insurance benefits designed by respective state governments. The beneficiaries under RSBY are entitled to hospitalization coverage up to ₹ 30,000 per annum on family floater basis, for most of the diseases that require hospitalization.

Varishtha Mediclaim for Senior Citizens

This policy caters to the need of senior citizens providing them with health care benefits. Its section I covers hospitalization and domiciliary hospitalization expenses and expenses for treatment of critical illnesses if opted for, section II diseases covered under critical illnesses areas under coronary artery surgery, cancer, renal failure, stroke, multiple sclerosis, major organ transplants, paralysis and blindness at an extra premium.

Critical illness cover is an optional cover under the policy. persons who will not opt for critical illness cover are entitled to hospitalization and domiciliary hospitalization expenses cover for those diseases categorized above as critical illness but up to the limit of sum insured under Section I, i.e. under hospitalization and domiciliary hospitalization expenses and the claim for those diseases will be paid on reimbursement basis or as cashless hospitalization. A person opting for critical illness cover may opt for claim either under section I or section II (if not hospitalized) or under both sections for those diseases categorized above as critical illnesses but claim under section I will be paid either on a reimbursement basis or as cashless hospitalization if it is otherwise admissible. If in any policy year a critical illness is diagnosed and claim paid after that, in subsequent renewals the person may avail cover both under section I and II but with the exclusion, both under section I and II, of that particular critical illness which has been diagnosed and claims paid in the preceding policy year.

Under the scheme sum insured is fixed per person. Under hospitalization and domiciliary hospitalization cover sum insured is ₹ 1,00,000 and under critical illness cover sum insured is ₹ 2,00,000. For fresh entry into the scheme, the age limit is 60 years to 80 years. However, for renewal, the age limit will be extended up to 90 years in which case the premium of 76 years to 80 years age band will be loaded by 10 per cent up to 85 years and 20 per cent up to 90 years of age. No medical check up is required if the insured was covered under any health insurance policy of national insurance company or other insurance companies uninterruptedly for the preceding three years.

Other Insurances

Various other insurances are also available to the elderly for their better future. Various private sector organizations are coming forward in provisioning health insurance benefits to the elderly. This includes the following:

1. HOPE – Health of Privileged Elder
2. Jan Arogya Bima Policy
3. LIC Jeevan Akshay
4. ICICI Lombard Overseas Travel Insurance
5. Aviva New Pension Elite
6. New Jeevan Dhara-I

Conclusion

The issues related to elderly is a serious concern in our country. Despite various policies and programmes, discrimination as well as abuse against elderly is a universal reality. Hence, there is a need to move beyond application, policies and programmes. Thus, the rationale of the society needs to change thoroughly wherein every person irrespective of their age should be treated with compassion and care. At the same time, age should be analysed not only in physical terms but should be measured holistically. Active elderly groups can be organized, or they may be given an opportunity to get engaged as per their terms. Finally, family members should be tolerant enough as ageing is an unavoidable reality, which everyone reaching old age has to confront and survive.

4

Elderly Diaries

The present book attempts to explore the plight of elderly population belonging to lower socio-economic background. In this regard a slum of Beleghata area of Kolkata has been chosen as the field. The basic idea is to describe, delve and explore the elderly interactions, aspirations, perceptions towards their age, life, family and the society as a whole. In this regard, we have been fortunate in getting our respondents who have believed in us and shared their thoughts. The field taken for research

A view of the field (Slum in Beleghata Area of Kolkata)

purpose is the 'Beleghata Slum' which was both a response to the increasing intolerance towards the elderly and an exploration of their despicable living conditions despite governmental measures and effort. Even after such relentless efforts made to mitigate the sufferings of old, execrable conditions prevailed. Our study attempts to depict the picture of rising deplorable situation of the aged people, who have to live under the mercy of their children and strive under acute poverty in unimaginable and difficult conditions and inconceivable social circumstances. We were initially at a fix and could not decide what could be the best way to understand their position in society. We wanted to take a perspective from a disadvantageous point of view, yet in a region where:

1. Government facilities were expected to benefit the elderly.
2. Different policies were considered essential to find an amicable solution to these distressful conditions.

Such a context was imperative to the study because this would help understand the situation better in how far these steps could make a difference in the lives of these people. It was not that easy to get a grasp on the idea at such a quick pace of time. It took days for us to finally decide upon the best possible place. This brought us to Beleghata Slum. We could contact a lady, Supriya Devi, who was the resident of this slum who assured us to get all sorts of help. Finally, our journey started through the mundane and dark alleys. It took some time to reach the spot; we were extremely intimidated regarding the whole research plan in the slum. The houses were in tatters and in tremendous unhygienic condition. However, our discomforts were eased off by Supriya Devi, the lady who was supposed to guide us through this entire journey. Admittedly, before the work began several warnings were given from people regarding the shabbiness of the slum, the uneasiness of the people out there, their unwillingness to comply, the darkness and gloominess of slum life and about the poisonous insects. However, we went there with open minds believing to capture the entire picture of the people living there. The first house where our quest started was a wide one, with sun rays hiding the darkness and lightening up every nook and cranny. We thought we would stay, learn, ask and analyse, but situation was not that easy, as initially our intentions were suspected by some. They believed us to be members of some organizations who have come with some hidden agendas and vested interests or desire, probably trying to uproot them from their households. However, quite soon their fears could be put to rest. So we sat in the room, a bit uncomfortably, waiting to strike the conversation and break the ice. Initially, we started interacting with the old ladies, who were sitting together and tittle-tattling about different ladies of the slum. However, it was a vast slum area where people believed the entirety to be a 'samsar' and their own house to be the samsars for the respective families. However, the word may imply only people in commonsensical term, conflicting with the real meaning of 'samsar' that they have attributed to. For them, 'samsar' is more than this. It included the material objects as well – the utensils, the deities, the beddings, the rooms, the room spaces, the showpieces, etc. These are the bindings without which they felt non-existent (Lamb, 2000). The people always expressed how much importance each item in their households carry for them and how they have developed a 'maya' towards them. They repeatedly mentioned that despite several hard times, they survive because of 'samsar ek maya' (attachment of the family). As found in Mangaldihi by Sarah Lamb (2000), the same connection between 'maya' bindings and that of the world could be observed in Beleghata as well. What seemed trivial otherwise, mattered to elderly, the most. Hence, we see that despite being old and believing that their 'end' is near, they could not relinquish their desires of 'samsar' and 'maya'.

Defining Old Age

> 'For age is opportunity no less than youth itself, though in another dress and as the evening twilight fades away the sky is filled with stars, invisible by day'.
>
> —Henry Wadsworth Longfellow

A person reaches maximum capacity once he reaches middle age, but after this optimum utilization of his own abilities and strength, these very faculties start to deteriorate (Desai and Naik, 1973). Ageing however, can be interpreted from different perspectives – sociological, biological and psychological.

Sociologically, ageing is the process by which the biological, social and psychological aspects combine and affect a person (Atchley, 2000). Similarly, other disciplines have different ways to define ageing. It might also mean the age which is close to or crosses the average age of individuals. Old age is contextual hence cannot be limited to a particular definition. The reason behind this is the fact that the meaning that is given to it varies from one society to the other. The advent of old age comes with certain change that takes place in one's participation in social roles and engagement in various activities. With old age, regenerative abilities decline which signals that one has become more susceptible to diseases and can have sickness more easily than any other adult. The study which deals with studying this old age process is called gerontology and the study of diseases affecting the elderly is known as geriatrics.

The western standpoint on old age states that it is a period filled with many negative experiences that one is bound to face in society. Some of the problems faced by elderly includes social isolation, senility, abuse of all sorts and vulnerability to diseases (Cumming and Henry, 1961). All cultures do not share this view. For example in Buddhist culture, old age is viewed with much optimism and is considered to be an age of maturity, where one attains wisdom and achieves stability socially as well as economically and also is satisfied emotionally. It is believed that with further ageing, an elderly person reaches spiritual salvation according to Buddhist culture (Ramamurti and Jamuna, 1992). There are many studies conducted and vast amount of literature is written on this issue which helps us to come to a concrete definition of old age. Chronological age as the basis of defining age is one of the most common approaches taken by people as a result of the socialization process. It gets more obvious with the emphasis the society gives on age, as an indicator, of how the different events that take place in life. However, age as such does not reveal much about a person and stands just as another marker of identity. Age therefore, becomes an indicator of the number of years a person has lived. An 18-year-old person might be entitled to vote in a country as in the concerned region a person is expected to attain political maturity by this age, though this hardly says anything about the actual level of maturity of the voter. While considering the age of retirement, a similar point of view can be extended, where the retirement age does not define the character, health and capability of the person who becomes eligible for a pension. In fact, it merely reflects the society's concern towards its people in believing a certain age to be old enough to get pension benefits. In some nations identifying people with age is not taken as a parameter in describing its people which showed that how people from Rural Hereo or Bantu pastoral societies were ignorant of age factor as a category to relate to its people (Harper, 2006).

There is no fixed activity which is stereotypically suitable or not meant for aged people, as they can do whatever they want to do at the age of 50 and continue doing that even 20 years later. Sometimes, participation in activities by old people gets restricted because of failing health, which can have a connection with increasing age, but that should not limit us into demarcating activities concerning age (Keith et al., 1994). Ageing is considered 'a process and not as a fixed point in life' (Pillai, 1987). The process of ageing is social and not biological. The major life events might not always be the real marker of age. Getting married or giving birth to a child or even having grandchildren has got nothing to do with age, but undoubtedly are part of the ageing process. Such life events undermine the crucial points for defining age. A girl is considered a woman when she gets married instead of when she, attains her puberty level. Similarly, a woman becomes old when her child ties the knot and not when she had her menopause (Rasmussen, 1997). There are culturally constructed groupings of age that people attain one after the other in the form of life stages since childhood till adulthood. Chronological age is not essential here to mark these transitions because age cannot determine the entry of people into these stages in life. Age groups and the respective chronological age attached to it varies depending on the age which connects the two. The young would consider delaying their entry into the old age classification (Giles and Reid, 2005).

Gerontology is a subject which has gained momentum in the last few years. What made it gain so much popularity is an indication to the fact that the population is ageing rapidly and that longevity has increased over the years with life expectancy touching 75 years for Western countries, with its Eastern counterpart following a similar trend. Gradually, the world is turning into a world of the old. It is expected that by 2030, Western Europe will have a population which will be half filled by people aged 50 and above and one fourth will be aged 65 years and above and about 15 per cent will be over 75 years of age (Harper, 2006). The situation in the developing countries is such that there is a vast population base and therefore, although the number of old people does not seem to be too high, it is greater than before.

As a result of modernization, globalization and urbanization, there has been a shift in the demography of the developing countries where modern family systems have replaced the traditional family structure often leading to poor social conditions. Increase in absolute as well as the relative number of elderly has caused an upward trend in fertility and a downward trend in mortality (Chakraborty, 2009). The question is whether ageing has been redefined in the twentieth century or not, or what has changed about old age. As we know, age is a necessary information required by today's bureaucratic arrangement and in a way to stratify society and this in turn, leads to age-based stratification in the society.

Various countries fix eligibility to claim a pension, but this age keeps varying at different points of time (Cooter and Pickstone, 2003). Ageing is inescapable and it is an inevitable truth of life. In the book *Unknown Women*, Ranjana Ray and others found that even in tribal societies, primarily the Santals have maintained their traditional roots of family structure and are still respectful towards the elderly. However, the effects of migration from rural to urban areas because of the various developments as mentioned above is ruining the economic position, the socio-psychological situation of the old people, creating trouble for their physical well-being and overall health. If we go by demography, then age group 60–65 indicates an entry to the old age group. Looking back at the 1950s, we will find that only 8 per cent people belonged to age group 60. The stereotypical images that define old age with grey hair, bent backbone and frailness can happen irrespective of age. However, Harper (2006) contested this view. He believed that although by appearance one might look aged much before their 60s or 70s, the old age acceptability will officially remain intact as defined by law, which means one has to quit getting involved into public domains for shouldering responsibilities.

Before further discussion on old age, we need to have an elementary understanding by what is meant by the term. Is it determined by the number, or it has got something more to it? Public perception of old age is that it is biological, which means biologically ageing is a natural process.

However, to understand old age a multifaceted approach is required. First, we should see how modernization was considered to have affected old age. One point of view is, old people could not draw any benefit from it and suffered from its advent. While the second view was seen to be more positive with its reforms bringing about some constructive changes for the old people with its social and political aspects and also intergenerational movements, varying from one society to the other (Harper, 2006). Like Mindy Greenstein and Jimmie Holland (2014) said, that some old people are hardly acquainted with their age.

Age can often mean 'slowing down', owing to the risks involved during old age. According to certain views, old age is the phase where people should be more apprehensive about whether to get involved in a particular work or not. For some old age means just being older than their age (Victor et al., 2009). Ageing can also mean the phase of life where the immunity power deteriorates so severely that people get affected by diseases very quickly until they succumb to death. Sickness is the only thing that makes the difference between the young and the old and except it, nothing varies in these two age groups. Contrary to this, sickness is not the only aspect that constitutes ageing, as it does not take into consideration the changes brought about mentally and physically. The athletes who retire by the time they are in their late twenties or thirties are no longer capable of using their reflex fast enough and are not able to run good enough to contribute to the concerned game. Whatever be the reason, they are not sick and yet are considered old to continue the game (Posner, 1997). In the military, the age of retirement was 50 years, because in case of soldiers their physical power was thought to be insufficient right after this age to carry out their service. Women were considered to have reached old age with menopause at the age varying in between 40–50 (Cokayne, 2013).

'Bodily decline' is also defined as ageing. The proximity to death, the issues of adapting to changes taking place around a person, the feeling of monotony as one remains in a particular job for long years are also the markers of old age. Somatic alterations can be a consequence of ageing but not necessarily a part of these age-related changes. The bodily declines involving one's physical well-being include the issues with reflex actions, energy, vision, hair colour, stamina, potency, immune system, etc. The declines involving the mental aspects are problems in solving puzzle and deterioration in other analytical abilities, unwillingness to adjust to changes and think over the old ideas, lack of physical courage, issues with sexual desires amongst others. Although with an increase in age, one becomes vulnerable to diseases and its connection to ageing may very well be separately analysed, the increase in susceptibility must be paid importance. With age, one becomes more prone to get affected by diseases and hence the need to finance these health issues becomes a requirement even if ageing does not happen like a usual process. To conclude that every person would age means that there is a difference in capability of the young and the old, where the old is deemed to be less able than the young. Ageing is not age specific, as it happens at different rates in different people (Posner, 1997). In the initial years of 21st century, in the United States, old age for women was considered to be 60 and for men, it was 65 (Cokayne, 2013). It varies, between 60 and 65 years old from a demographic point of view (Harper, 2006). In 1990, it was expected by United Nations that in India by 2025, 14.1 per cent of the population would constitute the elderly.

Our respondents in interacting mood!

However, in our current study, ageing for people in Beleghata Slum was not dependent on their chronological age. Many of them were not even aware of their age and they considered knowledge about age as possession of 'symbolic capital' (Bourdieu, 1986) in contrast to the big people living in the cities who are able enough to keep track of the number of years lived. A similar finding was found by Sarah Lamb (2000) in her work in Magaldihi. Beleghata people mostly calculated their age by their physical condition as was stated by Saxon and others who claimed that older people become more vulnerable to any disease when compared to young ones because of undergoing through some physical changes (Saxon et al., 2009). Old age gives rise to memory loss, decreased level of reasoning, not so active taste buds, problems in digestion, changes in hearing capacity and eyesight ability, amongst others (Radomski and Trombly Latham, 2008). The elderly populace of Beleghata felt that their physical weakness is directly proportional to the feeling of being aged. For some of them, son's marriage was an indication of stepping into old age. Some of them expressed their age in this way.

> *'koto r bayas hobe. Chele meyer biye r bacchakaccha hoe geche. Dhore nao ei shottor ashi hobe'.*
>
> ('How much will my age be. My children got married and had children. So you can consider my age to be around 70–80 years').

With old age which has been defined in these terms also for them was the time of comfort. The elderly irrespective of their genders felt that advent of old age meant that they should now rest for they have worked enough for their families and now their children and their partners should take care of their parents. The old people here wear white saris when they know that they have grown old with their eyes becoming weak, bodies becoming dry, legs becoming heavy and painful and hair turning white, face becoming fragile and wrinkled. They felt that they grow old mentally as well when their interest to carry out household activities or even activities outside home gets diminished as they no longer desire to engage in any work. I asked a lady that what does she do daily, to which she replied, *'Kichuina. Boshe thaki. R parina. Lokjon ashle kotha boli. Pa e betha, chokhe dekhina'* (I do nothing. I sit back. I can't do anything. If people come I chat with them. I have pain in my leg and can't see properly). I asked her age and she said, janina. *'Koto r hobe. Shat ki poeshotti. Dekhei bujhe nao'* (I do not know. How much will it be? Maybe 60–65. Look at me, you will understand). Another lady was there who seemed to be in her 50s, quite fit apparently told us her age to be 65. She said she is no longer willing to do anything as she ages – *'boyesh hoe geche. R icchai korena'* ('I have grown old. Nothing interests me').

Children are an integral part of their lives and ageing has got a profound connection with what they understand about getting old. For many of them, with old age, the behaviour of people change and old people are considered burden by the very close ones, primarily by one's children. It is then, one is supposed to understand that old age has arrived. It is at this juncture, the person is expected to realize that he/she has entered into old age.

While I was talking to the elderly people there, I realized that many of them are victims of separation where their sons have settled elsewhere leaving them in poor conditions as old age is perceived to be a burden by most of them in every respect with economic burden considered as the prime cause of such indifference. However, old age was not correctly calculated by most of the respondents who feared about the negative consequences of approaching old age. There is an existence of values in today's society which points out at the importance of taking care of the elderly as they need and deserve support, attention, counsel and honour. However, if we look at how far these values are respected and implemented in reality, then we would find how in practice it is ignored and neglected.

Various considerations like economic (elderly people for the loss of work are not able to contribute like before and this becomes more problematic with their increasing needs. It puts pressure on modern societies which are lacking in medical aids), health (old people have pressing issues related to their health) and social (sometimes problems are that elderly are separated from their close ones and are considered to be dependent on them). All this created a cultural gap between children and their elderly parents. Thus, this has made the situation quite tricky leading the old to be considered a burden on society (Steinberg and Rosner, 2003). We had a discussion in this area which lasted for couple of hours, gathering both the young and the old. The entire debate was about what does the young generation – the married and the unmarried couple – thinks about the old and how do they think they would take care of their parents and in-laws. The responses were unambiguous regarding the responsibility of children to take the responsibility of their parents no matter how ill or how aged they are. In the same discussion, the old women implicitly complained that some children have left their parents in the most needed hours of life and have even thrown them out. The ladies who have faced such humiliating situations were not much old and also were physically capable according to the residents. However, for most of them the very fact that they are in-laws and therefore 'old', creates such fears among the young that they feel getting rid of this responsibility right at the beginning would help them lead a peaceful life without much burden.

Old Age and Body

Ageing is often related to changes in physical appearances of a person which is unattractive and unacceptable in society drawing negative and prejudiced attention from people. On the other hand, a young, toned, fit body is considered to have more social value in a consumer society. The image of youthfulness is so significant to people that they are often led to buying make up and personal care that promises to have anti ageing benefits, which offer them the hope of not getting old, thus commodifying body more than ever. It is especially true in case of women whose value depends upon their physical appearance. Therefore unlike men, they are more inclined to retain back their youth as they do not wish to perceive as devalued, because of decline in the youthfulness of their selves. Dressing is a significant way of portraying selves to others and it is done in a socially approved manner. There is an 'age ordered' sartorial style, which means that particular clothes are considered appropriate for aged people which is often an informal way of policing that controls the styling, especially of elderly women. An aged woman would not be expected to wear something very much 'flamboyant', as it goes against the societal expectations and their dressing in society is acceptable if it is less loud and toned down (Twigg, 2007). They are expected to wear clothes that are toned down and not 'loud' as markers of age appropriate clothing.

In Beleghata slum, the old women irrespective of whether they were aware of their age or whether they were widowed or not, wore white saris. Men who were aged wore light coloured clothes. A lady in this slum had done a tattoo in her hand. We could see that she was treated like someone who is not mentally fit. Some commented that she is '*matal*' (drunk), some said she is '*pagol*' (mad), some even tagged her as '*shoetan*' (Satan). They gave derisive laugh and passed improper comments while passing by. She had a liquor business when she was young and a police raid took place for which she had to give up the same. Many years have passed since then, but such negative tagging has continued. We asked some of the dwellers there that what are the reasons behind calling her such names. The replies were of the same logic, i.e. she is very weird and is insane for she is different and does not behave normally with that tattoo in her hand and with such an awful past. I was asked not to approach her as she was supposedly always out of her senses. While I was questioning her, I realized that only half the story was true. The lady used to help her husband to carry out the business and with his death she continued it to sustain her family. She even built a two-storied house with her hard earned money, but had to quit the business after a police raid as mentioned by her neighbours. The tattoo which she had on her hand was of a God of whom she is a great devotee. Although, she wears white sari which was expected by her society, her connection with liquor and tattooing was sufficient enough to make her an object of ridicule. In a research done by Holland (2004) women who are old and have followed an alternative style like tattooing, piercing, etc. have attracted apprehension from people for trying to look young during this old phase when they are supposed to age gracefully. Hair dye, surgical methods like facelifts or even plastic surgeries can help delay ageing, which is ultimately unavoidable (Cavanaugh and Fields, 2002). In Beleghata also there were 3–4 aged women who could afford dyes in order to hide their grey hair. While I was talking to them I realized how this is not acceptable by her family members and neighbours. According to them she must not hide something which has come to her because of her age. They felt, trying to look young was unnecessary and unacceptable. She was even questioned on her intent that why does she want to look young and for whom? This lady has lost her husband many years back and so her desire to look nice was looked with doubts. For her she likes dyeing her hair, as it makes her feel good. She lives with her daughter and her daughter supports her and dyes her hair every month. However, her son and daughter-in-law are firmly against it along with the neighbours. They said, 'This is pure wastage of money. There is no need to dye your hair and show to people that you are still young when you are not'. '*buro boyeshe joto bhimroti*' (she has lost all her rationalities in this old age), '*shing bhenge bachurer dole dhoka*' (mutton dressed as lamb) were some other comments that came out during this discussion. This was not the only case that we found where an elderly wants to avoid looking old. As we moved further in the village to talk to others, we found another house which was a concrete building, considered as one of the richest households in the area, to be facing the same kind of reaction from the slum dwellers. Having the desire to look good and having enough money to do that have often been regarded as socially objectionable and these people as social misfits. The widowed old lady who was in her 60s does not wear white sari as expected from a widow, does facial and hair threading almost regularly. Unlike the other houses, not a single neighbour entered this house and while we tried to go in, they seemed to be kind of upset.

During the discussion, we got to know from the lady that the neighbours do not like her as she is financially superior to most of them and could maintain a good life. She said that she had worked hard to lead this life after the death of her husband which was not easy as she got widowed at a very young age and never felt wearing a white sari was essential enough as this reminded her of her loss. Also, as she had enough economic resources, she could educate her grandchildren, which many other residents could not and hence they envied her.

Poverty is indeed not only a threat to minimize our life chances, but also ruins our interpersonal relationships with others. 'Poverty narrows and closes life chances. Victims of poverty experience a kind of arteriosclerosis of opportunity. Being poor not only means economic insecurity, but it also wreaks havoc on one's mental and physical health' (Ropers, 1991). People who are relatively richer will have better life-chances compared to the ones who are poor and therefore have difficulties in having access to the valuable resources like property, proper medical facilities, money, etc. in society. These resources are not distributed equally in society and therefore happen to be a scarcity, which gives rise to unequal life-chances (Kendall, 2015). According to Etzen and Zina (1989), 'life chances' means, 'the chances throughout one's life cycle to live and to experience the good things in life' (Etzen and Zina, 1989). Tumin (1973) said, life chances are for those people who are better off to afford them in the form of good education, better occupations, good health care facilities and all sorts of extraordinary comfort, which makes life easy, comfortable and long and healthy (Tumin, 1973). The concept of 'wealth' varies between societies according to what they believe to be the good things in life and possession of these good things or ability to meet the expense of such things. The access to these good things depends upon one's life chances, lifestyle and experiences (Miller, 1992). This lady for possessing wealth although was able to utilize the best of things was not accepted well by her society. Her stigma was a societal construction, which was a result of being positioned in a 'discredited' social status. Her not being able to abide by the 'normal' societal expectations was a reason for public discontentment, where her behaviour took shape through the internalization of stigma (Parker and Aggleton, 2003). Local social world of people determines one's moral standing and meeting of social norms and obligations determines one's moral status. Each local social world has different codes of behaviour and inability to meet the requirements would mean decaying of the most valued assets of life including social relationships. This lady as well, for failing to do as expected could not develop or maintain social relationships.

Stigma can be the consequence of deteriorating health conditions as well. Old age is time and again just another way to relate to sickness or disease. Although it is not necessary to become sick and dependent with advancement in age, this negative stereotype is sustained by a mere assumption to associate age and reinforce such notions based on bodily declines and not on one's actual age (Barry and Yuill, 2011).

Giddens (1991) found that when people identify their selves in modern society with their bodies and with old age, existential troubles arise as this is related to decay and eventually death. Modern ageing is about how to adjust to the body which has been subject to changes over time with age. Death is particularly difficult for those people who are concerned about their bodies and relate their self-identities to it. They put effort to manipulate and design their bodies in ways with a particular image in mind hiding all their problems and anxieties behind it through the control of their look, revealing just the positive emotions. As if only 'exterior territories of the body' matters – slim, youthful and sensuous (Featherstone, 1982). Nearing death makes them realize that these created bodies which they have valued so much so far and which had helped increase their self-esteem would decay. The young are scared of ageing as that gives rise to the realization of an upcoming stage in life which reflects uncertainties and eventually the actual truth about inevitable death. The young is therefore, swirled around with thoughts of restlessness and try to pass up the confrontation with 'old age' (Vincent, 2003).

With increase in age, physical weaknesses get more pronounced. Tiger Woods won the Masters Golf Tournament at the age of 21. However, like all other athletes, his performance deteriorated with age as we saw in case of the most celebrated golfer Jack Nicklaus who gave his last shot of winning the Masters at the age of 46. In fact, the physical ability has been believed to diminish with age which led PGA (Professional Golfers Association) to create opportunities for professional golfers who are 50 and above by organizing a separate Senior Tournament for them. The physical changes easily noticed are wrinkles, change in voice-sounding weaker with trembling and imprecise tone and decreased volume.

In the current study, most of the respondents who thought they were 60 years or above assumed age is based on these physical changes. I met a very old lady, with a hunchback. Her condition made us believe that she is indeed more than 80 years old. However, to be certain, we asked her age. We do not know whether she had done any proper calculation or not but eventually confirmed it to be 74. At this age, she was sustaining her family, the only earning family member. She had a specially-abled child and an unemployed son and was working as a maid in four houses daily. Her age and physical condition were more than enough to let her sit back at home and relax, but her family pressures did not allow her to do so. She replied that she faces difficulties as she is not fit, but because of her age and visible challenges neighbours often help her financially and take her to medical check-ups if and when necessary.

There was not a single person who was physically fit. All had some or the other issues ranging from being hunched to being paralysed. Change in voice is often related to ill-health and not ageing. Therefore, this connection could not be confirmed. The people, who claimed to be old, did not always match with the stereotypical notion of voice change. Some surely sounded feeble and weak and could not even speak properly. However, at the same time, some had a healthy and robust voice which seemed as if they are in their middle age. The next change that occurs is a decrease in height and variations in weight during old age. Therefore, how far is age related to changes in one's voice is difficult to describe. Loss of bone tissues is also the result of ageing which is primarily a problem for women as their chances of such a failure is two times to that of men. It starts during the 30s, increases during 50s and then slows down during 70s. The bone fractures are not easy to heal during old age. The heightened level of bone loss can lead to osteoporosis among old women and at an advanced level can cause stooping posture among them. Rheumatoid arthritis can also be caused because of age as joint cartilage weakens with increasing age (Cavanaugh and Fields, 2002).

In a research conducted by Francis (2014), several factors were found to affect the elderly. Social factors included the issues in the provision of family support, food, health care facilities and other troubles. Health problems included blood pressure, hearing difficulty or eyesight impairment, arthritis, irregularities in the bowel, memory issues, backache, insomnia, cancer, diabetes, heart troubles, cough, etc. In this research, majority of them were suffering from eyesight impairment, blood pressure and backache (Francis, 2014).

In Beleghata several respondents had pain in their legs and waist. They were so much in pain that it became challenging for them even to visit a doctor. All believed that age had caused this difficulty in their lives, while even the young ladies in their 20s and 30s were complaining of joint pains. In fact, these young girls as a result of such body issues were regarded much older than their age just because their symptoms were stereotypically similar to the aged.

Purna (name changed) said,

> *'boyesher shathe shathe pa r komorer byatha barche. Kom betha chilo jokhn tokhon doctorkhana te jetam, akhon r hatteo parina, keo nie jawar o nei'.*
>
> ('with age pain in my legs and waist is increasing. Previously, when I had less pain I used to visit a clinic, but now I am just not able to and I have got no one to take me there').

Most of the old women interviewed were not able to walk or even move out of their house and had extreme difficulty with mobility. There was a difference in physical ability based on age, with the young being more fit than the old ones, but how far is it connected to age, in reality, is difficult to answer. They had no such proof of their age and the ID proofs that they possessed were made much later and therefore had a questionable authenticity.

There were also many people who said that they were in their 60s, but if we go by the connection of body and age, then their physical conditions suggested otherwise, disconnecting the age-body relationship.

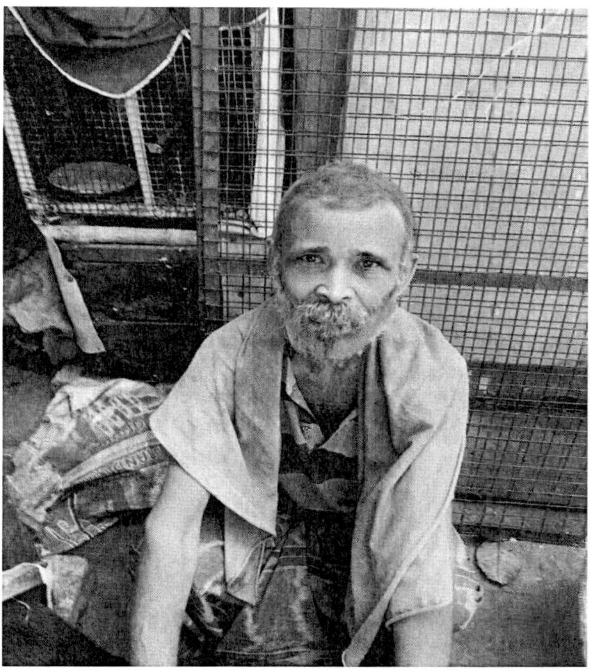

This man is aged 79 years old and a rag picker, working throughout the day without any physical hassles, thus negating the relationship between increasing age and failing body.

While some naturally looked one, few of them went for certain beauty regimens to retain their youthful body image with the help of the available beauty treatments available in the market. Turner (1996) said that to hold on to the young image, people disregard the look they develop during old age. Even Goffman (1959) has talked about the body as the prime aspect of society for the presentation of self. He said that body is something that people can have control over. They use it to make the progress of any social interaction easier. Body for him is a material entity which is involved in non-verbal communication as during this some non-verbal cues are taken into account to make sense of people involved, which is known as the body-idiom. It includes everything from how one dresses up to how one expresses emotionally and all these are considered together to categorize a person (Higgs and Jones, 2009). The village showed empathy and sympathy for the ones who are old and poor but lacked understanding towards those who wished to delay getting old and could meet the expense of comparatively better housing and living. Most of the people here did not consider these people's physical inabilities or psychological problems to be genuine and mocked at them. In some people, however, holding on to a youthful look was more like a compulsion. When we spoke to them, we unearthed that this fear of getting rejected during old age is so intense that to escape being under-valued and excluded from one's people, they discard the old look for a younger one, which they feel will be more tolerable and also a perfect solution to feel included, that trying to maintain a particular body image often leads to a conflict in perspectives between the young and the old. This discrepancy is found even among other old people, which makes the person trying to look young become a victim of ridicule and get into a stressful relationship with others and becoming unwanted for not being able to adjust with the old-image reality (Rosow, 1974).

Also, one of the most striking changes in the modern society is the rising concern about increasing life expectancy, which is known as the 'Life Extension Project' by Dumas and Turner (2007). This idea of prolongevism is advocated by the biogerontologists, according to whom medical interventions can halt ageing process and avoid death. For them very soon death in the advanced economies which are considered 'premature' would no longer be caused by cancer and other heart ailments, but by 'accident'.

The Ageing Population

When does ageing of a population occur? Well, it happens when in a population the number of elderly people increases. This has been adequately explained by United Nations in 1956, where it said that if the increase in population aged more than 60 years old goes beyond 7 per cent, then we can state that the population is ageing (United Nations, 1956).

Earlier, both the mortality and fecundity rates were very high. As a result, the population was young. Deaths were majorly caused by accidents and infectious diseases. The next trend was such that both fertility and mortality dropped and began to show stability. Age and degenerative diseases caused death. The mean age of life expectancy was considered to be 85 with little variations depending upon individuals were noticed and the population started to slowly shift from being young to old. During all these times attention to the health of the aged especially how they function was very much ignored and life expectancy above the age of 90 years was meagre. Robin and others carried out a study and found that the situation of the old in Europe was extremely appalling. The 'ADL' (activities of daily living) which involve the ability to bathe and dress, to move from one place to another, to do toileting tasks. It also consists of the ability to move from bed to chair and eat, seemed to be difficult to perform by the elderly during 1976 to 1994 (Grundy, 1996). Then slowly there started an increase of life expectancy at birth. In the 1970s it was 70.1 for males which increased to 77.2 in 2001. For females, it was 76.2 in 1970 with a sharp rise to 82.8 years in 2001 (Heiniger and Wanders, 2002). This change can be seen in countries with low mortality rates where the upward surge in life expectancy was attributed to the fact that there is a decrease in mortality in the aged population (Vaupel et al., 1998). In the 1980s the reason why this happened was thought to be because of improvements in medicine, but whether people will live hundred years or more with such advancements and will there be a healthy population in the coming future was still uncertain (Michel and Robine, 2004).

It seems that the countries which are highly developed and have witnessed a rapid and fast growth are the ones which showed a rapid rate of ageing. Japan and China are two of those countries which have achieved an increase in life expectancy. Japan could make it within 26 years of time with a fall in its rate of fertility and increase in life expectancy pushing the percentage of the aged population from 7 per cent to 14 per cent. Similarly, China could do this by minimizing its fertility rate with the policy of one-child and with an increase in life expectancy. With this, it is supposed to become the oldest society known. However, changes in age structure bring about huge effects on social and economic aspects of society; an issue which has not been paid much attention earlier.

The period that followed World War II was a time of acute labour crisis and because of war, there was low fertility and a high disproportion in the population giving rise to the old age group and lowering the normal working population, which led ageing population the focus of study among social scientists. However, the shortage was managed soon after 1960s and the ageing population was longer under focus (Thane, 1987).

In India as well, the focus has mostly been on youth and children and with a tradition of the joint family system in the country, it has for a long time protected the elderly and has taken care of their social and economic concerns. The elderly in Indian tradition irrespective of their gender were respected and looked upon with veneration (Biswas, 1987). The situation got altered with industrialization as it was no longer possible for people to continue their jobs in villages who had to move out to cities for seeking employment opportunities. It forced the elderly population to travel with their children and settle in cities. However, such a structural change had several negative consequences on the elderly (Joseph, 1988).

Everything for which they held a high position started to decline and their neglect began to rise. The social scene changed drastically within the last few years and had caused the elderly to witness a new family system in the form of nuclear family patterns. This change caused the elderly to face serious physical, financial and psychological issues. To safeguard the elderly, Ministry of Social Justice and Empowerment, Government of India framed a policy in 1999 to protect the welfare of the elderly through the provision of various services for people aged 60 years and above whom the policy has defined as 'senior citizens'. The reason why there is a rise in old age is attributed to the fact that there is a decrease in fertility rates as well as in rates of mortality. With this increase in the ageing population, there can be severe consequences for the nation as a whole affecting the economic as well as social aspects of the country. Expenditure on health, level of savings, pension, etc. all will be affected. It is expected that by 2026, with this ongoing trend, 12.17 per cent of the total population will be considered elderly having a different impact on the rural and urban parts of the country. After attaining the range varying between 60–65 years old, people who are from organized sectors get a pension and other retirement benefits. The condition of elderly at present is critical to making us realize that though the government is providing them with several benefits, a lot of work is ahead of them to make elderly feel safe and secure. Worse is the condition of women whose literacy rates are abysmal. Hardly do they own any property as such and the majority of women are not engaged in any labour force. Therefore, keeping in mind the situation where the people in India living for more than 60 years are growing which is equally apparent for the age group 80 years and above, policies should be framed accordingly. This should be done so that the alarming issues with regards to the aged are taken care of as soon as possible with gender as one of their top priorities (Situation Analysis of the Elderly in India, June 2011).

During 1901–2001 in the United States, it was found that more number of people are living up to 80 and 90 years old, with people living more than 80 years showing the highest growing trend (Thane, 1987). In the case of India, the rapidly growing population was amongst people above 60 years. They account for 7.4 per cent of the entire population with males sharing less proportion of this group compared to females. The rise is quite fast as it was just 5.6 per cent back in 1961. Right now, in West

Bengal out of the total elderly population of India the percentage share of the elderly is 7.1 per cent. There is a gap in male and female elderly in the state. The number of elderly varies depending on locality, as 3,808 old people live in rural areas and 1,892 of them live in urban areas of the state. In India, the percentage is expected to go beyond 12.4 per cent as we approach 2026. In 1951 the sex ratio of the elderly escalated to 1,028. It showed a downfall in 1971 indicating the ratio to be 938. It again gained momentum and recorded a steep rise reaching 972 in 2001. Change in dependency rates could also be observed, with 10.9 per cent rate in 1961 to an increase of approximately 3 per cent by 2001 touching 13.1 per cent. Female rate of dependency was higher than that of males. 65 per cent of the grey population is required to depend on others for carrying out their daily activities. The percentage of dependent population varied according to gender. About 20 per cent of elderly women are dependent on others and this percentage is in sharp contrast to the old men as many of them are financially independent. Old women are mostly reliant on their children with rate touching 70 per cent. A maximum 20 per cent of them depend on their husbands. There is a small percentage of these women who are dependent on people not related to them as family members and this percentage is just 6 per cent. In West Bengal 11.9 per cent of the elderly population is dependent. Nearly 11.1 per cent of elderly males are dependent and slightly higher, i.e. 12.8 per cent of elderly women are found to be dependent.

Rural elderly are less dependent on others than urban elderly, where for the former the percentage is 11.5 and for the latter, it is 12.9 per cent. Monthly per capita expenditure for half of the old people residing in rural areas lies between ₹ 420–775. People even above 60 years old seemed to be working and are part of economic activity, out of which the rale of participation of elderly male is equivalent to 66 per cent and elderly female's participation rate touching 23 per cent. Physical mobility showed to follow declining trend once one crosses 80 years of age. Where 94 per cent of elderly men were mobile in their 60s, the percentage dropped to just 72 per cent when one crosses 80. Locomotor disability seemed too common among elderly people and the overall disability rate in rural areas was .06 per cent. Women who remain married after crossing 60 years old were very much less able when compared with men. The percentage share of elderly men and women living with their children varied as well, with lower than 20 per cent men and approximately 50 per cent women living with them. More than 75 per cent of old men live with their wives, but this percentage seems to be quite low in case of elderly women with less than 40 per cent of them living with their husbands (Situation Analysis of the Elderly in India, June 2011).

As witnessed in the twentieth century, the entire world is ageing. Life expectancy has improved and is expected to recover more in near future.

The present statistics which reveals the elderly population to have reached 600 million is expected to go much beyond this number. The epidemic diseases have been controlled as public health issues have received the much-needed attention along with the improvements that have come in the world of medicine leading to such growth. The rise is 5.5 per cent to 7.1 per cent from 1961 to 2001 in case of elderly men, but for women, it is from 5.8 per cent to 7.8 per cent. This rise could be seen in India since 1951. Even in 1901, the elderly population was 12.1 million, but the percentage rose up to 77 million in 2001. By 2021 it is predicted to reach 140 million with females expected to be present in more number than males. The life expectancy is more for females than males as it stands at 64.2 years for the former and 62.6 years for the latter as seen from 2002 to 2006. For the same years in case of urban areas, it was 68.8, while in the rural areas 62.1 was seen to be the life expectancy. The expectation of life at birth varied across states. In Kerala, it was highest with 70.8 years for males and 76.2 years for females. The next state in line was Punjab which also had slight variations in the male and female life expectancy at birth with 67.2 years for males and 69.3 years for females. The age-specific death rate was more among males than among females and more in rural areas than in urban areas. Some states had lower age-specific death rates like seen in Kerala. However, age-specific death rates have decreased to a great extent as the fatal diseases which are infectious have been brought under control as much as possible through improvement in medical sciences. The illnesses which need more caution and medical intervention and that are the causes of death for a large number of elderly people are heart attacks, lung and circulatory diseases and last but not the least cancer. These kinds of diseases occur in both the genders once one grows old (Situation Analysis of the Elderly in India, June 2011).

In the elderly population, it is seen that number of women who remained married is more than that of men. The percentage shows that 88 per cent of men are still married and just 58 per cent of women are still married in the age group 60–64 years old. In this same age group, about 40 per cent of elderly women are widowed. As one moves higher in the age bar one would see this difference in men and women has been maintained. One reason behind such a gap may be because men used to marry women much younger to them as this was a usual practice in those days. This fact remains in both rural and urban areas (Situation Analysis of the Elderly in India, June 2011).

While we were interviewing in Beleghata, we tried to strike a conversation with elderly men as well, but we could hardly see them. There were some young and middle-aged men in this slum, but finding an old man on streets was an unusual scene. Also, another reason for not being able to see an elderly man can be because the slum dwellers did not consider a man old if physically he looked fit and fine. We, therefore, had to interview almost every man we came across and found only four of them who have crossed the required age bar. Out of these four, all were married but had some or the other health troubles. In cases of elderly men, as we saw in this village, all of them were living with their spouses. One of them has been abandoned by his son and was denied any financial help soon after he suffered a heart attack. His daughter-in-law also refused to take his responsibility during this crucial period. His daughter and son-in-law both were unemployed at that point of time but decided to stay with them as long as he needs them. This man worked as a plumber when he was healthy and gave his connections to his son-in-law. After that he is survived by his son-in-law and daughter who started working as a house-maid. In this village women said, they became widows at very early stages of their lives as a result of some health issues of their husbands which mostly according to the villagers is inevitable with old age.

In the present book we have attempted to penetrate the world of elderly scenario in slums and lower socio-economic background. There has been a considerable dearth of literature with reference to this. At the same time, owing to larger trends of elderly population, exploring elderly issues respective to classes becomes interesting. In the next chapters we will go into the details of the elderly scenario.

5

Elderly Life-Care and Social Constructions

What is status? Status is the position which individuals occupy in a social system. Every social position which an individual holds is expected to play specific roles. Thus, a role is the assimilation of a patterned behaviour which a person is likely to incorporate for being in the position (Merton, 1968). These expectations are nothing but cultural constructions and a reflection of a kind of relationship held by the person in the position and other members in the social structure (Rose, 1965).

Every individual in his/her respective society is unconsciously identifying with certain behavioural role pattern in coherence with his/her position in the society. These roles are as explained above expected to be properly adhered to and performed by the individual members. Every member is given authority so that the roles are played as expected. If we try to find out how this concept of authority works in a family, we will see that every member exercises it so that the family is maintained and smoothly functions. In Santhal society, people are respected on the basis of their age. Aged people are not considered as a burden. Instead, they are looked upon as valuable source of wisdom, values, knowledge and advice. They know the proper norms and customs and have high awareness about their culture. They are also considered to be the ones who can take care of the descendants responsibly. In this case, old age is not defined as a period devoid of problems that is an inevitable outcome of the ageing process. The aged in fear of becoming a burden on their family as a result of growing old feel the urge to keep working as long as they can so that they can contribute economically (Ray et al., 2003).

However, what position an aged individual would occupy and what role he/she shall play varies from one society to the other. A person, in accordance with a certain status, will have some roles to perform and specific authoritative power to exercise. With age, some of these are lost. In a civilized society, a person receives respect for the wisdom and experience he achieves with age. The aged is valued, as the society obeys him and considers him able enough to provide advice where needed (Gurumurthy, 1998).

Nevertheless, this valuable position that old age held in traditional societies is no longer the reality. For some anthropologists, respect is not given to a person just because of his age, but it depends upon the wealth he has, the power he holds, achievements he has accomplished. In Asian societies, though old people had a tradition to stay with the other members of their families, respect was not a compulsory element. In today's world life expectancy has increased and people are living longer. It is assumed that living longer indicates that people will now be dependent for a greater span of time on the younger members. Old age would inexorably be accompanied by failing health might not always be true. It is stereotypical thinking that exists in society mainly because of certain fear in people's mind (Cooter and Pickstone, 2003). Hence, the perception of old age being accompanied by declining health may not be true. Such a prejudice exists due to the fear in the minds of the people.

As discussed earlier, the population is ageing because of low rates of fertility and increase in longevity of life. Nuclear families are taking the place of joint families and several changes in the economic and social aspects of the country are altering the age-old patterns of the family that is eventually affecting elderly people (Sharma, 2007). These changes are not exclusive to urban geographies but have extended to tribal areas too. The infiltrations of different cultures in to the tribal society have altered the economic structure and the patterns of social value system. This is happening in tribal areas as well. With pressures that keep coming on this society from other cultures, have an impact on the socio-economic structure and patterns of the social value system (Sahu, 1998).

If we sum up these causes, we will understand the exact reasons that are responsible for the poor condition of the elderly people. With the change in economic production where the product shifted from household to factories, it becomes impossible to restrict young people from accessing these new forms of living. No longer are they dependent on their parental control over lands as means of survival, as was the case in traditional society. Therefore, with losing control over these productive resources, they lose control over their children as well. This also means that there will be a physical separation between the young and the old. The next change that has been taking place because of industrialization and urbanization is the participation of women in the labour force unlike in the traditional society. When they move out of their houses for jobs, they are not able to take care of the elderly family members anymore that used to happen previously. There has been a decline in fertility rates compared to the early period. Low rates of fertility has negative consequence on the elderly as there are less number of people to share the task of taking care of the elderly catering to their needs (Raju, 2002).

The family was perceived as a unit and source of shelter for all its members across generations. However, today without the income of the elderly in a family they are felt undesirable and are not given much care and respect. Therefore, strategies to provide the elderly with some work based on their past experiences, qualifications and potentials so that they can earn for their survival and contribute to their family will be a good step in maintaining their self-esteem and making them realize their importance in society (Kumar, 1995).

The modern patterns of living have brought about new modes of living for the elderly. For example, the development of old-age homes created with the intent of meeting the needs of the elderly, trying to fulfil their desires and value them, are also creating new hopes and meanings and a keen desire to accomplish them. It is only in the recent past that old-age homes have developed in India. What we found till date were the results of efforts made by the Christian missionaries who reached out to help the extremely poor and the communities of the Anglo-Indian communities. The old-age homes are largely seen to be situated in the urban centres. These centres are established for elderly people belonging to the middle-class or upper-class of the society. It is an outcome of the rapid demographic changes that are taking place whereby children are required to move out of their own countries to pursue their studies or jobs. As a result of this, nuclear family structures were increasing followed by degradation of elderly status which gave rise to old-age homes as an alternative.

While we were interviewing the elderly in Beleghata, we wanted to know about their situation regarding their relationships with their children, especially the widowed who have nobody to take care except their children.

In this chapter, we would like to depict the picture of elderly people's fear to stay at old-age homes, in spite of severe difficulties in staying with their children. Aparna (name changed), is 73 years old and has two sons. Both her sons are employed and married. Aparna lives with her younger son as her elder son has refused to stay with her. On asking whether she is happy with her younger son, I found her getting emotional and in no time she started crying.

Aparna said,

> *'tar boyish er karone tar shorir take r daena. Ora amae barite thakte dieche thiki. Kintu ami amar choto cheler shthe thaki ete shotti kotha. Kintu shotti kotha bolte kintu o sheta kokhonoi chaitona. Dhakka mere baere bar kore dite cheyechilo, kintu ei shobtai or bou er jale pore korte o baddhyo hoe, nijer theke kokhonoi chaena. Ami ok echini. Sharakkhon amar cheleke bouma ushakate thake. Ami to akhon boyoshko hoe gechi, r tante parina. Ja rojkar korechilam shobi cheleder biye r porashonar*

pechone dhele diechi. Kichui beche nei takakori. Thirish bochor age bor mara geche r tar por thele loker ghore ghore giye ghiye kaj kore berai. Akhon ki r pari bolo? R parina. R shombhob noe. Ami eta bujhina akta manush er pokkhe kotota oshubidha hote pare eta bojha je akta boyesher por manush r kaj korte parenatomader karone ami akhon baere berolam, r ami tomader bolchi oi manush guloke jigyasha koro jara oikhne darie ache j amar barir lok gulo amae kotota obohela kore. Ami dupur r rat er khawar o barir baere khai. Ami barir bhetore thkale bouma amake durdur kore. Ami oder atotuku birokto korina. Ami ak konae pore thaki aar akta fota kothao bolina. Ami amar natidero amar kache dakima kotha bolar jonne. Beshi kore khawar o daena khete. Sharadin khide pae. Amar shamne boshe bhalo monndo khae ar anondo kore. Majhe majhe bhabi ei ki amar chele? Kokhono kokhono bhabi hoeto oto mon die bhalobashte parini jar jonne hoeto o amar kache ki sheta bujhe uthte pareni'.

('It is true that I live with my younger son. But, frankly, he never wanted to stay with me. He even tried to throw me out. I know my son is forced to do this because of his wife. She is the one who provokes my son against me. Being an old woman, I am unable to live by myself. The money that I had earned so far has been I invested in my children's education and marriage. I have lost my husband thirty years back and since then I have worked as a maidservant. Now I have grown old and it is not possible for me to work anymore. I do not understand how much difficult it is for a person to understand, that after a certain age your body gives up. They have kept me in their house, but, you see even to give this interview I have come out. Ask the people out there; I have all my foods outside my house. The reason is she hates me if I stay inside. I do not bother them at all. I live in the corner of the house and do not even talk. I do not also call my grandsons to come to me. They hardly give me enough food to eat. I feel hungry throughout the day. They sit in front of me and have a right amount of food and have fun. I wonder at times is he, my son? I don't know and maybe I have not loved him enough to make him realize what he means to me').

Her condition was painful. Hence, we asked her whether she has tried to search for an old-age home or not and found her dead against it. She said,

'Apni ki pagol didimoni? Briddhasrom ejabo? Eta amader shongskriti na. Amake amar bari theke amar nijer chele meyera tarie dite pare, tobuo oder kachei fire jabo. Amar nijer bari ar shob kichur proti atotai taan je Briddhasrom er kotha bhabtei parina. Jader kono taan nei tarai briddhasrom e jae'.

('Are you mad Madam! Old-age home? It is not our culture. I might be thrown out of my house by my children, but still I would want to go back to them. I am so attached to this house and everything attached to it that I can't even imagine about old-age homes. People without any attachment go there').

Aparna was not the only person who dismissed the alternative of old-age homes. A number of them felt old-age homes must be avoided. Parvati (name changed) said,

> *'Briddhasrom briddhoder nirapotta dae, jotno nae, ar shob kichui kore. Shunechi ora onek beshi bhalo kore shebha jotno kore. Tobe ki boloto. Bridhasrome jawata akhono amader shomaje akta kolonko. Jei muhurte tumi okhane jabe, tomar para pritibeshira jene jabe tomar chele meyera tomae dekheni r tomae bar kore dieche. Tai bodhoe oikhne thai peyecho. Khub lojjajonok hoe jae. Emnitei ghorer karone onek manhani hoeche, are er cheye beshi omarjada pete chaina'.*
>
> ('Old-age homes provide security, care and all other amenities. I have heard they are better in treating old people. But, going to an old-age home is still a stigma. Once you are there, your neighbours would know that you have been thrown out by your children. This is very shameful to bear. Humiliation inside your house is already tearing you apart, further disgrace is not needed. Therefore, I have never thought of visiting old-age homes').

Although there were many like Aparna and Parvati (name changed) who disliked the idea of old-age homes, some of them found this option to be beneficial. One of the Union leaders whom we met during our interview told us that there are some of them who are in need of old-age homes. They have themselves tried to accommodate many in some good and reputed ones. But, he said the problem lays elsewhere,

> *'amra pari aar amra shobshomoy toiri jaate boyoshkora shombhabbyo shorbotyom bashosthan pae. onader jigyasha kore dekhun, amra ageo korechi erom kaj. AKta jinish jeta era bojhena sheta hcche je akbar Jodi eta rote jae je akjon briddho ba briddha ke amra shahajyo korechi tahole oder cheye beshi tader chele meyera amader baddhyo korbe tader ma babar shathe korar jonne. Boyeshkal e poribar chara briddhabash e thakata khub akta shomman er na. Briddhabash e tarai jae jara poribar er otyachar ar shojhyo korte parena ar jader rastae thele dewa hoe kono koruna charai. Apnara bolen shokriyo bashinda hishebe eta amader kortobyo oder pashe darano ar oder nirapotta prodan kora. Tobe amra jei akjoner jonne eti kori, poromuhurte arokojon ke aki bhabe dhakka mere tader chele meyera baere baar kore dae. Eshob amader bosthi te obhyash e porinoto hok sheti amra chiana. Boyoshkora amader opore bojha na. Oder dekhashona korata amader dayityo. Jodi amra dekhi je shahajyer karon ta khati tahole oboshoyi haat bariye debo. Ora sheta khub bhalo korei jane. Jothecchobhabe karon dekhalei kintu shob karon kei grohon kora hobena. Jeishob poribarera tader boyeshko shodoshyoder ke obohela kore tader onekbari shotorko kora hoe na korar jonne, jodio amra jani tate kono lab hi hobena. Jara boyeshkoder shathe durbyabohar korben shopoth neichen tader eishob shotorkotha kono kajei lagena'.*
>
> ('We can and we are always ready to provide the elderly with best possible accommodation. If you ask them you will know we have done

> this earlier. The thing that one does not realize is, once you start spreading this news that an elderly has been accommodated, more than the elderly their children force us to do the same with their parents as well. It is not graceful for an aged person to stay in his last days in an old-age home without any family member. The ones who have started living in old-age homes are the ones who just could not bear the torture anymore and were kind of thrown out on streets without any sign of mercy. You tell us, as active members of the village it is our duty to give them security. But, we saw the moment we did this for one elderly a number of them were kicked out in similar manner. We do not want this to become a practice in our locality. The people here must realize that old people are not their burden and it is their responsibility to take their care. Of course if we find that asking for our help is because of genuine reasons we are always there for them. They know it quite well. Random reasons won't be entertained and several warnings are given to those households who mistreat their elderly parents, although we know all these are of no use. Our warnings would not affect those who have taken an oath to maltreat the aged').

The ones who were willing to go to old-age homes were mostly of the opinion that they no longer want to live like a burden on their families. Shitala (name changed) told us how from being completely against going to an old-age home she has become one of the most desperate aged persons who finds this not only as an option but the best thing to do right now,

> *'ami amar shami ke hariechilam amar meyer jonmer por. Tokhon amar cheler boyish chilo char. Tokhon apni dharona korte parchen nischoi amar chele r meye dujonei amar dayityo chilo. Amar boyosh tokhon matro ekush. Eta noe je ami amar chele meyer theke ferode kichu asha korchi. Hya eta shotti je ami onek koshto korechi ar oder akta shabhabok jibon dewar cheshta korechi kintu parini ar amar rojgar khubi kom chilo. Tao oder poranor cheshta korlam. Kintu shobtai britha gelo. Amar chele nesha bhang korte laglo tero bochor boyish thekei. R sholo bochor boyeshei biye kore nilo. Ami chaichilam biyer age o age akta chakri pak. Kintu o shunlona. Biyer pore shabhabik bhabe or dayityo bere gelo, ar tai or amar theke taka chawar dorkar porte laglo. Apni i bolun ami kotha die ato gulo manush ke dekhashonar korar taka jogar korbo. Ami totodin e jotheshto boyish hoe gechi. Ei mote shat bochor age o akta chakti peyeche ar motamoti bhalo rojgar korche. Tarpor theke or byabohar amar prori palte geche. O onnyo kotha jete cheyechilo. Ami kakoti minoti korlam. Ami ebhabe beche thakte parbona janen. O amae roj bhoe dekhae je amae shobar shamne dhakka mere bar kore debe Jodi ami oi shomosto kaj gulo na kori jei shomosto kaj o amae korte bole. Or akhon duto chele. Ami ei boyeshe pach jon er jonne ranna kori, ghor muchi, bashon dhui, ar boumar pa, haat, ghar, r pith tipe di. Ami Jodi mana kori amae o bar kore debe. O bolto amae briddhasrome e pathie debe Kintu ami bhablam je na amae manie nite hob ear amae aposh kore nite hobe aar nijer loker shathe thakte hobe. Amar keo nei, shudhu orai ache. Boyesher ei shomoye*

eshe darie aka aka ke thakte chiabe apon joneder chara? Briddhasromer byapare shunechi, kintu poribar to poribar i hoe, r shorkar jotoi byabostha nik, ora kokhonoi poribar er jaega keo i nite parbena. Aki shomoe ami etao mani shongshar amoni akta jaega jekhane bhalobasha, anondo, ar akshathe thakar icchata thakata khub dorkar. Porabare Jodi bhalo kichu na thake tahole iota norok er thekeo jontronadayok hoe jae … tai ami thik korechi briddhasrome e chole jabo. Ete ontoto protiniyoto nijer chele r nijer poribarer galagalir theketo mukti pabo'.

('I lost my husband soon after I gave birth to my daughter. My son then was just four years old. You can hopefully imagine that both my children were my responsibility. I was only 21 years old then. It is not that I expected my children to give me anything in return. Yes, I did work hard to provide them with a normal life, but failed as I was very poor and had meagre income. Still, then I tried to educate them, but it went in vain as my son became drug addict from the age of thirteen. He married at the age of sixteen. I wanted him to settle down first, but he ignored my advice. After marriage, his responsibilities increased and he had to ask money from me. You tell me from where I shall get so much money to take care of so many people. I was very old by then. Just seven years back he got a job and started earning well. Since then his behaviour changed towards me. He wanted to go elsewhere. I pleaded and begged. You know, I won't be able to live this way. Every day he threatened me that he will kick me out in front of everyone if I don't do what he asks me to do. He has two sons. At this age I cook food for all

A conversation with one of our respondent

five of us, sweep the floor, wash the utensils and even massage my daughter-in-law's legs, hands, neck and back. In case I object doing these he will throw me out. He used to say he will send me to an old-age, but I thought I would try to adjust and compromise and stay with my people. I have no one, but them. Standing at this point in life who would want to live in isolation without the near and dear ones? I have heard about old-age homes, but I know a family is a family and no matter how many initiatives government takes nothing can replace a family. At the same time, I believe family is such a place which is supposed to be filled with love, happiness and a desire to stay together. If nothing positive is there, then it becomes worse than hell. Hence, I have decided to shift to an old-age home. At least I will be saved from daily abuses and insults from my son and his family').

We found that the desire to stay at old-age homes was not readily acceptable to the aged, despite being unhappy and apprehensive, they deemed it as their last resort. Most of them felt that these homes require the right amount of money. They believed that poverty leads to domestic strifes. With the money, they thought they can contribute to their family and will be considered an asset and not a burden and will be treated with respect and kindness. A study was conducted in and it was found that there are about 18 million elderly people in India who are poor and living below poverty line. The poverty line in 2007 decided by India was fixed at ₹ 356 per month per person for rural people. For urban people, it was a bit high at ₹ 539 (Ray et al., 2003; Liebig and Rajan, 2003).

The reason of this rising condition has already been discussed in the previous chapters. The breakdown of traditional families due to urbanization and modernization has made a number of things possible. For example, encouraging women to participate in economic activities in large numbers, the rapid rise in individualism and migration of young generation from one place to another. All these have disintegrated the very support system of the elderly (Knodel et al., 1992). The arrangement in living pattern where they used to live with their family members are now forced to live separately in a lonely world, where economic scarcity is one of the difficulties faced by them, pushing them into acute poverty (Sherlock, 2000).

A study found an increase of 20 per cent of elderly who are living in isolation or with their spouses from 1995–1996 to 2004–2005. As one's age increases, expenditure increases as well, but the source of income reduces. Most investment goes out to meet health expenses. Focusing on health matters means that expenditure on other things will decrease and when it is too much costly to handle the various costs people fall into the trap of poverty. Poverty is therefore connected to old age, as medical expenses are more during this time and is also permanent because of its long-term pricey affair. This holds true for aged people from both rural and urban areas. Households which are larger have higher poverty levels than the ones which are smaller. This means that households with two family members are richer compared to the ones which have near about five to seven family members.

In a study it was found that 10 per cent of people with two family members are below the poverty line, and as the number increased to five or seven members, the percentage went up to 30 per cent and then went further up to eight family members or more. The scene is same for both rural and urban India. However, in case of rural areas which are poorer have more than three or more elderly present. While meeting the people, I found this is true for people over here as well. There are some families where some elderly women live together. When the elderly, live with other non-elderly members, the scenario of living below poverty line is not so much seen. However, the elderly in rural households are the poorest of all. Out of 17.7 million elderly in the country, as found by this study in 2007, 12.8 million were residing in the rural area of the nation. Some states where in the rural areas the elderly population is stuck in poverty are Assam, Rajasthan, Kerala, Maharashtra, Uttar Pradesh, Madhya Pradesh, Haryana, Rajasthan and Tamil Nadu. In West Bengal the percentage calculated was 13.7 per cent (Srivastava and Mohanty, 2012).

Old people do not have resources to exchange with others and are disengaging, though have strong urge to lead an independent life and live longer. A study was conducted in Andhra Pradesh on people between 60 years to 80 years. Out of 450 elderly people, 180 were females and 270 were males and 50 per cent of them have lost their spouses. Large number of them were not literate. The 69 per cent of the elderly were under poverty line. Majority of the people were illiterate with total number of family members ranging from two to six and seventy six per cent of the households had earning members. Fifty-five per cent of the family members lived in kuchcha houses. Proper sanitary facilities and tap water were lacking in most number of cases. The psycho-social aspects of the people ranged mostly from health issues to economic issues and 60 per cent of people suffered from these very problems including marriage-related issues. The percentage of old people who had maintained good relationship with people living in their neighbourhood or the ones who have least associations with them are almost equal in number though number of people who had friends were slightly more. These elderly people with health-related problems generally go for government medical services and also visit private practitioners as alternative options. On asking which relationship they considered for spending time – spouses or grandchildren, their primary choice was that of spouses and if children allow and if cordial circumstances prevail in family then their choice was of grandchildren. Most elderly were either idle or were involved in activities within the domestic sphere. Access to newspapers or television or other sources of mass media was still quite less. Social problems which affected them the most were joblessness, the aggression which erupts during election, financial crisis and problems because of scarcity of food. Their health conditions varied from having normal health, or reasonably fair health to having poor health conditions while some of them suffered from vision problems and physical deformities. The relationship that they had with others was mostly pleasant and very few had negative social relationships. They have little say in decision-making process. The only areas where their decision was considered significant were during marriage or religious functions and funeral rites. Most of the elders feared about their future in terms of economic condition, health, proper living, health, jobs and marriage of their children, property (Kumar, 1995).

Decision-making power related to marriage, budget, property and other ceremonial functions are the best that which indicate the status of the elderly. The decisions taken in the fields of marriage or religious rituals by the aged are often obligatory for the family to adhere to, but other areas where budget or property is in question, it is not the elderly who take the decision, but their sons do have the final say. Even in Santhal society, the respect that the elderly once received is now declining leading to hopelessness among the aged of the society for the sufferings they are currently required to confront (Ray et al., 2003).

In general, the elderly rarely suffer from loneliness and only a few who have these issues either suffer from the negligence of their child/children or have lost their husbands/wives. Elderly people believe in superstitions like black magic or fortuneteller. However, according to Kumar (1995), most of the elderly exercise their voting rights. He also found out that there is a low level of awareness among the elderly about old-age homes and the fact that even they can play constructive roles in society despite their age (Kumar, 1995).

In Beleghata slum we found that majority of elderly were illiterate and maximum education received by them was upto third standard. Earning members in most of the households were in average two and therefore most of them had financial crisis for not being able to sustain the entire family of a large number of people. Most of them lived in proper *kuchcha* houses and had severe problems in gaining access to tap water facilities. Beleghata dwellers have maintained a cordial relationship with their neighbours, especially, the elderly have maintained close relations with fellow elderly. They felt that they have similar troubling stories to share. The problems that they mostly had were marriage issues, food scarcity, lack of employment opportunities for their children. The loss of jobs generated fear of financial crisis among the elderly. For health issues, almost all availed government health care facilities, which are very close to their slum. They mostly wished to spend time with their partners, but as most of them were widowed their wishes, as they said, 'remained unfulfilled'. The people here did not have a good relationship with their children and their family and although some of them wanted to develop and improve their bonding most of them were scared to do so as they felt it might lead to further humiliation. There were some aged who craved to spend time with their grandchildren, but as they and their children have a hostile relationship, this wish also seemed challenging. We noticed access to media was possible in just three to four houses in this entire slum, but that was for the children or grandchildren of the elderly and not the old themselves. The point is made here, to indicate the varied characteristics of the slum dwellers. They were spending their life almost in isolation. Most of them had physical ailments. They did not have any say in any issue and for many, even the decisions of the marriage of their children were taken by the children themselves. The majority had no property.

Is being Old a Burden

The problem of the elderly is quite intense and is surrounded by various interpersonal issues as well. Besides having a failing health and income, there is also a loss of social capital. Social capital 'is productive, making possible the achievement of certain ends that in its absence would not be possible' (Coleman, 1988). It specifically involves the engagement in social networks, interpersonal trust embodied in those networks and living in a community and exchanging mutually beneficial relationships with one another (Bourdieu, 1986). Securing social contact can harness a number of positive results for the elderly. There are various positive impacts that social capital can have on the elderly. For example, when elderly are able to live in a neighbourhood with high social capital, they become actively engaged and more secure (Lim, Lee and Hwang, 2011). Also, from medical perspective, research says that elderly with declining cognitive and physical abilities depend more on social capital and this often heavily influences their health status (Cannuscio, Block and Kawachi, 2003). The grim reality of the elderly population has been often translated into various films, songs and stories. One such very famous and popular song will take our readers through the traumatic emotional experience of the elderly parents when they are left in old-age homes.

'Chele amar mosto manush mosto officer
mosto flat e jaena dekha epar opaar
nanan rokom jinish aar ashbab daami daami
shobcheye kom daami chilam ekmatro ami
cheler amar amar proti ogadh sombhrom
amar byaboharer shei almari aar aayna
oshob naki besh purono flat e rakha jaena
or babar chobi ghori chori bidae holo taratari
chere dilo kaak e khelo posha buro moyna
amar thikana taai briddhassrom
shami stri aar alseshian jaega boroi kom
amar thikana taai briddhassrom

nijer haate bhat khete parto nako khoka
boltam ami na thakle ki korbi re boka
thot fuliye kaadto khoka amar kotha shune
khoka bodhoy aar kadena nei bujhi aar mone
chotobelaae shopno dekhe uthto khoka kede
duhaat diye buker kache rekhe ditaam bedhe
duhaat aajo khuje bhule jaae je akdom
amaar thikana akhon briddhassrom
khokaro hoyeche chele du bochor holo
taar to matro boyosh pochish thakur mukh tolo
aksho bochor baachte chaai akhon aamar shadh
pochish bochor pore khokar unoshaat
ashrom er ei ghorta choto jaega onek beshi
khoka ami dujonaate thakbo pashapashi
shei dintaar shopno dekhi bhishon rokom
mukhomukhi ami khoka aar briddhassrom
mukhomukhi ami khoka aar briddhassrom
mukhomukhi ami khoka aar briddhassrom'.

—by Nachiketa Chakraborty

'My son is a big person and a renowned officer
He lives in a big flat from where the two ends cannot be seen
Various things are there along with costly furniture
The least costly present there was I
My son has immense honour for me
That is why my address now is old-age home
For my usage there is only almirah and mirror
These things cannot be kept in old flat
His father's picture, watch were removed hurriedly
Crow ate the old pet myna
For husband wife and Alsesian the space is too less
That is why my address is old-age home
Son could not eat rice with his own hands
I used to say what you will do if I'm not there
My son used to pucker up his lips after hearing me
I don't think my son cries anymore and remembers me now
As a child he used to see dreams and wake up crying
With my two hands I used to tie him close to my chest
Even today my hands search for him but forget that
My address now is old-age home
Now my son also has a son who has grown into two years old
His age is now just 25 years old, God please look up
I want to live 100 years and that's my desire
After 25 years my son will be fifty nine
This room of this home is small but there is ample space

My son and I will stay together side by side
I dream of that day too much
I and my son facing each other and this oldage home
I and my son facing each other and this oldage home
I and my son facing each other and this oldage home'

—by Nachiketa Chakraborty

Many movies, novels, daily soaps, etc. have been mainly dedicated to old age. The above song is on 'Briddhasrom' which means old-age home. This poignant composition by Nachiketa Chakraborty devoted solely to an aged widow who has been neglected by her son and therefore had to accommodate herself in an old-age home for her importance and requirement evaporated once they got well settled. He wonderfully explains how a mother does everything possible to provide comfort to her children who grow up just to throw her out of their lives (Nachiketa, 2001).

The movie 'Baghban' is another effort to show, how insignificant parents become when their children grow up. Amitabh Bachchan who played the character 'Raj Malhotra', after retirement gets insufficient income and therefore he and his wife had to depend on their children. They in return get disappointed as they realized how unnecessarily they waited to expect a part of their father's share and to top it off have to now look after them. The aged couple were detached from each other so that the responsibilities are equally shared and no complain arises from any of the children about overburdening themselves. However, even though they shared the liability, all of them were similarly indifferent to attend the needs of their parents (Trehan and Trehan, 2010).

A work from literature which beautifully portrays old age is through the poem 'Mirror' by Sylvia Plath. It is a beautiful depiction that how a mirror perfectly reflects the imperfections of an aged lady who gets hurt and is terrified to see the look that old age has brought to her (Rahman, 2014).

These are all a reflection of how media and literature depict old age as a source of pain and discomfort. These are poignantly depicting the experience of an old lady in coming to terms with her aged body. People from Beleghata showed how genuinely such picture exists around us.

Old Age and the Next Generation

According to Talcott Parsons, a family is a place, an institution that functions to play two crucial roles. One is Primary Socialization and another is Personal Stabilization. The first one refers to how when a child is born a family helps it in inculcating the values of the culture of which it becomes a part after its birth and thus helps to develop its personality. Personal Stabilization means the family plays the role of providing emotional support to its adult members. One way of maintaining the healthy relationships is a marriage of an adult man to an adult woman. Before the advent of industrialization, joint family systems were dominant which acted as a source of support among the kins. Industrialization created a detachment among these kinship ties. According to Parsons, nuclear families are dominant in the age of industrialization, where a husband should play the 'instrumental' role of working outside the family and the wife should take care of the children and others in the family and thus play the 'affective' role. Feminists criticized such a point of view of the domestic division of labour. They held the opinion that a family is a place where the egalitarian relationship should exist and should be harmonious in nature (Giddens and Griffiths, 2006).

Since the advent of urbanization and globalization, second generation members are moving out of families. For this reason, the elderly people are forced to survive themselves. Increasing competition and entry in job markets has a positive correlation with the decrease in birth rate, as more concentration was devoted to children's overall development. Both parents are required to do jobs, to facilitate material comforts and meet the increasing financial needs. The care taking roles performed by the elderly are getting replaced by services and institutions which are built solely to serve the purpose, like crèches and paid caretakers. With women's entry into the job markets, they are no longer able to play the effective roles. It is eventually giving rise to the withering of emotional bonds among the family members, where the second generation parents are not able to take care of both their parents and children despite trying their best to do so (Sudha et al., 2007).

According to Soneja (2004), a vast majority as much as 90 per cent of the aged population belongs to the unorganized sectors and therefore their source of income is uncertain when they reach the age of 60. Most of them are from the rural areas as a result of which they have inadequate access to health care facilities and other such services. A micro-level perspective will show how this affects people as individuals and as families. From a macro-perspective, it will demonstrate the effect at the national level. The income of these families is so low that which is also 33 per cent live below the poverty line. Another section of the population which is also about 33 per cent lives above this poverty line but their income is too low and therefore they are considered to belong to the lower income group. Almost 50 per cent of the population is that of aged women and more than half of them are widowed (Soneja, 2004).

A study was conducted in Bhubaneswar's urban fringes with 148 middle class aged men and women. The study found out that the aged people were considered a burden by their sons and daughters-in-law both socially and economically. For the elderly population, the fact, that they have aged was not as distressing as the other social and economic factors were. The study opines that breaking up of traditional families is one of the main reasons of their suffering. Other reasons stated by them are increased cost of living and an adaptation of the education system of the West. The authors of the study have suggested that an improvement in their condition can be brought about if socialization which can be carried out at the community level can make the people of the place go through proper socialization where they will be taught the appropriate values to behave and deal with the elderly people. Community-level punishments should also be implemented for those who do not abide by the laid down value system which deals with one's treatment with the elderly. Moreover, NGOs can be established to provide counselling to people who are non-compliant (Behura and Mohanty, 2000).

Another study was conducted in West Bengal, Burdwan district to find out their situation. It was seen that the old Santals are engaged in work and hence are not too often considered as a burden by their children. In fact here, one becomes old when one ceases to work and earn. The study was conducted on 418 Santals of Benkuli. As already mentioned they receive just ₹ 100 per month under District Rural Development Project which is so less that economic problems consistently bother them. There are other distressing factors as well which are equally responsible for degrading their lifestyle. These people were found to have a fatalistic attitude which means that such an outlook and their already poor financial situation has been enough to push them into an unhealthy life. The position once the elderly held in society with regard to the power of decision-making, experience, knowledge, advice, wisdom and respect has started to wither away leading to intergenerational conflicts and negligence on the part of children towards the elderly people (Dasgupta and Ray, 2000). According to Bhatia (1964) also, societal changes have taken place with industrialization. Developments which are taking place in communities has ultimately eroded the high status that the elderly had in society as an advisor or as someone who had prestige and respect for the wisdom and experience achieved with age (Bhatia, 1964).

Agricultural societies are also experiencing similar trends. There too, the elderly are facing unsympathetic attitude and hatred. Here, though neglect is a new adverse change which came about lately, it is something that unfortunately could not be avoided (Pillai, 1988). Elder people in majority are facing the problem of adjustment. The various changes which are taking place in society are creating trouble for aged people to adjust with them. Western culture and the different foreign elements, to which the young generation is shaking hands with, have collaboratively brought about a drastic change in their mentality and have also shifted their point of focus. This has again changed the youngsters' way of caring for the aged that has faced deterioration as their level of consideration for the old has decreased with such transformation in the society. When the aged are faced with such depressing attitude, they feel isolated and abandoned. However, to cope with such negative feelings, they choose to depend upon religion which gives them a ray of hope in helping them overcome the grief faced in return of peace and satisfaction (Kapoor and Kapoor, 2004).

Traditionally, the care taking tasks of the aged were handled by women, which were expected by them to do as a duty as homemakers. The primary caregivers were mostly the daughters and wives of sons more than the sons of the aged people (Bromley and Blieszner, 1997). Since primarily women are the ones engaged in attending the needs of the elderly, they are the ones who feel the burden more than the sons and often slip into depression higher than them (Raschick and Dayton, 2004).

Often if a woman is into a job and is in a situation where her children have left the nest to pursue a career, they find it burdensome and trying to take care of the elderly, especially if that requires her to leave the job (Cox, 2008).

As per a report because of increased in life expectancy more number of elderly people are living up to 80–90 years old. When women reach the 40s which are the most productive years of their lives concerning work, they often face this challenging situation to balance between elderly care and work life. Sons provide the primary care in terms of financial support, but women do the primary task of looking after their health, food and comfort. Elaine M. Brody, a very popular researcher of this field, said, 'And it's going to be primarily women for a long time'. Brody added, 'With many more very old people and fewer children per family, almost every woman is going to have to take care of an ageing parent or parent-in-law'. Ladies can go out and earn to the best of their abilities, but they still regard these care taking works as jobs which 'women' should do and ignoring all the pain and burden she takes, she must go on nurturing and providing care to her family. According to the reports, women find this so complicated, that they often go for part-time jobs, consider pass up promotions or even consider quitting it all together to be a better option than to struggle with this daily burden of finding the right balance between job and household works. This double burden of work and taking care of the aged family members often become triple when they have children also. Travelers Corporation surveyed in 1985 and found that 20 per cent employees who have crossed the age of 30 are taking care of elderly people, especially of widowed mothers and these employees were mostly women taking care of aged relatives including mothers of their husbands (Lewin, 1989).

Who will take the responsibility of the aged parents, is often a source of conflict among siblings. The one who is observed more in this task often find it frustrating when the other siblings try to take advantage of this attitude and care less for their parents. The ones who take less responsibility might often suffer from guilt feelings for they are well aware of the fact of not carrying out their part of the task. The one who cares more becomes irritated as it does happen that when they try to get help from the other siblings for their parents, they are often refused. This declining of providing advice generates such anger that they get involved in fights over who should be given more significant share of the estates of their parents. Children who took more care of their parents often feel that they deserve more than the other siblings, thus giving rise to conflicting relationships between them. However, sometimes children do provide care to the elderly, but because of parents high expectations the concern seems to be less to the elderly who then experience dissatisfaction (Cox, 2008).

In our study, Saswati (name changed), a young resident of the slum, 28 years old, told us something similar to what Cox, 2008 has observed. Saswati is a married woman but has been separated from her husband because of dowry related issues. She was tortured physically and emotionally daily for money and when situations could not be brought under control, she decided to leave her in-law's house and settle with her parents for the rest of her life. Her mother, Basanti Devi (name changed) was happy with the care taken by Saswati, but was dissatisfied with regular discords. Basanti Devi is a widowed woman and depends entirely on her daughter for survival. Although Saswati does a brilliant job in helping her family and supports it in the best possible way, they often get involved in great deal of dissention. Basanti Devi finds Saswati's behaviour upsetting feels she has become a burden for her. Also, she accepted that Saswati is under deep emotional pain as she could not be with her husband unlike the other ladies of her age and instead of enjoying her life is taking care of her only son and aged mother. This she believes is the bone of contention. She also added that it is difficult to forgo every iota of pleasure for the sake of family members and yet be cool, calm and collected. However, she said the regular fights that take place between them are eroding their relationship and Saswati does not understand that only financial comfort is not the sole requirement in life. Basanti Devi expects her daughter to take care of the psychological distress she goes through because of all this. When asked, Saswati explained,

> *'didimoni, apni dekhun, ma apnake bollen apni apran sheshta kori khushi thakar. Ami jibone shob hariechi, kebol ache bolte oi ma r amar shat botshoer ak chele. Ami oder jonnie beche achi, oder khushir jonnei beche achi. Eta shotti kotha je kokhono shokhono ma er opore chechiye feli, kintu jighyasha korun kano. Ami dokan e jai akdom thik notar shomoe. Ar creta der bhir er jonne bari firte firte deri hoe jae. Kokhono kokhono doshtar pore o firi. Tokhn prar lokera ma ke gyan dite chole ashe je meye hishebe amae koto bhodro bhbe thaka uhit, shalinota kake bole ityadi. Ma tarpore amar opore chechabe, jeta shunte amar khub koshto hoe. Amar ma hishebe amar choritrer opore angul tolata ma er shojyo korata uchit na, jeta roj roj cholte thake, ar ami mone kori ma er to ruche darano uchit. Ami jokhn nijer matha thanda rakhte parina ma er opore chechiye di. Ami khub kothor pporisrom korechi jober theke ei chakri shuru korechi, kajei nijer ma er shindeho mene nite parina. Oitai akmatro karon jar jonne ami jhogra kori. Amar ato kajer chap er jonne*

ami ma ke shomoe dite parina jotota dorkar, kintu ami ekhane amosh korle rojgar ta ke korbe? Ami i to khali roj kori ei shongshar e. Er cheye beshi ar kichu korte parbona. Amader ak bhai ache. She biye kore shukhe shongshar korche tar bou baccha nie. Ma tader biruddye apnake kichu bolbena kokhono. Kanoki janeto oder bolle tarpor ki hobe. Je oder jonne ato kore shei shob shomoe bhul. Tumi jotoi korona kano, sheta kokhonoi jotheshto na'.

('Madam, you see my mother told you I am trying my level best to be happy. I have lost everything in life except for her and my seven years old son. I live for them and their happiness. True that I often shout at her, but ask her why. I go to my shop at 9 am sharp and because of customer's pressure I usually get back late, sometimes even after 10 pm. The neighbours then come to my mother and lecture her on how and when as a woman am I supposed to behave. She will then shout at me and I find that painful. As a mother, she should not tolerate my character assassination that goes on daily and I believe she must fight back. When she does not, I lose my cool and bite her head off! I've had my nose to the grindstone right from the day I started to work and I can't take it when my mother doubts me. That's the only reason for which I fight. Because of so much workload, I fail to give her quality time I agree, but if I compromise here, who will earn? I am the only earning member of this family. I can't do more than this. We have a brother who is happily married and stays with his family. Mother won't ever go or complain to you people against them, as she knows what will happen after that. The one who does so much is at fault. No matter how much you do, it is never enough!')

Another study was conducted on the aged women in Calcutta Municipality Corporation situated in Kolkata in Ward No. 6 consisting of 65 people and in Ward No. 88 consisting of 115 people. These elderly women as per the study were found to be very much dependent on others and were not actively involved in the workforce with a poor health condition. These women reported that they were not satisfied with the nursing care they receive. Also, sadly they are disheartened as decision-making powers in families are longer in their hands. There is a possibility as the study suggests that since these ladies lack economic independence their status in families have degraded and they are not regarded as the head of the families anymore (Basu, 2000).

A study was conducted on employed women who were aged and has almost reached the retirement age and on unemployed women who belonged to this same age range as well to see the difference in their mental state. The employed elderly were found to be anxious and disheartened. The unemployed women, on the other hand, showed some other psychological issues. They displayed feelings of inferiority and were suffering from mania and fear (Asha, 1991).

Another study was conducted amongst the elderly both men and women in rural and urban areas to find out what are the differences in their levels of adjustment that they are expected to do with age. 206 women and 348 men were selected as sample for this comparative study and it was found that women faced more difficulty with regards to adjustment compared to that of men. However, there was no significant difference in their adjustment capabilities concerning rural and urban areas except for that of social adjustment (Asha and Subrahmanian, 1990).

We tried to find out the extent of the disintegration of joint families into nuclear families amongst people of Beleghata slum. Our respondents often told us that the change has been drastic which has altered their lives more than ever. Availability of jobs outside the rural areas has forced their children to move out of their house and settle in the cities, which in turn has broken the families. Sons because of low income often take only their wives and children and leave aside their parents. Also, they reported that how these elderly people as daughters-in-law have taken care of their family members and how they have exhausted themselves regularly just for the sake of their happiness. They even told that the society was arranged in such a way that children could never imagine about neglecting their parents as they were their duty and responsibility. They showed disappointment about how this very feeling is dying out slowly and how parents are increasingly considered burden. One lady aged about 65 years told us what she feels about young generation's attitude towards the elderly. She said,

> *'nijer chelemeyera kibhbe tomake obohela korche sheta dekhte parata khubi durbhagyojonok. Eta shohorer lokeder probhab. Shekhane abeg er kono jaega nei. Takar lobhe e manish douracche. Beche thakar jonne gramr manush gulo o akhon oi poisha bananor lorazi e jog dieche. Taka to bilashita ene dae kintu shukh ar shanty ke shongsgo kore dae, thik jeta amader shathe hoeche. Tar chahidar kono shesh nei. Tomar joto thakbe tumi toto aro pete chaibe. Tobe tumi khoroch korte chaibena. Kintu durbhagyocrome amader moto kichu manush nijer chele meyeder badhyo kori jaate tara tader rojgar amader shorirer pechone, khawarer pechone r jama kaporer pechone khorcha kore. Etai ora ghrima kore. Karon amrai karon jader jonne oder rojgar kora taka opbyay hoe jacche, tai amader theke nistar pete parle ora beche jae. Oitai oder mone hoe shobcheye bhalo shomadhan. Ar jokhn tara parena tokhn tara tader biroktir karon amader opor prokash kore. Etai desher boyeshko manisher bashtobota'.*
>
> ('I feel this is unfortunate to see how your children neglect you. This is the influence of the city people. The emotional bond is missing there. People are just after money. To survive villagers are now forced to join the money making race. Money brings luxury but destroys happiness and peace just like it has done to us. There is no end to its demand. The more you have, the more you would want to have. You won't like spending it. People like us force our children to spend it on our health, food and clothing, which is something they hate. As we are the reason why their income gets wasted, they feel getting rid of us is the best

solution. And when they can't, they vent out their frustrations on us. This is the reality of aged people of the country').

Many others blamed their demeaning status on the changes in the value system. According to them, today's value teaches people to have a safe living uninterrupted by any hurdle. Like Durga Devi told us how she has been pushed to a level of least priority by her son and daughter-in-law and how little wishes have been continuously ignored. She told us that even when she suffers from some serious health issues. It is not until someone other than her alerts them, that they pay her attention. She said,

> *'dukhyojonokbhabe, amar shashtho kokhono sherom Sadly, my health never gets any gurotyo paean. Ora oder taka poesha niei beshi It is their money about which they are shocheton. Jokhn doctor bole amae hashpatal e bhorti korte hobe ora tokhono oshudh khaiye thik korar cheshta kore. Amra amader shomoe bhabtei partam na baba ma kimba shoshur shashuri ke obohela korbo. Amra eta ke amader daityomonei kortam. Ami nijei to koto jhamelar shaman korechi bouma hishebe kanoki tokhon to akkebare jotota chotobelate biye dea shombhob sherom chotto boyeshe biye hoe jeto.*

In Mangalore, husband aged 70 years and wife 65 years lived a secure life where their life revolved around their children. Taking their care and making them independent and self-sufficient were their primary focus. Also, to avoid being a burden, they have utilized their own economic resources and constructed a house for their children on their land. Despite such efforts they have been thrown out of their house by their daughter. She did not scruple to push them out on the streets, along with their belongings which were scattered here and there on the road. This couple has six children, but none of them was there with them at that moment, as sons have left before the incident. Instead of being grateful, she even legally claimed the land of her parents. One of the neighbours said, 'The daughter showed no sympathy when she drove the parents out, making use of the court order as a weapon. The pleadings of villagers have not influenced the police who expressed their helplessness in front of the court verdict'. This elderly couple refused help from any neighbour who wanted to support them and said, 'We will live and die here.' (Daijiworld, 2013)

In Adilabad, an elderly couple, Mandati Veera Reddy, aged 70 years and Radhamma aged 65 years old were shown the door by their sons. They then went to live with their daughter. Later, they went to State Human Rights Commission who decided to counsel the sons. However, despite the case being posted their attitude remained indifferent. Counselling did take place, but eventually the third son also turfed them out of their house and finally their daughter gave them roof over their head. However, they were so aggrieved by their son's behaviour that they committed suicide, by jumping off a bridge. They were run over and despite the locals' effort of taking them to a hospital, they could not be saved (Express News Service, 2011).

> *Chelemanushi buddhite thelae koto bhulbhal kaj korechi jegulo amar kora uchito hoeni r sherom bhabei shashti peyechi tobe kokhono protibad korini kanoki tokhon manusher adorsho onno kichu chilona eta chara. Chelerao shasti peto Jodi ora dayityogyanhinotar udahoron ditto ar bari theke onek shomoe bar o kore dewa hoto oder kanoki tokhon amader shanskriti te erombhul pothe chole gele porabibar er pokhye ta mene newa shombhob hotona. Eta khubi lojjajonok je kibhbe sheta palte geche ar prottekta barir nishthur shotyo hoe darieche'.*
>
> ('They try to cure me through medicines even when doctors prescribe them to admit me to hospital. In our times we could not even imagine about neglecting our parents or in-laws. We regarded this as our duty. I have faced so many issues as daughter-in-law as at that time we used to get married at the youngest age possible. Out of immaturity, I did many things which I wasn't supposed to do and therefore was punished, but never protested as that wasn't the norm then. They punished their sons also if they went astray and they always bowed down to then out of respect. Moreover, the society was such that the sons who showed signs of irresponsibility were thrown out by the families as it was not in our culture to accept such forms of deviance. It is shameful how this has changed and has become the crude reality of every household').

Is Ageing a Curse?

Margaret Trawick highlighted that in some societies conflicts might arise in between generations. Trawick in context of families of Tamil societies said, 'At certain times in his or her life, these different kinds of bonds are likely to pull an individual in different directions. As one bond grows closer, another may stretch and break and someone may be left out in the cold'. She said that to balance these bonds one should be involved in some bonds, but at the same time try to maintain harmony between them so that none of the bonds breaks apart (Trawick, 1990). The different generations were bound together by some bonds, which get disturbed or have chances of breakdown when each generation moves to a new phase altogether. When a son marries, his love and attention are more for his wife than for his mother. Similarly when a woman gives birth to her children her focus shifts from her parents-in-law towards her children, just like when a daughter marries she becomes the 'other' for her parents (Lamb, 2000).

During fieldwork in Beleghata, we realized people related old age with their children's abandonment and with health problems. We also approached young women who were either the daughters of the elderly people or were daughters-in-law, where Tanima (name changed) said,

> *'jokhn boyish hobe tokhn borera more jabe, thik jamon bostir baki boyeshko mohilader borera mara geche, r chele pule thakle tarao chere chole jabe morar jonne. Ei shomoe tae ele bujhbo shotti karer boyesh hoe geche ar nijederi lokera amader bojhar moto mone korche'.*
>
> ('Once we grow old, we will lose our husbands just like the other elderly women of the slum and if we have sons they will leave us to die just like

their sons do. When this happens we would know we have grown old and have started to be seen as a burden by our very own people').

Like Tanima, almost every resident had qualms about reaching old age. This age is not only a period which receives less attention from their children but also a phase which is viewed as a burden by old people themselves because of society's way of looking at them. The portrayal by media regarding the expensive affairs of taking care of elderly people, or even the depressing imagery on birthday cards, or entertainment programmes, that represents old age are all shreds of evidence of the fact that society indeed considers old age to be a dark phase of life. From Spain, an elderly person said that dignity of an individual is maintained as long he has the ability to tend to himself. With withering away of this power, the dignity is lost, where one becomes dependent on others for everything. A lady, 83 years old from Slovakia said, how cold people's smile towards the elderly is, meant only to serve one's duty, utterly devoid of any feelings and emotions, reflecting old age is undeniably a burden. According to professionals, dignity gets diminished from the time one is no longer able to do things on their own and needs the help of others. One's sense of self is lost and there is a rise in the development of a negative self-image. There can be a sense of loss of dignity when the arrival of old age is seen as an age which needs care and dependency on others and the chance of being assisted by others is regarded as shameful enough as if not being dependent is a yardstick to measure one's dignity in society. The negative associated with old age face are sometimes enough to hold a disregard for themselves, with a loss of dignity and self-worth (Nordenfelt, 2009).

In Beleghata, elderly people often described how they experienced a loss of dignity and self-worth with old age and how they faced negative labelling. People over here left work before they were in their 60s because of health issues. Most women with whom we had the opportunities to talk to were in more than 65 years old and mostly widowed. Majority of women went to work after the death of their husbands and a good number of them are out of work for more than ten years. Therefore, these elderly women are entirely dependent on their children and other people as the death of a spouse and physical inability made it impossible to be independent. Dependency has given rise to several troubles. Their own children have left many of them, have regularly abused them, have compromised with their foods, shelter and clothing, had deliberately stopped talking to them as that might make the elderly communicate their concerns and also have in some cases denied taking terms like *'Budhi'* (old), *'pagli'* (insane), *'khitkhite'* (irritable), etc. are often used to demean old people. People pop off at the elderly when they try to protest against such derogatory remarks as if this is the appropriate way to address them. There were many incidences where old people were time and again been made to believe that they are good for nothing and that they are not needed. Some complained of being told by their children that it is better to die than to be in someone's pocket. Some complained of being beaten up by sons and daughters-in-law for being a ball and chain. She said,

> *'khawar khawanor kotha bhule jaan, jamar dewar kotha bhule jaan, bisram newar moto thikthak jaega dewar kothao bhule jaan, ora amae ato ghenna kore je amar shathe thik kore kotha porjonto bolena r amae eriye jawar cheshta kore. Jokhon ami amar oshyosthir kotha janai oder jokhn oshyoshthir karor chorom hoe darae ar poristhithi mene newa jaena amar chele bhishon rege jae ar tokhon aro durbyabohar kore. Ora shobshomoe rege jae jokhoni ami amar moton kore ektu thakar cheshta kori. Amar ghumanor jonne ghorer kebol matro akta kona ache. Shiter shomoe to ar beshi jama kapor nei tai chordi kasha badhe. Iota nie o oder shomoshya. Ami oder boli oshudh ene dite kintu ora enena. Dupure ghumonor cheshta kori, kintu oder oi muhurte oi jaegatei lage jeita ora amae dieche bolechilo boshe goppo dewar jonne. Jokhn ashe pashe nati natnider dekhi tokhon oder golpo bolar jonne cheshta kori kintu tokhn chele r bouma khub rege jae amar opore. Amar shobshomoe lage ora amae asto gile khawar jonne opekhya korche bodhoe. Amitotai bhoe peye achi amar jiboner theke je ami bhogoban ke roj prarthona kore boli jaate tini amar ei jibon er oshanti chirokaler moto akbare shesh kore dan'.*
>
> ('Forget about being fed properly, forget about being provided with clothes when needed and forget about being given proper space to rest. They hate me so badly that they avoid conversation with me and they do not talk to me properly. When I try to convey my discomforts, as at times situations arise which are unbearable to tolerate, especially to my son as I feel he might understand me better, he becomes like a bear with a sore head. They blow a gasket whenever I try to live my way. I have a corner to sleep. During winter because of insufficient warm clothes, I often suffer from a cough and cold. They have a problem with that as well. I ask them to bring me medicines, but they will not. I try to take a nap during the afternoon, but they want that very space that they allotted to me, to sit and relax. When I see my grandchildren around, I try to tell stories to them, but my son and his wife come down like a ton of bricks. I feel they always wait to eat me alive. I am so scared and cheesed off with my life, that each day I pray to God to end this forever').

In some cases, elderly people toss and turn every night for the torture they face daily. Some elderly were abused physically by their children for reasons too painful to bear. In some cases, adult children of elderly parents wanted money to meet the costs of drinks and cigarettes at the expense of their parent's health and violently reacted when refused. An aged lady in her late 60s told us how inhumanly her son treats her and how year after year she has put up with this torture in meek silence. This lady is ill and has spondylitis along with heart issues and is also a diabetic patient. For this, she needs to visit a doctor. She said,

> *'Amake korakoribhbe shuparish kora hoeche je jano ami mashe akbar kore dactar dekhai. Kintu amar taka kori nei Karin amar chele amar shob joma kora taka amar bag theke chinie nie baje jinish er opore khoroch kore. Jodi oke ami amar sharirik shomoshyata je kotota gombhir sheta bojhai tahole o amae marte porjonto didha bodh korena Onekbari o eta koreche ar o amae mere felar o humki dieche ei bole je amae mere debe Jodi ami kauke nalish kore di or naam e. O amae prayi bole je ami onek bechechi ar akhon amar shob taka or howa uchit, ar amar shorir er jaegae jeta or kache tuccho byapar or dorkar guloi beshi daami ar gurotyopurno. Ami or kache akta bojha jar kono shomman nei or kono mulyo nei, ar ami kono bhalo kichuro jogyo noi'.*
>
> ('I have been strictly recommended to visit doctor once a month. But, I have no money at the end of the day because whatever I earn and try to save is snatched by my son out of my bag and spent on worthless things. If I try to make him understand the seriousness of my health, he will not hesitate to beat me. He has done this many a times and he has warned to kill me if I try complaining about this to anyone. He keeps saying that I have lived enough and that now all my money should be his and instead of my health which is least significant his needs should be prioritized. I am a burden who deserves no respect and has no value and I am not worthy of anything useful').

Such hopelessness surrounded many such elderly people who were unwanted and felt their families are bearing the burden of their lives. India ranks third with 10 million elderly people in the world, aged 80 years and above. The different changes as already discussed have eroded the long history of strong intergenerational bond that once existed through the joint family system, caste groups, strong kinship, panchayats, religion and traditional values and ethos, letting the young respect the elderly indisputably. The changes in society have degraded such value systems and compromised with these intergenerational relationships (Phillipson, 2002).

Food is not the only necessity to live, people need and desire to be surrounded by others and share a feeling of belongingness. The more one is with others, the more one will be in peace and satisfaction. Modern society has witnessed a shift in family structure leading to the growth of nuclear families and therefore elderly people who have no source of income are becoming burden for families with a limited financial resource. In a study, it was found that mainly the middle sons, about a quarter of them were the ones who felt the elderly to be a burden. Such feelings were not much severe in case of elderly people staying with the eldest or the youngest ones. Elderly women reported being neglected by sons of middle order over and over again. Neglected 'often' and also 'occasional' neglect was frequent maltreatment faced by elderly women living with their middle born sons, with 'occasional' misbehaviour by these sons reported to be second highest in number. In a study, it was found that almost half of the sample studied has neglected the elderly often and intermittently by their middle order sons. However, elder sons were not too far in the race to avoid and neglect their elderly parents with 36.1 per cent of them in this study showing such disregard for the same if all forms of neglect were summed up and analysed in totality.

The youngest sons' show of neglect towards their elderly parents was the least with just a 5.2 per cent of them seem to be ignoring them 'often' and none showed to disregard them somewhat 'repeatedly' or 'occasionally'. Youngest sons were the ones according to the study more safe to be with compared to the middle sons in terms of showing disrespect and neglect. Once a person ages, he faces certain difficulties ranging from motor disabilities to certain psychological issues. As a result, aged people become dependent on the younger ones with advanced age and require their help in carrying out their daily activities. Therefore, the sons on whom they become dependent often regard them as a burden for not being able to take care of themselves on their own. When situations are difficult, these sons often lose their patience and are up in arms about the trouble encountered to bear the burden of their elderly parents. Elderly people faced abuse over and above neglect by their sons, which is unfortunate enough to believe but a harsh reality.

People who live with their 'only sons' face such treatments in less number. The sample on which the above statistics were found showed more than 30 per cent of the 'only sons' never abused their elderly parents. Eldest sons also showed similar behaviour with almost 30 per cent of them choosing to be respectful towards them. In case of abusing elderly parents about 27 per cent, youngest sons showed to have never abused their parents. As perpetrators of elderly abuse, middle order sons were reported with 76.7 per cent of them exercising such behaviours. Aged parents staying with their middle sons were the ones most scolded as their abuse rate was four times the abuse faced by the elderly living with the 'only sons' and three times the abuse inflicted upon them by the eldest and youngest sons. This showed that the elderly were more protected and well taken care of by sons other than that of middle order (Gowri et al., 2003).

In Beleghata a similar situation could be observed. The youngest son seemed to be more responsible than the eldest or the middle. In terms of abuse as well middle sons were more aggressive. We tried exploring the underlying reasons behind such a pattern. It was found that the middle order sons felt that when their elder brothers are present, they must not pass the buck. They felt that for being born before them, the elder sons are more obliged to shoulder the responsibility. Some thought that the eldest son is more pampered for being the first child of their parents and the younger ones are the ones who survive on things already used by their elder brothers. They, therefore, felt elder sons are supposed to return anyways the love showered upon them. In case they have younger brothers who have taken their parent's responsibility, answers were pretty much the same. For most of them, elder and younger sons receive more love and affection for their birth orders. The younger ones for being young need extra care and attention and their mistakes are often considered childish and ignored. The middle sons felt that all this extra attention is always received by children who are elder and younger than them. Therefore, they often feel less loved and wanted. Eventually, when their parents need them, they are either not able to connect with their requirements for being emotionally detached or are merely ignorant for being ignored themselves. However, these are not the only reasons as others factors like less income, problems in accommodation, adjustment issues between mother and daughters-in-law, are also equally responsible. The younger sons took the responsibility more often than the other order sons because most of them have witnessed the plight of their parents when left alone by the other elder sons. They have themselves suffered for being neglected by their elder brothers and are aware of the displeasures associated with such maltreatment. Therefore, sympathy and emotional bonding is more among them and their parents which often is the reason why most of them are less abusive towards their parents. The eldest sons though too less in number are still compassionate and kind and less abusive compared to the middle order sons. The main reason found was the fact that they are the eldest of all and hence they felt it is their duty. Some of them despite several hurdles squared their shoulders to carry out this responsibility.

The Responsibility of Parental Care

Nowadays, family members show negligence and indifference towards the elderly and their problems. The kinds of conflicts aged people face can be categorized into four groups as done by Sarah Lamb (2000). The first category where such disputes occur is in the relationship shared between mother and daughter-in-law. The second category is the conflict between mothers and their sons who have got married. The third category is in between the fathers and their sons and the last type where such fights take place is between daughters who are married and their mothers (Lamb, 2000).

The first focus would be on the first category, which is about the relationship shared between mother and daughter-in-law. Sarah Lamb (2000) in her research on the aged people in Mangaldihi in West Bengal found similar findings. She observes that when mothers get their sons married, they become aware of the fact that right from when the new bride has stepped into their lives their well-being will be in the hands of their daughter-in-law. Whether it is cooking of food, or serving it, or whether it is washing of clothes or massaging the painful legs everything is taken care of by this new member. They after few days start taking control over their lives and it is upon them to decide what kind of tasks are they willing to perform and how. They may even manipulate the sons in their favour and can influence the idea of settling elsewhere in a separate house. These are some of the qualms that elderly people experience during old age. Thus, their expection from daughters-in-law who would maintain their loyalties towards the older people of the house. As a result, the elderly people cannot accept them as their own daughters. On the other hand, their sons drift apart from them. Thus, there is a profound sense of insecurity at this age. However, this stands in stark contrast to the previous literature findings, which was also supported by Sarah Lamb's work (2000). For example, traditionally, in the initial years of marriage, newly-wed girls controlled and dominated by their mothers-in-law. The domestic activities that are to be performed by daughters-in-law and they going to their parental households and even whether they can have some alone time with their husbands or not are all decided by their mothers-in-law. Sarah Lamb found that many of the ladies there who got married at a very early age had shared years of affectionate bond with their mothers-in-law. Some ladies told her that they are treated like servants by their mothers-in-law and are restricted by them regarding how much time they can spend with their husbands so that they do not develop bond only with their husbands but also with others in the house. She also narrated how the mothers-in-law used a stick to have an eye on what the daughters-in-law do especially to restrict her movements so that she does not get the opportunity to interact with other males (Lamb, 2000).

Daughters-in-law are no longer willing to get up before everybody else and engage themselves in works which are heavy or are dirty in nature. Though the attitudes of daughters-in-law have changed, one thing that remained same was the expectation that the mothers-in-law have towards them. For serving their mothers-in-law, they felt they deserved the same treatment. Therefore, there remains a gap between the mindset of the two which gives rise to family troubles in the form of scuffles and daily disputes. Huang (2010) has cited some examples to show how much and to what extent difference in opinion can create huge disturbances in a family. In one of the narratives he mentions a story of an elderly couple with two sons. Neither were interested to live with their parents. A room had to be made from an old pigpen where this elderly couple accommodated themselves and lived with their younger son of course in a different setting situated at the back of his house. However, this sort of living was disliked by his wife who thought that the old couple should not solely depend on them and the elder son and wife should also share the responsibility of their parents. The distance where the elder son and his family were situated was quite far and hence going there was not possible for they could not walk for so long. This agitated the younger daughter-in-law who started calling names and abuses her in-laws in front her husband. This made the old couple seek help from the village authorities (Huang, 2010).

Right behaviour with the in-laws can be learnt through ones' mothers or other female members in the family or can learn overtime by staying in one's in-law's house and understanding the family culture. Daughters-in-law played roles according to what they wanted in return from the family members, depending on what position they occupy in the family and how their husbands treated them. Thus, daughters-in-law behaved as they were treated. Sarah Lamb's work (2000) on Mangaldihi has tried to explore, whether the daughters-in-law found it easy in trying to play their roles in their in-law's house. The ones who said that they had learnt how to play this role as socially expected was by following their female family members, especially their mothers and grandmothers. However, they said that unless they stepped in and started playing the role of daughters-in-law themselves, they did not realize the difficulties one can have. They initially thought it to be easy to treat their in-laws like their parents, but soon they realized that it is much problematic. In the study, one of them opined that she was made aware of the expectations that her mother-in-law had from her when they got engaged, often this acted as burden for the future bride.

Some of the respondents told about the strategies they adopted to deal with the disputes they had in their in-law's house. 'Let it go' approach was used by some who did not wish to confront the situation as for the majority of them this might worsen the situation or might put the marriage at stake, or even trouble the husband. There were about 16 per cent of the respondents in the study who did not confront their mothers-in-law but wanted to resolve conflicts to speak about the issues they have with each other, but it was seen that often, when the mothers-in-law did not want to understand the latter's problems. Often, the daughters-in-law stressed that the mothers-in-law did not want to resolve the issues and this resulted in further confrontation leading to family feuds and disturbances. For some, conflicts need to be resolved right from its roots and hence confrontation rather than 'let it go' tactic is essential. For some, they keep quiet when there is a dispute, but they confront with situations which are too much to bear to avoid mother-in-law's interference. Some thought that despite warnings from husbands, they feel only this can clear the misunderstandings between them. There was only one lady who was a bit aggressive in dealing with her mother-in-law. There was another 16 per cent, of whom husbands took the stand of defending their wives in such conflicts and according to some of them, change in the behaviour of mothers-in-law often occurred because of sons intervention. Father-in-law helped one of the respondents to resolve the dispute. Some manage the situation differently, for example through a physical separation which means staying away from the in-laws, some use drugs to keep themselves calm, some said to behave in a way as if they are paying importance to their in-laws while at the same time ultimately doing what they want. For some of them, the relationship will remain bitter as no strategy can improve the bond between the two. Some of the daughters-in-law told that with time and growing familiarity with their mothers-in-law they changed their approach from ignorance to confrontation to sometimes just talking it out. Their relationships remained more or less the same but certain changes in their behaviours did take place as they entered into the middle years of their married lives (Merrill, 2007).

During this time the sons and daughters-in-law take over the control from their mothers-in-law. This, taking over of power is especially true for the eldest son and his wife, continually competing and fighting mainly because all of them at this point are able enough to speak up and fight for what they feel is right. This greed either to sustain power or to take over the power, in Mangaldihi, has been a huge reason for a fight. Then comes a time when finally the mothers-in-law fail to maintain their control in the affairs of the house. When the brides first came in, they were completely dependent on their mothers-in-law as they were yet to learn about the rights and wrongs of their households and since in Mangaldihi girls got married at a very young age, sometimes even at the age of five their dependency continued for an extended period. With mothers-in-law giving up their authority over the family affairs, they become dependent on their daughters-in-law just like the way they once were. In this village at the time of Sarah Lamb's visit, a firm opinion among people prevailed – that daughters-in-law are never their 'nijer lok' ('own people'). This tendency of distancing daughters-in-law means that they will never become an integral part of the house only when they get into the position of mothers-in-law of their sons' wives (Lamb, 2000).

In Beleghata as well, mothers-in-law have often addressed their daughters-in-law as '*porer ghorer meye*' which means daughter from another household. They often told us 'we do not expect them to love us as they are from a different house and we also don't love them as we know we did not give them birth. It is as simple'.

This kind of hostile attitude is however, not confined solely to mothers-in-law only. In a recent case in April 2015 in Uttar Pradesh, evidence has come to focus where a lady has been caught on CCTV to assault her mother-in-law brutally. The CCTV was installed by her husband who suspected that she beats his mother in his absence (Tupaki.com). In 2013 a report came out which stated that India witnessed in every hour at least one woman died because of dowry since 2007 till 2011 (NDTV, 2013). In various states of the country as counted in 2012, there were 8,233 dowry deaths reported. These cases are increasing with years. Also, this is not limited to the upper and the middle class strata but has also extended to lower socio-economic households.

There are cases, where women felt that their mothers-in-law control and spend more time with their sons and make it a point to create situations where sons will be with them for long periods of time and not with their wives. For example, a lady stated how despite a business which had no future regarding earning profits was continued by a mother-in-law who wanted her son to help her out to manage it. According to the lady the mother-in-law did this so that the son and the mother can be together. The daughter-in-law strongly believed that this was a plan to distance the son away from her who has been married to him for about fifteen years. Another lady told how desperate her mother-in-law becomes when she sees any trouble in between her son with his wife or her daughter with her spouse and tries to take advantage of the clashes that the couples have so that she can intervene and ask her children to get back to her. This lady narrated how one incidence of fight where she asked her husband to leave her house became days of a nightmare for her and worse than that when her mother-in-law threatened her over the phone to send divorce papers soon. However, the daughter-in-law managed to resolve her issue with her husband and return back, only in the absence of her mother-in-law. However, when the mother returned, she tried to convince her son to stay away from his wife. Eventually, the husband took his wife's side and went back with her (Allinson, 2004).

Some studies were conducted on Bangladeshi women to learn about their point of view about mothers-in-law. There was a case where a lady named Naveen Mannan told, how her sister's married life got a bit affected because of her mother-in-law. According to Mannan, every woman has some expectation from marriage. They are brought up in a family and are accustomed to it and find it difficult when they see different things and do not understand the reason behind this difference. Her sister had to face similar situation as she could not adjust to her mother-in-law's conservative thoughts. The relationship was filled with hatred as she was expected to do what her mother-in-law wanted her to do, but with time she had known her position and could speak for herself. Another lady named Nazma also described how mothers-in-law try to assert their authority especially over the kitchen which she felt is every woman's area of control. For Nazma this has been happening all the time as every mother-in-law would want to show and teach the ways of cooking irrespective of whether her daughter-in-law knows the art or not. However, even if she does, Nazma felt the girl would not escape the criticism that would go on over every little thing. This same interview revealed that in London, girls from Bangladesh are thrilled if married to boys of Bangladesh. The main reason is they are not required to stay with their in-laws (Young et al., 2011). According to HelpAge India (2014), abuse by daughters-in-law on elderly was as high as 61 per cent.

When we started interviewing people from Beleghata, we realized that mother and daughters-in-law issues existed here also. We did mention in parts about some of them in the previous chapters. However, we felt the need for a separate section to cover this issue for the gravity it carries. Every household we went to was full of such familial tensions. Most of the aged complained about how the daughters-in-law became a problem. Most of the sons, post marriage lived separately and did not care for their aged parents who were then a liability for them to take care of. In an interview, an elderly named Bijoya (name changed) told us how tough it was for her to stand the regular family issues. She said that her son married a girl of his choice. Bijoya had no problem with that, but she said,

> *'Amar or shobhab nie oshubidhe chilo. Amar iccha chilo je amar chele amar pochondo moton meyeke biye korbe, kintu jokhon ta holona ami akta shobdo o uccharon korini. Kintu akhono mone hoe Jodi ektu kortam bodhoe bhalo hoto. Amar shami mara jawar por cheleke joto shombhob cheshta kore jotota perechi bhalobhabe boro korechi. Ferod e ami khali etai cheyechilam je chele amae manoshik shanty ontoto debe, kintu amar durbhagyo je sheta pawar kono ashao ar nei. Amar chele erom kichu mash ageo chilona. Amar mone hoe or bou oke amar byapare ja pare bole jae, ar o ektu bholabhala tai biswas oke kore nae. Akdin o mithye bollo je ami naki oke diye amar pa tepano koriechi char ghonta dhore. Amar kono shurak o khuje pelam na je o ki bollo. Amar chele or kotha biswas to korloi ar amae bollo je ami jano amar shimana na charie jai arbollo jano erom bhul poroborti kal e ar na hoe'.*
>
> ('I had a problem with her behaviour. I wanted my son to marry a girl of my own choice but never uttered a word for not doing so. I wish I had done that. After my husband died in an accident, I brought up my son in the best way possible. In return at least I expected some amount of mental peace, but unfortunately, I am not even left with the hope of getting any. My son was not like that even a few months back. I feel his wife keeps saying whatever she wants to against me and he innocently believes her. One day she lied that I made her massage my leg for hours. I had no clue what was she saying. My son believed her and asked me to remain within my limits and dared me not to repeat such mistakes ever').

While she wanted to continue her friend was sitting right beside her, aged 65. She said,

> *'ami bujhina o Jodi or bouma ke eta korte boleo tate khoti ki? Amader boyish hocche ar amader shorir e akhon byathao hoe. Kokhono khonono byathata oshombhob barabari rokom er hoe jae ar tokhn ar newa jaena. Bijoya to thik kore darateo parena. Or bouma ki andho naki? Tar cheyo boro kotha or chele ki andho? Boro howar por era bhule jae eder jonno amra kotoki boshorjon diechi. Ora nirjhonjhater jibon chae. Ami asha kori akdin eshob ora fire pabe'.*
>
> ('I do not understand that even if she had asked her daughter-in-law to do that what the harm is! We have grown old and our bodies do ache. At times it becomes unbearable. Don't they realize when they see us that what extreme physical problems we are facing on a daily basis? Bijoya can't even stand properly. Is her daughter-in-law blind? More importantly is her son blind? After growing up, they forget what all we sacrificed for them. They want to live a trouble-free life. I hope they get back everything one day').

Out of so many women interviewed, there were just two women who told us that they have a good relationship with their daughters-in-law. Among them one's daughter-in-law kept telling us about the health troubles her mother-in-law faces every day and that how every medicine and doctor has failed to find a solution to it. We found the daughter-in-law takes her to the toilet. The mother-in-law very gladly told us how her life would have been difficult without her and we realized that she indeed loves her and shares a good bond with her. However, she paused and said that this daughter-in-law is the younger one and the eldest one has left their house and settled elsewhere and her elder son has never come to visit her ever since he got married. The reason that this old lady gave us was financial reason. She said that her elder son does not earn well and is ashamed to come to her as he would not be able to help her with such a small salary.

We visited another house where again there was a problem which as a bit different than others. Srija (name changed) told her husband passed away a few years back because of kidney failure. She used to live with her parents-in-law. The death of her husband created a greater rift in their relationship. She was thrown out of her house, beaten up severely. Without anything to hold on to, it turned her into a beggar and eventually get her into this slum as her final destiny. Similar things happened to her daughter as well who has been a victim of family violence, due to dowry. The lady said,

> *'ami nijei amar shashurir otacharar er shikar hoechilam bole amar mathae shobshomoe chilo jano amar meye kokhono eshob onyay shojhyo na kore ar ami jeta korini sheta jano she kore Jodi poristhiti sherom hoe. Amra gorib, ar amader shomaje eshobe hamesha hote thake. Amar meye akdin mar khelo. Ami oke bollam akhoni bari chole ashte ar bollam oke shob rokom nirapotta ami debo. Akhon ami amar meyer shathei achi. Oboshyoi onek shomosha ache, tobe amra onek bhalo achi shei shob baba ma e der theke jader tader cholera bari theke dhakka mere pothe fele rakhe morte dewar jonne. Tobe jei shomoshyar jonne amar ar amar meyer moddhye prayi jhogra badhe ta holo ami or jibone beshi nakgolale. Tobe bhalobasha ato beshi amader moddhye je eishob monomalinyo khub shiggiri thik hoe jae. O amar meye bolei amar or proti bhalobasha ta bojhe r ei abeg ta amar mone hoe akta meye i bujhte parbe'.*
>
> ('I being a victim of my in-law's torture, always had it in my mind that my daughter must never tolerate such unjust activities. Unlike me take steps against if needed in case she faces similar things. We are poor and in our societies, such things keep on happening. My daughter was beaten up. I told her to come to me right away and assured her all security. Right now I am staying with my daughter. There are problems, but she is better than the sons in the nearby households who throw their parents on streets to die. The only issue for which we fight often is my daughter simply scolds me when I interfere too much into her life, but then there is too much of love and differences get sorted

out in no time. She being my child somewhere understands my love for her and I feel only a daughter can understand this emotion').

There were different issues related to mother and son relationship in this slum, but most of the mothers believed sons to have changed after marriage because of their wives' influences. However, some thought improper socialization, or blamed their fortune and some others felt the sons are meant to throw elderly parents in distress as they are never much connected with them, unlike the daughters. Monika (name changed), said,

'Ami amar bouma kibhbe dosh di Jodi amar chelei omon hoe? Amar mone hoena Jodi o amae bhalobashto prithithibite konokichu or proti e bhabe probhab felte parto, jar modhye or bou o pore'.

('How can I blame my daughter-in-law when my son is like this? I don't think that if he had loved me, anything on this earth could have influenced him, which includes his wife').

There were some elderly whose sons are not yet married but still, do not take care of them. Some people observed that this is largely due to their unemployed status and some others believed that most of them are addicted to alcohol and drug, while some thought this to be the influence of bad company. Like Madhura (name changed) commented,

'amar chele age erom chilona. O porte chaito. O jokhn class eight e uthloor baba mara gel oar or babar bhai ra shob ak bari te boshabash kora shuru korlo. Etai shomosto kichu palte dilo. Ors shobai neshakhor chilo. Ato olpo boyeshe amar cheleke ora oder shathe nie jeto. Ora oke ato probhab korte shuru korlo je o class kamai korte laglo. O dubar fail korlo, ar tarpor monojag haralo puropuri bhabe chole gelo porashona theke ar sheshe giye iskul chere dilo. Akhon or bekar er moto ghure beae ar amae gali dae je o choto thakte kano kichu korini. Ami ma hishebe shob kichu korechilam amar cheler bhobishyot bachanor jonnyo. O amae tokhono bujhtona ar aaj o bojhena. Oke nie amae roj cholte hoe. O mod khae, nesha kore, ar tarpor bari fire e amae gali dae ar mar e'.

('My son was not like this. He wanted to study. When he was in class 8, his father expired and his brothers settled with us in this same house. This changed everything. All of them were drug addicts. They used to take my son along with them at this tender age. They influenced him so much that he started missing his classes. He failed twice and then eventually he lost all his concentration and dropped out from school. Now he roams around unemployed and abuses me for not doing anything when he was young. As a mother, I did everything possible to save my son's future. He did not understand me then and not even today. I deal with him regularly. He drinks, gets drugged and then comes back home to abuse and beat me').

There was another mother, aged 77, who also sounded miserable, not because the son abuses her, but because he avoids to acknowledge her as his mother. Here is what she said,

'Ami or ma. O amae bari theke bar kore dae or biyer kichu mash porei. Amar khub oshohae lage, kintu ami konodin obhijog korini. Ami arekjon briddhar shathe thaki jaake karor dekhar nei. Kintu amar bhoyanok lage jokhon ami amar cheleke rastae tar poribar er shathe anonde dekhi, ar amar shathe jaate dekha na hoe jae shaman shamni tai nidarunbhabe amae eronor cheshta kore. Amar or proti kono raag nei ba obhijog nei, ami or kache khobor pathiechilam akbar dekha korar jonne akbar. Kintu o kokhono asheni. Dosh bochor kete geche jokhon or shathe shesh kotha hoeche. Or obhab bodh hoe khub, or chele meyeder, or bou er. O amar nati natnider o amar kache ashte daena. Akbar ami oder dekechilam jokhon oder parae khelte dekhechilam, kintu or bou oder deke nie chole gelo'.

('I am his mother. He threw me out of his house few months after his marriage. I felt helpless but never complained. I live with another elderly who has nobody to take care of her. But, it feels terrible when I see my son on the street happy with his family, yet desperately trying to avoid any confrontation with me. I have no hard feelings for him. I had sent a message to him asking to meet me once. He never came. Ten years have passed since I last spoke to him. I miss him, his children and his wife. He does not even allow my grandchildren to come to me. Once I called them when I found them playing in my neighbourhood, but his wife took them away').

Such is the situation of the elderly. Many elderly people complained of not getting enough food even after pleading for it with their sons. Some complained of not being taken to proper medical checkups by them even when situations were alarming. As told by the person there was a situation, where on one rainy night a son forced his mother out of the house. This inhuman act agitated the neighbours so much that they beat him up to teach him a lesson and continued beating unless the mother intervened and took all the blame on herself to save her son from public rage. Though the son allowed the mother to stay with them a week after the incident, they started living in two separate households eventually.

> In 2012 in Delhi, a similar case came into limelight when a son who was a businessman threw his mother out of the house at night in the open air, took away her property. When she was booted out and not allowed to enter, the mother had no choice and so she lodged a complaint and the son was put behind bars. The mother, however, requested to grant the son bail (NDTV, 2012).

Many elderly women in the slum said that sons often harass them for money and go to the extent of physically harming them if it is not given. Often this money is refused to be provided, as according to most of the people these amounts are spent on alcohol, drugs and *bidis*. These refusals often were followed by warnings and threats from sons. Monika (name changed) said,

> *'ami jani amar chele biri r mod er opor e taka khorcha kore. Or uchit shongshar er proti kichu khoroch dewa kanoki amar rojgar atoi shamanyo je shob shamlano besh jhamelar hoe jae. Tobe or kono hush nei. Akdin o bollo o amae mere felbe Jodi or dabi ami na mani. Ami oke bollam kore felo. Amae nishchoi marte pareni tobe khub merechilo'.*
>
> ('I know my son spends on alcohol and *bidi*. He should contribute to this family as my earnings are so meagre that it becomes difficult to make ends meet. However, he doesn't care. One day he said that he would kill me if I do not pay heed to his demands. I asked him to go ahead and do it. He definitely could not kill me, but has beaten me hard').

Abusing a parent, especially mother, or threatening her, were ubiquitous in this slum. Cases of abusing parents are not confined to this slum only. A report by HelpAge India shows that in Bhopal 70 per cent of elderly are abused by their sons, in Patna the percentage is 57 per cent, whereas in Kolkata the abuse rate is 54 per cent. The overall abuse rate for elderly was 59 per cent from sons. Almost 41 per cent of the abused elderly remain silent and tolerate such treatment. Out of this 59 per cent of them believed this is important for 'Maintaining confidentiality of the family matter' (HelpAge India, 2014). Therefore, I asked the elderly people whether they have complained about this abuse to anyone or not. Most of them held the opinion that these are indeed family issues, which can be solved only when there is no third party interference. Some felt that when such conflicts are out in the open, they will hold up the matter to ridicule.

One thing that could be easily noticed was old women as mothers were very much reluctant to discuss their problems that have with their sons. In case of conflicts with daughters-in-law, they were much open and irritated and willing to share. The ones who were hesitant to talk out their clashes with their sons or ready to share their bitter experiences with their daughters-in-law told us, that sons were expected to respect their mothers. It is a question of their upbringing when they do not do so. For some, sons were not at fault as their wives influenced them and for some unemployment was the cause.

Now, next, we went to explore the relationship between fathers and sons. The problem we faced was, elderly men were too less in this slum. As already mentioned in the very beginning we could find only four of them. One of them could not be approached because of illness. Out of the remaining three elderly people, one was childless. The other two old people were in their late seventies. Here, one of them has been deserted by his son when he needed financial help to deal with his heart attack. We asked him how it all happened. He told us:

> *'Ami ar amar stri khub shukhi chilam amader rojgar nie. Beshi chilona, kintu jotheshto chilo beche thakar moton. Ami chele meyeder biye dilam. Kintu hotat akdin ei heart attack hoe. Onek taka lagto. Amar stri amader cheler kache gelo, kintu o tokhoni mana kore dilo. O konobhabe taka*

jogar korlo nijer goenagati beche. Akjon heart er patient er onek sheba susrushar dorkar pore attack theke beche jawar poreo. Amader kache kono taka kori kicchu chilona. Tai tokhon dhar nite holo. Amader chele oi nie oshubidhe chilo. O shojhyo korte parchilona je takata amar opore khoroch hocche. O tai thik korlo amader bari theke chure felte, kintu amito shokto thakbo mon theke thiki kore niechilam. Ami age kichu korini, kintu or durbyabiha er jonnyo bhablam oke chole jete bolatei manoshik shanty ana jabe. Ei shomoe amar meye ar or bor amader shathe thake, jara ei puro pothe amader sharakkhon shahajyo kore geche'.

('Myself and my wife were pleased with our income. It was not significant, but enough to survive. I got my children married. However, one day I had heart attack. We needed huge money. My wife approached our son but was immediately refused. She somehow gathered money by selling off her jewellery. A heart patient requires a lot of care even after he has survived the attack. We were flat broke. We started taking loans. My son had problems with that. He could not stand the fact that money was spent on me. He then decided to throw us out of the house, but I was determined to stay strong. I did not cast the first stone, but because of his misbehaviour I thought I would ask him to leave my house is the way to go to bring some mental peace. Right now, my daughter and her husband live with us, an immense source of support throughout our journey').

The other elderly person was living happily with his son at the time we conducted this study. He was not well, but extremely delighted to say how lucky he was to get such a beautiful and supportive family. The people told us that since elderly men are not present much in this village father and son rivalries are also visibly absent.

Exploration of mother-daughter relationship was also important since a majority of the elderly people used to live with their daughters. A typical feature found here was the abandonment of women by their husbands. Their husbands left most of the women who got married within 5–6 years of their married lives. The reasons ranged from dowry, the birth of daughter, unemployment, second marriage and alcohol and drug abuse. After being left by husbands, they generally come back to settle with their parents. After their parents grow old, they take up their responsibility. We did not find any elderly women in the area who had complained of not being helped financially by their daughters. Most of them opined that their daughters are their source of mental support as well. One of them told us,

'Amar meyer biye hoechilo jokhon o khub choto chilo. Or bore r bari oke prothom prothom besh bhalobashto. Kintu shomoer shathe shathe shob bodle gelo. Okarone taka chaite laglo. Amader boyish hocchilo, ar tai ei shob chahida metano khub beshi i mushkil hoe daracchilo. Tarpor tara taka marte laglo. Akdin oke ghore ora atka dilo jaate kore oi ghor ta ora agun die jalie dite pare. Bhagyochrome amra or i shoshur bari jacchilam tokhon ar tai shomoer moddhye pouche jai. Amadero galagali kore ar

> *mare ora, kintu tao oke oi norok theke amra baar kore ani. Kichu mash porei amar shami mara jaan. Amar meye porashona shekheni, tai kono chakri khuje amader shongshar chalano tar pokhye khub mushkil hoe daracchilo. Akhon jodio o beautician er kaaj kore akta parlour e. Akta beauticianir opor porashonao korechilo nijer takae. Ja taka rojgar kore sheta amar ar or dhosh bochor er cheler opore khoroch kore dae. Ami janina, kintu nischoi ami tamon kono khub bhalo kaaj korechi jaar jonne oke nijer jibone peyechi. Oke chara jibon ta boddho kothin hoe jeto'.*
>
> ('My daughter got married when she was very young. Her husband's family initially loved her. With time, however, everything changed. They demanded money unnecessarily. We were growing old and their demands were too much to meet. Then they started to beat her. One day she was locked up in a room to be set on fire. Fortunately, we were on our way to her in-laws' house and could reach there in time. We were also abused and beaten, but still, we managed to bring her out of that hell. Just a few months later my husband died. My daughter is uneducated, so finding a job to sustain our family was very difficult. Now, however, she does the work of a beautician in a parlour. With her own money, she had completed a beautician course. Whatever she earns is spent on her ten years old son and me. I don't know, but I feel I must have done something good for getting her in my life. Without her, my life would have been hard').

Almost every family had similar stories to share. There was another family where a daughter not only takes care of her mother but takes care of all her aunts who have been abandoned by their sons. A research took place in India, which showed how daughters sacrifice their happiness to take care of their mothers. One such daughter who was unmarried because of her family responsibility was asked what she will do when she grows old. She replied that her brother has passed over the duty of taking care of the mother to her. And she took it as a challenge and is happy that she can meet the responsibilities quite well and is entirely okay with the fact that she could not marry because of this (Kumar, 1995).

In a study, it was found that a lady in Ukraine chose to emigrate and take care of her sick mother, her widowed daughter and another daughter who was married but whose husband met with an accident, with regular sending of money and monthly visits. In another case, a married lady with two children also takes care of her elderly mother in Peru from Switzerland and manages to take her home whenever possible (Baldassar and Merla, 2013).

In Beleghata slum, there were some households where women after marriage took time to take care of their parents from in-law's house. They pay a regular monthly visit to their parents even if the parents are settled with their sons. Daughters often send letters and money when they are not able to go themselves. Daughters often are trapped in unfortunate situations like that of domestic violence and poverty, but according to the people of Beleghata, daughters manage to bear this responsibility with utmost courage and determination. In one of the cases mother said,

> *'Amar meye paribarik otyachar er shikar hoeche and some ar sharirik bhabe. Ekhane ami amar cheler shathe thaki je amae roj galagali kore chotokhato jinish er jonne. Amar meyesheta jane. Tai o nijer koshto amar shathe alochonao korena, karon o bhabe ami chintito hoe jabo. Akdin o thik korlo nijer shoshur baric here debe ar amar shathe thakbe chirokal er jonnyo. Ami oke prothome jor kore ferod pathalam, kintu pore bujhlam o ki oshombhob jontronar moddhye die jacchilo. Ami thik korlam amar cheleke bolbo chole jete kanoki shesh shat bochor dhore amar meyer biyer pore o bekar, amar shob taka nie nieche ar amar dekha shonao korent, aka chere die chole jeto. O oi haat ke mereche je oke atodin khawar jugieche, ar tai bhablam shomoe esheche oke boli nijer dik dekhe nite'.*
>
> ('My daughter has faced domestic violence in the form of regular mental and physical torture. Here I stay with my son who abuses me regularly for every little thing. My daughter is aware of it. Therefore, she refrains from discussing her issues with me as she feels I might get worried. One day she left her in-laws and decided to stay with me forever. Initially, I forced her to go back, but then I realized what pain she must have gone through. I decided to ask my son to leave as for the last seven years since my daughter's marriage he had remained unemployed, taken all my money I earned and left me unattended. He had bitten the hand that fed him and now it was time I felt to ask him to make his way').

Strangely, such scenes were not confined to a few households. Majority of the families, about 85 per cent of them were staying with their daughters and 5 per cent of them were dependent on their married daughters. In 1900, in the cities of America, almost 50 per cent of the widowed elderly lived with their daughters. It was found that more than 33 per cent of elderly people who were widowed lived with their daughters in America and 20 per cent of widowed elderly lived with their daughters in Canada (Dillon, 2008).

With an increase in life expectancy, there are several changes taking place. The first change is the increasing plausibility of families to live with more than two generations. However, most families have less number of siblings leading to a horizontal shrinkage. Less number of siblings implies that there are fewer caretakers of the elderly generations. Technological advancements have provided the scope to the younger generations with more jobs, making the older generation dependence on the young for direction, leading to a reversal of roles. These changes, in turn, are disintegrating the families. However, the relationship that each generation shares with each other is the result of several forces. Both generations belonged to different times, which mean both have been brought up in atmosphere which are different from each other. Hence, there are conflicting interests, choices and mentalities, values, family culture, attitudes. Whatever, the disparity is, these generations are tied to each other through transmission of values and ideas, knowledge about appropriate behaviour and lifestyles, leading to narrowing down of gaps between generations. However, there are changes taking place in today's society, impacting the aged significantly. In a study out of 37 joint family households, it was seen that 20 of them had a member from the second generation as head of the families highlighting on the fact that in joint families also there is a gradual shift of power from the first generation to the second generation. The study conducted showed that there were elderly who were asked to make arrangements for themselves, there was an elderly who said that she did not get any room to sleep at hours of daylight for other family members used them during this time. She had grandchildren's room, but did not have permission to use it. As many as 73 per cent of the second generation parents confessed that they were trying to take care of their needy and elderly parents, but somewhere facing challenges because of the needs of their own families which seemed more concerning to them because of the rising competition. Health was getting compromised and their security at the metropolis was at stake because of rising crime rate in these places. Parents left by children all alone were victims of seclusion, gloominess, uncertainty and were compelled to meet the basic necessities of life like marketing, visiting clinics when required, etc. (Sudha et al., 2007).

6

Leisure Moments

> Work is about a search for daily meaning as well as daily bread, for recognition as well as cash, for astonishment rather than torpor; in short, for a sort of life rather than a Monday through Friday sort of dying.
>
> — Studs Turkel

What does work mean to us? Work has got several meanings and recognitions attached to it which varies in importance from one person to another. Often people associate work with prestige and many a time it is more about social recognition. Sometimes it is connected to one's self-worth. For some, work is creativity, while for others it is an opportunity to make use of oneself to do something constructive and thus add meaning to it. However, for the majority of people work is a source of income. From this, it can never be perceived that it is the exclusive element that people find rewarding in a job, in fact, there are other factors as well like friendship, self-worth and power awarded to execute at one's will, etc. which are equally important. The most recognized meaning of work is earning money to buy the necessities of life and few luxuries if possible along with bringing about one's overall growth (Cavanaugh and Fields, 2002).

Herein, we are focusing on understanding the relation of various dimensions of the discourse of leisure in association with the elderly. In case of elderly population, after retirement when people are out of work, they get ample amount of time to sit back and relax. This is what leisure is all about. For researchers, the meaning of leisure is enjoyment, a flexible and innovative activity that people take up to relax (Gordon et al., 1976).

Leisure activities can be many, but researchers have divided them under certain heads. These are cultural, physical, social and solitary. The following fall under cultural head – visiting churches, concerts, meetings and going to sports events, etc. Physical activities involve playing, gardening, etc. Social activities include meeting friends and going for get-togethers, hitting parties, etc. and solitary activities mean engrossing oneself in music, television, reading (Bossé and Ekerdt, 1981).

Leisure activities often involve emotional aspects, cognitive as well as physical associations. Sexual activities are of high cognitive, physical and emotional intensity and these are also included in the category of leisure. Creative works, nurturing children and teaching activities are often classified as leisure in spite of their serious nature. Visiting events, travelling or clubbing including soft interactions with others, reading for enjoyment or even socialization are activities of moderately low level of intensity can also be categorized as leisure, just like low intensive activities of solitude, taking rest and nap, etc. (Cavanaugh and Fields, 2002).

Different perspective on leisure pursuits have stressed on the notion where preoccupation has been separated from interest. Preoccupation is similar to that of daydreaming, which often turns into interest when it is treated with more focus and seriousness. Interest for a person is something which includes all those activities which he/she likes doing, or is inquisitive about or is interested in, like jogging, fishing, etc. Leisure activity could be known in more depth, when the people involved in it are taken into consideration, to understand what activity means to them or what value it has in their eyes. A gourmet meal can be cooked by different people with different meanings attached to it. For some, it is an area of interest and liking, a part of one's leisure activity. While for others, it has got nothing to do with leisure, such as for professional chefs, cooking a gourmet meal is their work (Rapoport and Rapoport, 1975).

People engage in different leisure activities depending on how much competition they feel in comparison to other people of their age. It also depends on how much mental satisfaction is reached when the targeted goals are met and on how much income one earns from its performance. It may also depend on how much interest a person has in pursuing it and whether one has proper education and ability to practise it. Other things which are equally relevant are whether one's health gets affected or it requires transportation facilities too. Downhill skiing can be taken as an example as it is one such activity that can very well explain this. Skiing is costly, requires a more or less fit body with reasonably good physical coordination and also proper transportation to enjoy the sport. On the other hand, if reading is considered then with the help of public library the cost of accessing books can be minimized and also it does not require any physical effort. Taking up of leisure activities might be dependent on many or some such factors. During adulthood changes often take place regarding which leisure activity will be taken up by people as they might get influenced by any of these factors mentioned above. For example with age, physical prowess might face decline. One thing is to be noted that the exact connection between them and leisure activities are yet to be found out (Burrus-Bammel and Bammel, 1985).

Leisure activities vary depending on age as seen in cross-sectional studies (Howard and Bray, 1983). Young people engage in more number of intense activities like scuba diving, etc. in comparison to middle ageds, who engage in simple activities. With further increase in age, strenuous activities are performed less and they become more interested in sedentary activities like reading books or enjoying television programmes, etc. When one reaches old age, the intensity of work gets further reduced (Gordon et al., 1976). However, whatever the age may be leisure activities have been reported through one's engagement in these experiences of freedom (Larson et al., 1997).

Very little research has taken place on the leisure activities of the elderly. A few quantitative studies which have been done in this regard have mostly highlighted that the elderly are increasingly living in depression and isolation. Most of these researches have shown that old people usually spend time in watching television and listening to the radio. For Tokarski (1991), there is an inclination in focusing more on how old people become less productive or less active with age and also how they gradually become incompetent. Such a negative portrayal is not always true, but what is alarming is that it has a harmful consequence as well, as elderly starts internalizing such an image by recognizing this as their fate (Ateljevic et al., 2007).

Among elderly people, the most popular forms of leisure activities are watching television and meeting friends. There are other involvements as well in which elderly involve themselves, like gardening, reading, walking, caring for animals, travelling, etc. Kelly and others tried to find out how with increasing age, activities tend to follow a declining trend. Two such activities are – decrease in physical activities and recreational activities outside home (Kelly et al., 1986). Although they observed this declining trend, what they also found was stability in physical jobs inside home (Nussbaum et al., 2013). In a study, it was found that elderly people also like to take the pleasures of gambling by visiting poker clubs at night, which not only was a source of fun but was also a source of making money if played with wit and skill (Stone and Kalish, 1981).

A book by Mundorf and others (1997) is based on how older people get adapted to computer technologies. The authors stressed on the importance of workshops based activities which had proved to enhance their intellectual abilities and improve their access to information and knowledge. The elderly seemed to have a very positive outlook in their dealings with computers and it was found that computer programming interested them more than anything else, although a gender difference could be noticed as elderly males were found to be more interested in this field than the elderly females.

In this regard Furlong and Kearsley (1986) did not find any difference in the level of pickups that these elderly people had, or the number of mistakes that they committed, or in the level of excitement and enthusiasm, they experienced when compared to people of lower age groups. Probably, this is the reason why sites meant for senior people are increasingly gaining popularity. Example can be cited of Cyber Senior or Senior Net. It is interesting to note that elderly people also find the online world very interesting as this is where they can connect with new friends. Findings suggest that such a connection deters isolation (Mundorf et al., 1997).

In Beleghata slum, an interesting thing was noted, related to computer and mobile technology. Most of the young people here have mobile phones but very few of them have access to the computer. The elderly people told us about the benefits that such technologies could provide and also expressed their dissatisfaction at the fact that their illiteracy and lack of minimum knowledge refrained them to utilize the benefits, unlike the young ones. They also expressed on the positive consequences of access to ICTs, which inherently will help them to spend their time constructively. We were quite excited to know that people of 80–85 years were also equally interested in these technologies despite the fact that they were staying away from their young generations. Their answers were quite sorted as they told us how their children at the time of their stay with their parents would often ask for money to take admission in computer courses or how some children of their neighbourhood would come and share what computer is all about. They also told how television nowadays is always showing the potential benefits of this technology and how all these sources are making them aware that it has become an inevitable part of people's life.

However, not every person will be engaged or interested in the same kind of leisure pursuits. There are various factors which affect this. Money and time are two such variables. One who has money will have plenty of options to explore and will be engaged in leisure more than a person whose level of income is inadequate. The time factor is equally important. Sometimes because of availability of time after retirement, one can pursue leisure of one's own choice. However, for some elderly, time is a constraint even after retirement and hence pursuing leisure activities are often out of question for such people. Another significant factor that has a substantial influence on taking up of leisure activities is one's state of health and potential of mobility. There can be some preferred activities of an elderly, but health condition would play the determining role in finally allowing or disallowing him from engaging in these. Healthy people can take part in a wide range of activities compared to that of an unhealthy person. Mobility is also a significant factor which enables or disables participation in leisure activities. Inability to move can obstruct a person to travel. For this reason, many of them remain dependent on others for purposes of transportation and in some cases if proper transportation facilities are not available they fail to commute to the places of their choice. Family and friends also are an essential part of an elderly person's life. When they live with their children and grandchildren most of their leisure time is spent with them.

Those elderly who are married find the company of their spouses good enough as a way to spend their time. But, when children get separated and spouses die, the family environment gets threatened. In such conditions they find pleasure in spending time with their peer groups which means friendship also plays a vital role for people during their old age.

Subculture theory explains that aged people form their own groups. Rose (1965) was the first one to propose such a theory. In this group, they have their own beliefs, norms and values. They have certain expectations and habits which are different from people of other age groups. They, therefore, form their subculture where they have this separate identity which confirms to their age. The theory also says that once a person grows old, he gets to experience that the bonding he has with his society is loosening. Therefore, instead of attaching himself to people from every other age group he tends to be associated with people of his own age group. Formation of such an aged subculture is primarily because of the degrading status of the aged. There is a negative way to view the aged in the United States of America, where negative labelling is so severe that people do not want to be regarded old. The aged subculture endows on its members the status based on aspects which were not previously relevant, like educational attainment, financial condition, or occupational status. Instead, it is based on health and mobility issues. Rose (1965) said that there would be one positive outcome of such a subculture which would strive to replace the negative image that serves the old age people's status presently with the one that is more positive and that would change the definitions that have been ingrained into the culture for so many years (Rose, 1965).

In Beleghata, the percentage of people who loved to be with people of their age group was as high as 80 per cent. Majority of them were of the opinion that aged people would best understand their concerns and would be able to relate more easily to what, they as elderly, are going through and through discussions can decrease the levels of depression reached due to the daily turmoil. A person's environment also is critical along with his location and background. A person from a particular background might be exposed to a type of activity while a person from some other background might not be familiar with, which restricts him from pursuing it. This we find in our study as well. In the city, the elderly might be quite familiar with the use of modern technologies, but people from Beleghata slum are aware of it as they cannot use it and given the background and money that most of them have, they are not in a position to make it a part of their lives. Like Shobita (name changed) said,

> *'Amar akhon bochor shottor hobe. Ami amar nati natnider theke sheke shob notun projuktir kotha shuntam. Amae ora hajar hajartakao dite bolto kanona oder ma baba eishob chahida guloke kokhono pattai ditona. Oder jokhon ami jigyasha kortam je egulor shubidhe ki ar ato dorkari kano eshob ora bolto eshob khali dorkari i na egulo akhon beche thakar*

> *joneo khub guruytopurno. Ora bollo duniyar shob kichu oikhane ache ar computer na thaka mane tumi bakider theke pichiye acho. Amar mone ache ami oke amar nati ke jomano taka theke du hajar taka diechilam. O amae akta chotto jinish er moto ki akta dekhalo, bollo iota naki mobile phone. Amae o bollo landline phone jeta ami telephone booth e dekhechi tar shathe mobile phone er parthokyo ta ki. Tarpor ami tar prochondo boro jei shubidhe sheta janlam, oitake naki ak jaega theke arek jaega nie jawa jae shathe kore, jena landline er khetre shombhob na, ar mobile phone e naki chithi o lekha jae. Amar mone hoe Jodi amaro orom akta thakto. Jodi amar kache computer thakto, akhyorik gyan thakto, ar shadyomoto taka thakto tahole ami ei nanan shubidhe gulo nite partam ar jibon ta onnyo bhabe katate partam*'.
>
> ('I am about 70 years old. From my grandchildren, I used to hear when they lived with me about these modern technologies. They often requested me to pay thousands of rupees to buy them as their parents never paid any heed to their demands. When I asked them about the benefits and why is it so much important, they explained that nowadays it is not only essential but a necessity to survive. They told me that almost everything in this world is available there and not having a computer forces you to lag behind the rest. I remember I paid my grandson ₹ 2,000 from my savings. He showed me a small object like thing which he told me is a mobile phone. He also made me familiar with the differences between a landline which I have seen in Telephone Booths and the mobile phones. I then got to know its immense potential for it can be carried from one place to another unlike the landlines and also he said one could write down letters and send to others. I wish I had one. But, who will I call or what shall I do with it. If I had the computer, knew letters and enough money to avail the different facilities it has, I could have spent life differently').

However, such desires were found not in too many households even though knowledge about the existence of computer and mobile was found among most elderly, probably because of their awareness about their inability to use them.

In a study which involved few focus groups, it was found that religion was something which most of the aged agreed to stay associated. Although here women irrespective of their age believed that increase in age increased one's religious performances, survey brought to the fore that no such increase was observed and in fact, a decrease in religious activities was reflected both among men and women after the age of 55 (Hareven, 1996). In another study which was conducted to learn about the religious activities of elderly above 65 years old, it was found that in this sample 61 per cent of them visited the church at least one day in every week. Added to this percentage about 59 per cent of them were engaged in listening to religious events broadcast by TV and radio no less than one day a week and a higher rate of about 79 per cent was involved in reading religious books such as bible at least once a week. 43 per cent of the respondents reported praying at a fixed time every day. Another 31 per cent in this sample opined that they offered continuous prayer to God during the entire day. Only 3 per cent of them did not engage in prayer at all. In this sample, women's engagement in religious activities was more than the males (Palmore, 1985). There are some other studies as well which show that with an increase in age, people get absorbed in religious activities more intensely. Opinions have been collected from public polls to understand the relationship between religious activities and increase in age. It has been found that there has been a consistent rise in levels of attending church, reading of devotional books and offering of prayers for people aged 50 or above compared to young people (Toch, 1953).

In another study over 597 protestant homes, elderly women aged 65 years old or more were studied to explore religious inclinations and dependency. It was found that with increase in religious engagements, religious dependency increases as well. These old women had bitter relations with their family members and were not much connected with friends or with their relatives or even with people from lower age groups and were also not much interested in participating in group activities (Pan, 1952). Idler and others have shown that advent of old age brings with it the inclination to visit their religious places of worship. Studies have also revealed the difficulty for people to visit churches and offer other religious services once they reach this age, the reason being ill health and deteriorating physical ability (Idler et al., 2001).

Herein, it can also be said that irregular presence of the elderly people in places of worship is often as a result of failing health condition and incapacity to travel which necessitates them to shift their attachment to religious activities from there to more available forms of engagement like through electronic media or prayers (Mindel and Vaughan, 1978).

In Beleghata, most of the elderly spend their time in religious activities. A majority of them have been abandoned by their children and lived all alone. For them, spiritualism turned out to be an epitome of peace and solace from the ongoing upheavals in life. Most of them are suffering from various physical ailments, like vision problems, arthritis, diabetes and heart issues, they are not able to spend time in activities that require physical and mental efforts. Some of them expressed that since there is nobody to talk to they feel God is someone with whom they can share their sorrows and get blessings in return. They feel if they communicate with God their wishes will be fulfilled soon. They also think that because of their faith and prayers they can fight in the most adverse situations.

We asked the respondents about the different ways in which they wish to spend time. Almost all of them said that they want to spend time with their family members. However, for most of them, this is not possible because of their children's attitude towards them. As a good number of them lives in isolation separated from their children they are not able to lead their lives according to their own will. Spending time with grandchildren seemed to be a distant dream for most of them, as even getting a glance of their faces was barely possible most of the time. For those who were surviving alone told that for most of the day they cook and do household activities like sweeping and washing clothes and utensils and during afternoon try taking a nap. In this slum, it is a part of people's daily routine to gather outside during evening and spend time in each other's company. When they meet, they discuss and share each day's work. Also, this time is perfect to know what's cooking in other's families. Elderly people generally meet separately and often we heard young women complain that these get-togethers are merely a way to gossip about daughters-in-law.

Negotiating Death

Death is an inevitable part of life and cannot be avoided even if we try. Death of parents are something which we would never like to witness but it is inevitable and obvious. When we reach the middle years of lives, we are forced to confront this reality of losing our parents or that of our partners. However, it does not happen so quickly. It is sometimes an expected fact that when people reach their middle age, they are required to take care of their children and aged parents and the time spent on both is often the same. Couples living together might find it stressful when ailing and aged parents come to settle down with them as it can sometimes create strains on their married relationship. This happens because of a mature adult person whose responsibilities are already too much and therefore when they are to take it up, they find it too much burdensome. However, this can be viewed from a positive angle as well. It is seen that since parents and children belong to two different generations, there can be conflicts in their thoughts that might have existed for years. When parents age it gives an opportunity to both the parties to resolve such differences. The time and energy spent might require extra effort, but the closeness and intimacy brought about by it are worth it sometimes. Also, it helps a person grow as an individual by developing patience. Elderly people often feel great in providing care to kids, hence if a family can accept them well then they can often prove to be people who can share their wisdom and love with them. It has been seen that adults who provide the care to the elderly parents get depressed more than the elderly themselves at a rate four times higher. The reason can be a fear of one's nearing future of ageing and also that of ultimate demise that every old person reflects in him through his frailty, weakness and helplessness. When a baby is born, a mother takes her complete care and nurtures her. As she grows old, she is no longer able to be independent and take care of her child. Instead, the opposite happens, there is a kind of role-reversal when the child is now a grown-up adult and in a situation where her so long self-sufficient mother needs her help like she required when young.

This role-reversal is often very confusing to understand. Couples might find this stressful to see how their parents slowly become dependent on them and they might become depressed to comprehend this fact. To come out of such depression support groups might often prove to be helpful (Steffen et al., 2011).

Old people often with spend more time with friends than with their family members. An immense amount of pleasure often accompanies a friendly relationship and there is flair of frankness and honesty in this bond which helps in eliminating all sorts of worries and daily problems which the elderly face. When there is an intimate relationship with an elderly with his friends, he feels wanted and valued by them. Old age often brings with it several changes and friendship does the magic of dealing with it and helps to overcome the crisis that this age has brought about (Papalia, 2004). Friendship is not about carrying out any task or meeting specific needs on a daily basis which happens in case of families. Friendship is a bond which is full of excitement and leisure (Antonucci and Akiyama, 1996). Friendship becomes essential especially when the elderly start feeling that they are losing control of their lives (Adams, 1986). Old age means there are bound to be specific physical changes and other issues, so this might give them a feeling of being unwanted and not valued. However, when they have friends, it gives them a kind of reassurance that their existence matters and they are still appreciated (Essex and Nam, 1987).

In case of women, self-disclosure and emotional expressions might be related to increasing life expectancy (Weg, 1987). However, friendship does not increase contentment in life if seen from overall perspective, as compared to the satisfaction brought about by spending time with spouses. The essence of friendship lies in the fact that friends are occasionally meet and for a brief period. Instant delight springs from friendship, unlike family which is the primary source of emotional support and security. Therefore friendship plays a constructive role in ushering upon the aged a feeling of well-being, but in case of absence or issues in the family, aged people are led to deal with its range of negative consequences (Antonucci and Akiyama, 1996). However, often the task of giving care to an elderly, or in cases of emergencies neighbours take the place of family members if they are far away from aged person and friends in these situations fulfil these responsibilities. It is true that friends will not be able to take the place of family members and spouses but they can compensate for their absence. In Netherlands, it was found that among 131 old people, who had either never married or are widowed or have been divorced are living a life devoid of loneliness in the company of their friends. In fact, friendship seemed to be so crucial that it affected them more than being single and pushed them into solitude (Dykstra, 1995).

Friendship in old age involves spending time in leisure activities which are shared among aged people, for whom friends are often exceptionally carefully chosen and revolves around interaction which goes beyond the daily routines, thus giving a positive feeling to the people involved (Larson et al., 1986). Life is full of transitions which shift from one form of the goal to the other, where childhood is deeply connected to the roots of its family, middle childhood days and even in the initial years of adolescence, family and emotions become less critical compared to goals combined with knowledge. Then gradually during the late years of middle age, one's priority becomes family once again. The reason why such a shift happens again is that by the time a person reaches the late middle age he has already accomplished the goals of selecting a partner, developing a career path and forming an identity, along with the realization that death is a definite destiny of every person. Such happenings push people to cling to their emotional goals all over again, however, in this age they become quite choosy regarding interactions and selecting people with whom connection will be emotionally meaningful (Schaie and Lawton, 1997).

In United States, people have a high probability to live for long years till one becomes old. If 65 years is considered as the onset of old age, then it will be evident that 33.3 per cent of one's adulthood is spent in this phase and for people who cross ninety spend 50 per cent of their adulthood in old age. At a particular point, a person retires, becomes weak and all these changes can often come along with feelings of loneliness. However, some relationships do not die out even when one ages and hence are a source of varied benefits to people. Close social ties provide comfort, happiness and healthy life and also makes one live longer compared to the ones who do not have such close ties (Miller, 2003).

Toni Antonucci and others surveyed to study about social networks of old people and found that adults who are older have less number of social partners compared to the younger adults, but both have an equal number of close ties and the former's relations with family are much extensive when compared to the latter. Younger adults are connected more with casual relationships and people who are not part of their family and the opposite is true for older adults who have stronger bonds with family and friends (Antonucci, 2001).

Older adults tend to be more connected with family because after retirement they lose their connection with people they met during their work life. According to Carstensen and her colleagues, with an increase in age-old people realize that the time left is short and as a result, they feel good to spend time with their closest ones (Larson, Mannell and Zuzanek, 1999). For young adults, it might be feasible to make new friends and move in romantic relationships, but for aged, family relationships and already existing friends seemed to be more critical (Miller, 2003).

Forty-eight per cent of the time is spent by healthy elderly people in leisure pursuits and other social activities. The jobs which are obligatory constitutes 38 per cent of their time which includes taking care of oneself, carrying out household activities, doing necessary shopping and other such similar tasks. Such activities are often performed by the aged people alone comprising about 60 per cent (Walker, 2004). Kosberg said that people after retirement often take to religious pursuits and a good number of them are engaged in taking care of the young ones, attending family functions, performing domestic works, etc. (Kosberg, 1994).

People stop working during old age because of physical problems mostly. The second reason why aged people do not work is that of assurance of help from children and relatives. However, even if they are engaged in paid work, significant time is spent on unpaid work as well. This includes cleaning of the house, taking care of livestock, carrying out the responsibility of caring for grandchildren, repairing household stuff, growing vegetables and the like, that can help in consumption for the family members, gathering firewood and collecting water, etc. In five villages, studies were carried out on old men and women and they were questioned about their daily routine and the role therein and it was found that there is a gendered division of tasks where aged women carry out the care taking roles and other works such as cleaning and cooking. In all these villages every aged woman did the job of cooking, excluding the very ill and frail ones. Financial management was all taken care of by the aged males who had control over the income earned by the family members, distributing them at times of need. This role was played by elderly females as well, who besides being a banker of household perform tasks which earn them income. Taking care of animals and other burdensome jobs were carried out by elderly males. They are allowed to work on their terms, once the expected jobs are already performed. On the other hand, despite such obligations, women seemed to be worried about every little thing and took care of everyone. Old men without wives or dependent on them carry out broader responsibilities (United Nations Economic and Social Commission for Asia and the Pacific, 2002).

People involve themselves in leisure pursuits to eliminate all sorts of stress and age gracefully and efficiently. A study was carried out to determine leisure activities of elderly people. They divided the activities into groups – physical and solitary ones. These include reading newspapers, watching television, listening to the radio, reading devotional books, or watching movies, etc. These also include activities which are cultural and social like spending time with friends and relatives, taking care of grandchildren, etc. There are other ways also to spend time during old age, like performing household tasks, going for walks, or engaging in personal hobbies. It was found with an increase in life expectancy, time spent in leisure activities also increases, where aged people from 76–80 years old were highly interested in leisure activities, but people aged between 66 to 70 years showed disinterest in such pursuits (Francis, 2014).

A study on 287 elderly individuals was done to find out their change in advancing lifestyles with an increase in age. About 59 per cent of the respondents replied that there had been specific changes in how they are leading their lives as unlike their past they can spend more time with their family members including their children. There is a rise of 7.7 per cent respondents' involvement in religious activities. Among them what constitutes significant part of such activities are reading religious books or worshipping. In this study it was found elderly men are more interested in religious performances than elderly women. About 19.3 per cent of the respondents felt that there has been a decrease in their interest in work and family affairs. Their roles and responsibilities as breadwinners got reduced with an increase in age. The disappearance of joint families, decrease in the number of children, economic insecurity, the increasing rate of migration of people to the urban areas and inadequate accommodation facilities in cities and other complications of the modern world are the primary reasons why the elderly are facing so many problems (Nasreen, 2009).

In our research study as most of the households had no television or radio and a majority of them were illiterate, hence instead of reading religious books their interest was more on praying and worshiping God and spending time in nearby temples. The next activity in which they participated was household functions and the third activity where many of them were involved was going for walks with other aged ladies, gather together and enjoy each other's company. However, worshiping God was the most enthusiastic activity that gave pleasure to the elderly who participated. Most of the respondents told us how difficult their lives are and how God has been there all the time to support them at times of need. Some of them have managed to find some space to accommodate idols so that they can offer their prayers, which is a source of both hope and relief. The next major activity that interested them the most was gathering together with other aged people and chatting with them. However, friends with whom they felt connected were mostly of their age group and only those people whom they have known for years. They seemed to show no interest to share their feelings with men or women who were new or younger than them. The reasons they told us revolved around the fact that aged people are best to understand each other's situation and nobody else, they will know the various changes and problems that this age group faces. The younger generations according to them are responsible for putting them in bad circumstances and therefore are not in a position to identify with their plight.

Household activity was something that according to most of them was forceful. None of them was willing enough to engage in household works because of their age and wanted their children and their spouses to help them. Unfortunately, not many of their expectations could be fulfilled as several of the elderly from the Beleghata slum were deserted by their children. Therefore, household work was not an area of interest, but it was an unavoidable activity which they had to do in order to survive. Ashalata Devi (name changed) explained her situation with regards to what she loves doing and what she dislikes the most, yet is thrown into a situation where her leisure interests are buried deep under her daily necessities. She said,

> *'amar akhon akashi bochor, ar amar biye hoechilo baro bochor boyeshe. Thik oidin thekei ami jantam amae shoshur shashurir jonne kaj korte hobe. Ami shob kichu puro mon die kortam, kintu akhon amar cheler biyer pore ar would jonne bhebechilam ferode kichu pabo bhebechilam ar amae ato kaj kort people who are eligible but did not e hobena are ato barir kaaj nie chintao korte hobena. Kintu, janen, or biyer por kajer chap aro bere geche, karon akhon ami boumar jonneo ranna kori, je amar boyish ar shashther jonne ektuo bhabena. Ami amar cheleke bolechi je boyesher shathe shathe khub mushkil hoe jacche amar pokkhye raana, porishkar, dhoya mocha ar bajar kora. O pattai daena. O atotai udashin je o bollo nijer jaega dekhe nao Jodi oshubidhe hoe ar nalish korona. Amar baki bondhuder shathe goppo korteo bhalo lage, kintu shomoe hoena ba shorir bhalo thakena'.*
>
> ('I am 81 years old and got married at the age of 12. Right from that day, I knew I would be required to work for my in-laws. I did everything with all my heart, but now after my son's marriage and because of my age, I thought I would get something in return. I thought I will not be required to work any longer in relation to household activities. But, you know after his marriage, I am burdened with more work. Now I cook for my daughter-in-law as well, who hardly cares about my age and health? I told my son that with days it is getting difficult for me to continue working as at this age cooking, cleaning, washing, pulling up to the grocery store, etc. is very hectic. He doesn't care. In fact, he is so indifferent that he asked me to make my way if I have issues and not complain. I love chatting with my friends, but either I don't get the time to do that, or I am not well').

Therefore, people here even in their old age are involved in physical activities and are hardly able to take rest and are always doing something or the other, like cooking, cleaning, washing, or even going for walks. In fact, such activities have a positive side as they are said to be good for one's health irrespective of age. It brings about an overall development by reducing stress and depression and also helps in getting rid of the chronic illness. As mentioned earlier, increase in age brings with it difficulty in mobility and ability to function properly, but if regular physical activities are done even the very old and frail adults can improve such skills (Butler et al., 1998).

Research shows that there is a decrease in the level of physical activities with an increase in age. It was reported that people within the age group of 65 to 74 years old and more than 85 years old vary from 25 per cent to 11 per cent with a slight increase in percentage in between 75 and 84 years old people during 2007–2008. Elderly men aged 65 years or more than that (28%) are more into physical work than elderly women (18%) (Federal Inter-agency Forum on Aging-Related Statistics). However, their involvement during old age reduces in intensity as they are forced to retire from a job after a certain age. Health-related issues are also equally important for them to minimize their level of involvement. There are certain cultural norms as well which regulates the Do's and Don'ts with regards to one's roles and activities. So when this involvement reduces there must be some other means via which they engage themselves and that becomes an important part of their lives (Hareven, 1996).

In this slum, we find that most of the elderly population yearn to talk, stay engaged and valued. In fact, everyone desires to spend time with family members, but in most cases they are not able to do so, as they are forced to live an isolated life far away from near and dear ones. Like already mentioned, old people are not able to spend much time with their children and grandchildren, despite their longing for their love and company. The ones whose husbands were alive were seen to be engaged in traditional gender roles like that of cooking and cleaning. Another thing that could be observed in this slum was the difficulties faced by women because of their husband's death. First, this absence caused immense emotional turmoil and since, most of them were still earning to survive themselves and other dependent members, their leisure interests were forced to be kept aside. This means that there is excessive pressure on them even at this age, for which they are tapped out, making the situation extremely frustrating to tolerate.

7

Economic Situation and Aged Populace

This chapter shall throw light on the financial situation of the elderly in Beleghata Slum. Before that, we need to know whether they have any knowledge about financial literacy or not. Literacy here can be understood as the skill or ability of people. While considering financial literacy, we should look at it as ability or skill in the area of finance.

Organization for Economic Cooperation and Development (OECD) defined financial literacy in relation to a person who is regarded as a financial literate if one can utilize information and take advice and understand products and concepts related to finance, has the skill to recognize the financial risks and also have an understanding about it and is clued-up on taking financial decisions. We have a general understanding of financial literacy, as a condition where chances of failure are minimum and a high probability of success, so that marginalization due to lack of economic resource can be prevented and therefore obstructions for social participation does not come in the way. That means prosperity of individuals will increase as a consequence which when taken together will make a society affluent at the same time (Rabušicová, 2002).

However, this form of financial literacy usually lacks in elderly population, women and people with low educational levels (Honekamp, 2014). Research has shown that many a time the elderly lack definite idea about how the financial market works and regarding its various components including interest rates and because of this they are not able to take any independent decision regarding financial matters. They look up to other members of the family to even sign a contract or for financial advice. It is seen that the elderly people have a helpful nature, who in times of financial difficulties of their near and dear ones try to interact and extend a supporting hand to other family members. However, they are themselves very much dependent on others for various reasons like health, living, low pension. They have poor education level as well, which enables the corrupt banking staff and sometimes their family members, to swindle money from them. Therefore, the aged people must be provided adequate legal protection and be assisted in enhancing their financial knowledge so that they are a part of the consumer society (Niemi et al., 2009).

Many studies including EFM (Education for Ministry) show that people of 65 years and above have shown signs of diminishing degrees of financial literacy (Moody, 2013). This has interested the economists who are now trying to find out the cause and result of lack of financial literacy, because only then can they understand to make proper retirement plan and financial security at the time of retirement.

A finding suggests that people are unaware even about the basic concepts related to finance that are vital to making any decision in an investment plan or even in saving. This is found among both the young and the aged of America and some other countries as well. No doubt, to deal with this situation several NGOs and even governments have taken initiatives, such as the saving campaign in Japan, the pension privatization scheme in Sweden (Lusardi and Mitchelli, 2007). However, making retirement compulsory for people after they have attained a certain age has placed old age to be regarded by the governments of the West as 'social problem'. Retirement policies aimed at replacing the old employees with the new and young ones in economic positions. This was done to achieve a smooth departure of the elderly people at a time of health deterioration or death, which would save the society from the hands of instability and disorder (Bond et al., 1993). Therefore, attention was drawn towards the problems people face when they are out of a job.

Thus, retirement was a natural solution which was socially engineered to eliminate the problems that ageing population can bring about and as a result shake the equilibrium of labour-market. Talcott Parsons has well explained this in his strain theory. He focused on the social isolation that individual faces, as a consequence of loss of job which also makes the people lose the contacts of the workplace and become detached from the workplace structure and eventually are pushed into a condition of 'role less role'. Therefore, when people are reincorporated, it is just another way of adjusting oneself to society that helps them drive a level of mental satisfaction which so long was drawn from one's job. This organized comradeship is compensation that is considered to be efficacious sociologically (Parsons, 1942).

Disengagement theories say that old age is a period which is followed by a period where one was occupied with work and the activities and culture surrounding it. Stepping into old age is the start of a time when such culture would be absent and therefore they will have to readjust through disengagement from previous roles to the new patterns of life which may not generate income (Cumming and Henry, 1961).

Disengagement is a natural process where both society and the aged individuals engage in a mutual withdrawal and this means that when people grow old and die the order in society is not disturbed (Neugarten and Neugarten, 1996). The process cannot be avoided, as during old age this is what expected to happen. According to them, disengagement is essential so that society does not need to go through any chaotic situation. The disengagement process limits the range of activities in which an elderly may wish to participate. The theorists claim that this is how the society rearranges itself while old members die with new ones to replace them with their 'new blood' (Cumming and Henry, 1961).

As per Bromley, with old age, people face decreased levels of psychological well-being and biological capability. Therefore, according to him with this phase's arrival, disengagement helps in adjusting people to the new roles that perfectly fit their age (Bromley, 1966). While the retirement was evident in job sectors, the employers were prepared for the loss of their senior employees after a certain age to be replaced by new ones (Kunkel and Morgan, 2015).

During old age, people are no longer able to follow the scripts that cultures have written for them for the early years of their lives, instead, at this stage they live with scarce resource and create new scripts and perform them. In some cases, the days are passed in loneliness and feeling of worthlessness waiting to see its end (Blau, 1973).

However, this theory does not suggest that advent of old age will toll the death knell. Old age means loss of income for the ones who had to retire from work. Therefore, according to the theory, despite carrying out daily responsibilities, old age should be occupied with jobs that are more relaxing, flexible and voluntary. It says that the elderly to be less involved with the environment and gives a logic which is biologically based on supporting the idea that with age, interest in activities is lost. It also asks the elderly to withdraw oneself from playing the central role in a family. Therefore, before someone falls off his perch, he very slowly cuts adrift from the bonds and roles that he so long treasured. He then silently bids goodbye to not to rupture the tranquility of society. Disengaging oneself from the essential spheres of life might come about to different people at different ages, but the ultimate reality of disengagement is real and inevitable. In fact, for Henry and Cumming, people who do not sever the ties and actively remain a part of everything, are going to be labelled as 'unsuccessful disengagers' for not being able to respond to the universal way in which elderly people should withdraw themselves. Hence, their reactions would be deemed dysfunctional (Cumming and Henry, 1961).

In Beleghata, we have seen some people who at different age are wilfully withdrawing themselves from daily responsibilities and trying to voluntarily be a part of activities that would not interfere with their ill health. Pratima (name changed) said that she is 67 years old with lots of physical issues, which compelled her to leave her job. She now spends her entire time worshipping and also wishes to be with her family, especially with her grandchildren. She said,

> *'Amar akhon gona din. Amar jibone ja ami sharirik shomoshyar shathe bhugchi ami amar shesh din gulo shanty te katate chai amar priyo manush gulor shathe ar oi kaj gulo korte chai jei jinish gulo amar korte bhalo lage'.*
>
> ('My days are gone. With the number of health issues I have, I want to spend these last days of my life in peace with the ones I love and through my engagement in works I love to do').

According to activity theorists, ageing should be seen with optimism rather than in such a negative light. It evolved as a criticism of disengagement theory. Ageing can be successful if the values and way of living in middle years can be carried out in old age. By starting something new and fresh at this phase can also help to keep oneself well absorbed and promote activities that would improve overall well-being. They promoted the idea that social roles must be continued and interactions must go on to be happy in life. If one is disengaged at various levels of life, dissatisfaction cannot be avoided. For them, it is mandatory to find a replacement for the relationships that are lost, for the works that have come to an end. Instead of considering old age to be the end of all happiness, it should be considered as the new beginning of a new chapter in life. A new leaf should be turned over to embark on their journey of post-retirement days (Lemon et al., 1972).

People who lived in Beleghata quit job only after they knew they are no longer wanted/desired to continue, for their declining health. Most of them were into temporary works when active and when they were out of the job, to feel productive, they engaged in works which were more temporary. When they felt good, they worked and when did not, they stayed back home. They were more into carrying out household activities, gossiping with other aged people, worshipping and for the ones who did not have too many issues with leg and joints went out for evening walks. While conversing, they said, after work these are the things that made them feel good about themselves. Those jobs which earned them their living were also the reason for their physical strain. However, most of them considered it essential for the level of economic security it provided. Kanchana (name changed), aged 72 said that she used to work as a maidservant in 4 houses but then because of health problems had to quit, now she has a teashop in a nearby place, which she maintains on her own and attends it only when she is physically fit. She does other works as well as she said,

> *'Amar akta cha er dokan ache adh kilo metre dur e barir theke dur e. Ami motamoti roj i eta khuli, kintu oshushtho hole khuli na. Bhalo jinish etai*

eta amar opore nirbhor kore, je amae keo kichu bolte parbena Jodi ami kamai kori. Amar iccha nah oleo jaina, kintu eta khub kom shomoe i hoe. Akhon eta akmatro ae korar upae amar. Eta baade ami puja kori ar baki boyoshko der shathe adda di. Eshob kore ami shanty pai ar amae eshob shukh dae'.

('I have a teashop just half a kilometre away from my house. I generally open it regularly, but if I am sick, then I do not. The good thing is, it depends on me and nobody can tell me anything for being absent. I am also absent if I do not feel like going, but this happens rarely. It is now the only source of earning. Other than this, I generally worship and gossip with other elderly people in the slum. It gives me peace and makes me happy').

However, both these theories were criticized. Disengagement theory was criticized on the ground that it was a way to encourage unequal policies that favour the idea of retirement and showing old age as unidirectional and something that is inherent and universal. Old age faces a crisis regarding economic resources, health and thus is unable to perform various activities. There is hardly any income generating source in which they can participate. However, activity theory does the work of impractically encouraging aged people to prosper despite these short-comings (Hochschild, 1975).

Therefore, we can as now see that in old age one of the most critical problems is financial crisis. To study about their economic position in society the main aspects that are taken care of money earned, or expended and saved. In India for the poor economic condition, widowed elderly women are in the most inconvenient position and this is so because of their gender, age and the fact that they are widowed. Although in India, taking care of elderly parents by sons is considered an obligation but as mentioned earlier because of the various developments, this is no longer a reality. The only solution left, therefore, is employment. As they are not much educated and because of the country's social system and culture they suffer from the marginalized status of which they become a part from the very beginning. The sufferings of women in patriarchal societies are looked down upon and this marginalized position has multiplied manifold. In case of older women, since they are mostly dependent on others for financial support, are often considered a burden in society. Old age is therefore not an age where mental worries diminish and in Mumbai, Raju found that 70 per cent of poor elderly have anxieties because of different issues. Widowed women seem to suffer from depression more because they are dependent on others followed by their husband's death (Raju, 2002).

In a study, it was found that among the widowed aged women, 57.9 per cent of them from slums were still working and earning a livelihood and when non-slum areas were studied only 17.8 per cent were found to be earning. In a particular age group from 58–70 years old, these aged widows were earning more than the ones who were more than 70 years old, as the percentage showed to be as high as 65.2 per cent. With an increase in age, they have increasingly chosen to refrain from work and therefore earn no more. In non-slum areas, 80 per cent of the widowed aged women were not working, hence adding nothing to the economy, irrespective of their age. The reason is economic uncertainty and insecurity that is more severe in the slum areas compared to the non-slum areas which force these women to work even when aged, but of course, after a certain age, they lose this status. The study showed that within 58 years to 70 years 54.3 per cent of the aged widows were working in service sector such as a cook, or as a maid. 45 per cent of elderly women in the slum areas worked as a maid. However, with age, when their physical condition deteriorated, they were no longer able to continue working. The same research revealed that no aged widowed women were engaged in service in the non-slum areas. In case of household activities, the study showed that in both the areas, women continue to work as long as their health permit and quit only when they are no longer able to because of physical incapability. In case of getting a pension, 11.6 per cent of the slum aged women are pensioners and in case of a non-slum area the percentage is 17.8 per cent, but in case of the former those women are the old-age pensioners and for the later, a pension is earned because of husband's death. Therefore, economic condition is a serious issue in the slum area, but definitely, age plays the determining role in constraining one's capacity to work. The independent status was more in slum areas compared to non-slum areas, as one widowed woman aged more than 81 years old was still working when the study was conducted. However, age is a big factor which does restrict the aged women from working in later ages. As age increases, they start becoming dependent more and more on others, especially on sons. Some elderly are dependent on married daughters and some rely on their brothers. There were some aged widowed as per the studies who were dependent on their grandsons as well, while others survived on charity. Therefore, as we can see elderly people's dependency, especially that of widowed elderly on others is very common. However, there is a difference in a slum and non-slum areas, where slum elderly are less dependent than the non-slum elderly with increased rates of dependency with an increase in age. In non-slum areas, the culture of traditional India is one of the main factors why elderly females have stayed away from engaging in any social activities and have confined themselves to the household activities. While in the slum areas, it is the economic burden that forces the aged women to engage in income-generating activities to provide additional income to the family in which many a time they are not willingly participating and which is beyond their physical capacity. The study showed the dependency percentage of widowed elderly of non-slum areas and it was as high as 91.2 per cent. In slum areas, the percentage of dependency is increasing as well. In the slum areas, about half of the respondents (46.4%) were earning from their present source of employment for example as a maid or cook. This scenario is absent in non-slum area as not a single widowed elderly was earning from the current employment. Other than current employment the next source of their income was the pension. This scenario was slightly higher in non-slum areas as the percentage was found to be 17.8 per cent and for slum the percentage was slightly low, standing at 11.5 per cent, where the main source of financial support of the elderly are their children, which is not the case with slum area elderly people. However, 11.6 per cent of the slum and a little less than that which is 9.9 per cent of the non-slum area have no income earning source. This is the reason why dependency on children is a common feature among them, though slum area people's main source of income is still their employment. The study has also included the nature of asset that is possessed by widowed elderly such as land, jewellery, cash and utensils. In the slum, about 88.7 per cent possess no asset as such. In case of non-slum area elderly widows, the percentage is 58.7 per cent. This is, therefore, the source of data which shows the poor condition of elderly regarding their dependency on others. 68.1 per cent of the widows from slum are under debt and for non-slum areas it is just 14.8 per cent. The reasons behind taking loans are mostly for daughter's or son's marriage, for meeting medical expenses, or for some other familial responsibilities and this is higher in the age group of 58 years to 70 years elderly widows as the percentage for this group is 76.1 per cent. Also, in a slum, loan repayment becomes an impossible probability as their income is too poor to meet it. Therefore, their condition is always quite stressful. The responsibilities that they have to bear with regard to acute financial pressure, marriage of daughters, or even the unemployment or underemployed status, their indebtedness and even the taking care of disabled member, increases one's level of liability and at this age it becomes a tough road to travel which is a reason why slum's elderly widows are forced to be a prominent part of families, as it can help reduce the huge economic instability (Ray et al., 2003).

The problems of widows were quite severe until the time the world had witnessed one of its most significant wars of all times – World War I. Widows had to sustain their families despite their age, condition, number of dependent children and fluctuating labour-market. However, income generated from available employment used to be too meagre to fulfil their daily needs. Therefore, they were left with no choice but to rely on others, like relatives or local authorities of places where the widows lived who could provide them with supplementary income. Elderly widows because of their age often became physically ill and therefore it used to be too tiring for them to work as full-timers. However, they were forced to be part of some part-time work, to avoid their communes and relatives consider them as burden. When widows became frail and weak because of their age, it became nearly impossible for them to participate in full-time jobs. For example working as maidservants, or in factories, or surviving without any financial assistance and working as day labourers, or laundrywoman during summer was difficult for them (Moring, 2015).

In a study in Rome and Los Angeles, it was found that old people take care of the elderly people as caregivers, indicating that old people are the ones who care for the other elderly people. Also, it was found that job preference depends on age, where the young are more into caring for children and other domestic works. Since this routine care of the elderly is monotonous, slow and a bit isolated, young people avoid doing it. It is creating a form of social inequality. Among the elderly, the ones who get the benefit of getting cared by other elderly are posited in a better position compared to those elderly who are not economically well-off to afford the care. This kind of division is a kind of an international inequality among the aged concerning the elderly care and will become a part of many countries (Parreñas, 2015).

In Beleghata, we find that out of 50 women respondents 45 elderly women were working as maidservants. Unfortunately, most of them were physically weak with many health issues and were working beyond their capacity. As already mentioned in the previous chapters, these women were mostly widows and have been discarded by their children, most of their source of income was their work. They have almost no savings as whatever is earned has been spent on various occasions, as on children's marriage, on health-related matters and also on their husband's or son's addictions. We found in a household, a disabled lady. The mother of this lady was more than 80 years old and was extremely unwell. We asked her about her sons, to which she replied all of them are married and settled in separate households. She had asthma, arthritis, vision problems, hearing troubles and diabetes. Looking at her daughter and her health condition made us ask how she is managing, to which she said that she works in five houses and earns ₹ 2,500 per month, with ₹ 500 paid by each household on a monthly basis. Another lady, with pain, was lying on her bed, unable to sit and answer us. We went in to see how this elderly lady is leading her life. She told us that she is out of work for the past few months because of a severe form of rheumatoid arthritis. She has a son, who has left her and right now she is living on the little saving she has which has almost come to an end. She said,

> *'Amar kache ar more kichu hajar baki ache, jegulo ami amar kajer theke bachiechi. Akhon ami kono kaj korina, ar akhon jinish porter daam bere jawate ar akhon amar oshushthotar karone amar shob ae berie jabe khub shiggiri. Tai akhon ami oishob barite kaaj khujchi jekhane amar shorir er koshter kotha ora bujhbe ar amae shei bujhe kaj korte bolbe. Ami sherom bhabe kono kaaj i korte parina, tobe aaj o ranna korte pari, kitu shobji kaatte parina karon churite katte ami obhyostyo noi ar boti diei katte pari. Kintu amar mone hoena kono bari amae eitukur jonne rakhbe. Tai*

> *amar mone hoe akdin amar takar obhab hoebi ar tarpor ami akdin khider jalae mara jabo'.*
>
> ('I have hardly few thousands left, all of which I have saved from my work. Right now I do not work and because of the present situation of high priced commodities and my health, I will be very soon drained off all my savings in no time. Therefore, I seek work only in those households which will understand my health status and ask me to work accordingly. There is hardly anything I can do, but even today I can do cooking excluding the task of cutting vegetables as I am not used to with knife and I cannot sit and cut with the help of Boti. However, I do not think any household will keep me just for that. So I will probably run out of money one day and die out of starvation!')

There are a considerable number of problems that aged people face in society, where financial insecurity is one. In a study, most of the respondents were from unorganized sector and their retirement happened before they could secure their financial position. The researchers found that the elderly were economically dependent on their sons. However, the sons were not much stable economically for their low level of income. Hence, it became difficult for them to sustain not only their children but also their elderly parents with necessities of life. One important aspect that was taken care of was the housing condition of the elderly people which will help to understand both their economic and health condition. In this study, many retired people were suffering from health problems. Therefore, they were mostly staying back at home and the utilization of the various amenities like the sanitary facilities or living space was essential in influencing the conditions of their life and in providing them satisfaction and comfort. The elderly people of slum suffered from the unavailability of sufficient space and unavailability of required facilities. Moreover, the poor people suffered from various problems like shared bathroom, water facilities and sanitary provisions. The poor, elderly people unlike the rich aged people, who owned their own houses, lived mostly on shanty constructions built upon public lands and claimed their ownership right. Almost 94 per cent of the elderly from poor slum areas share toilet and other bathroom facilities with other families. Although it is desirable that the elderly should have a separate space which they can utilize as per their requirements and needs, they should also be able to accommodate their belongings and essential items so that they can access them without much difficulty. However, the study showed that 60.3 per cent of people had no such facility and number of elderly females had to share spaces with others compared to elderly males. Only 6 per cent of elderly poor got this facility, but it was available only to male aged people. However, a large number of the elderly male in the study were still married and was given the privacy they needed to be with their wives. For the absence of separate rooms, the elderly poor especially elderly women with about 98 per cent of them used passage or some relative's house to sleep. Another significant element was their professional involvement which often plays the determining role in influencing their health status and kind of medical facility they can avail. The study done here mostly included those elderly who were from the unorganized sector as already said and therefore, were not entitled to share, the pension and other benefits that a retired person. For this reason, their source of financial support was absent during old age. Since, problems are many at this phase they need money to meet their daily requirements, which compelled them to continue working either as full-timers or part timers, even at late ages. 30 per cent of poor people have worked in factories and more than 50 per cent female elderly were still earning during the time of research. Out of this 6 per cent were working as a daily wage earner, 6 per cent as a factory workers and another 6 per cent were into some small business, all of which indicates their financial burden and compulsion which is pushing them into workforce even at such an age. 84 per cent of the respondents said their present low income does not meet their needs and 60 per cent of female elderly were old enough to work and were dependent on their children. There is a belief in countries which are patriarchal that sons are the only ones who can help their parents when they are old. Only sons are given higher status in such societies and not the girls. Taking financial help from sons is acceptable which is not so in case of daughters. What seems more appropriate is taking help from daughters after they got married. This study showed that some elderly were staying with their sons and therefore were in favour of such a practice and 43 per cent of these elderly regarded taking daughter's help to sustain themselves to be inappropriate. This view comes with the belief that after marriage, daughters no longer belong to their parents but become part of their in-law's families. Hence, taking their assistance is against a society's expectation and such a strong view against daughters was more common among elderly females. Elderly males felt, if all other doors are closed then they might have to seek their daughter's help. A large number of respondents said that one of the sons can take the responsibility of their elderly parents and rest of the children can divide the expenses amongst them. Staying with different sons in rotation throughout the year was disliked by most of the poor elderly, where 50 per cent elderly males and 38 per cent elderly females supported this kind of a living arrangement (Raju, 2002).

Developed countries took almost 50 years for its population to age and increase the percentage of aged people above 65 years old from 7 per cent to 14 per cent, developing countries are expected to show in a time much less than that. However, the fast pace at which such a pattern is taking place is not able to provide the aged population with adequate facilities in terms of economic security and infra-structural developments. For this reason pension benefits are still insufficient and health care is poor. The aged population is striving in acute poverty with a quarter of them living in the developing countries.

Approximately 50 per cent of Asia's population is striving under acute poverty. The basic requirements of sanitation is absent and unavailable to most of the people living under such circumstances. 75 per cent of people from Afghanistan, 55 per cent people from Bangladesh and 45 per cent of people from Pakistan are deprived of health care services and availability of safe drinking water is also absent for 88 per cent of Afghani people and about 60 per cent of people from Nepal. 300 million people are not literate in India and 48 per cent are not literate in Pakistan. Therefore, situation in these and other developing countries are so extreme that problems of aged have never received much attention by the governments. Schulz has identified the reasons behind which issues of the aged are undermined. According to him, first, the aged population comprises of a small proportion of the entire population. Although the amount of deprivation the elderly faces and the poverty under which they are required to live and its susceptibility to various other problems are huge, the governments find them barely to be a major national concern. Women, children, disabled and aged are considered to be those sections of societies which are vulnerable and among them the aged receive the least priority by the government. World development agenda must also be considered responsible for devoting so less attention to the elderly population along with the governments of these countries (Harper, 2006).

Most of these countries are rural in nature, where most of them are part of informal labour force, which means they do not belong to the formal wage economy. They continue to work until any physical problems arise. For such countries old people are mostly supported by their family members and any kind of financial support which they need are provided by their extended family members and such is the case with more than 50 per cent of the world's aged population, where even their basic needs are often ignored. Next reason according to Schulz is that young people have long-standing potential which is deemed important by the nations and therefore investing on them is listed under their development priorities. The last reason was, old people are quite unwilling to welcome change and reluctant to adapt with the changing nature of societies, proving to be quite inflexible. All this is not desirable if development is needed, therefore the aged people are considered an obstruction in the path of development (Schulz, 1999).

However, old people should be understood as the ones who are vulnerable to many problems and therefore they must receive due attention. Their needs should be considered important in the developmental agendas. The problems faced by them are physical troubles, weaknesses, ill health and inadequate health care facilities. Dependence of a large number of family members on the elderly, insufficient financial resources or land, limited skill and potential and lack of money to spend on new constructive ventures are other issues faced by the aged people. Besides such problems they also possess a low status in society for being old (Gorman, 1999).

In his study Harper found, that in Africa a majority of elderly people are deprived of any regular income and they do not receive any pension and availing formal health care too is full of difficulties. For lack of enough nutrients, there is a presence of malnutrition among a large number of elderly people. There is also a rise in abuse of elderly because of erosion of traditional values firstly which meant that providing care and protection to elderly was a cultural practice and secondly because of a new myth according to which people who have HIV/AIDS can be cured of the disease if they have sex with elderly people. Therefore, because of the disease, the elderly take care of their children who are affected by it and often succumb to it. They also take the responsibilities of their grandchildren who have lost their parents and therefore frequently fall victim to this ailment (Harper, 2006).

More than 50 per cent of the elderly population in Asia lives in two countries – India and People's Republic of China. In India, where 70 million people have been calculated to belong to the elderly population aged above 65 years old, there 80 per cent of them are living in rural areas of the country. Among these people, 40 per cent are too poor and live below the poverty line and 50 per cent are dependent on others and only 10 per cent claim they are not entirely dependent (NSSO, 1998). A large number of elderly people live with their families, which means they are dependent on their families' economic resources. At times of instability, they are bound to face the crisis because then the young people are taken care of and protected and not the aged (Vijaya Kumar, 1990).

Beleghata slum dwellers consist of elderly who are mostly self-sufficient, despite the acute physical troubles faced by them on a regular basis. All of them were abandoned by their children and were living in a secluded state for years, but still had hopes of being accepted by their children and daughters-in-law sometime soon. Economic issues were very much the cause of such a detachment, where anything that an elderly needs seemed to cost the other family members, especially their children an arm and a leg. After having interviewed several households and after months of observation what we found was children expected their old parents to keep contributing to the families irrespective of their age and capacity. The moment there were signs of impossibility on the part of elderly parents because of poor health conditions, they were discarded just like an unwanted commodity. In many situations, the elderly therefore make arrangements for themselves, because most of them as we saw wanted to live the last phase of their lives with respect until they leave this vale of tears. Also, the fact that their children have thrown them out of their lives is something that most of the aged people were not able to bear as time and again they had tears while remembering the days of humiliation.

The respondents in the study were willing to cooperate and adjust as much as possible with their children's family but were scared whether anything will ever be enough or not. In a study, an old lady, Damayanti (name changed) expressed how bad and unhappy she was for staying with

In conversation with our respondents in a common chat point!

her brother-in-law's family after her husband's death and son's departure to the United States of America. Her son's connection with her happens mainly through money which he sends her often for her maintenance. Damayanti gives this money to her brother-in-law who is quite happy with her contribution, but this is a source of her unhappiness as she knows all the respect that this family has for her is because of the money she contributes to them. In another case, an elderly couple's children suddenly decided to form separate arrangements for them. They felt that the responsibilities of their elderly parents are becoming too difficult to handle, which is an unnecessary financial burden. Also, there were space problems and therefore as a solution, they decided to divide their elderly parents amongst themselves. However, despite their unwillingness, the elderly couples were forced to live separately with different sons and when the elderly lady was interviewed, she expressed her discontentment. She could not talk adversely about her children as that might give rise to arguments. She was extremely displeased to see how badly money mattered to them. They did not hesitate to compromise with their parent's emotions, whose entire life was spent in each other's company and got separated at this phase (Panda, 2005).

The most vulnerable groups are elderly women as they become widows and because of low level of income and assets, become dependent on others (NSSO, 1998). In case of India, the population is greying at a rapid rate. In 1991 the aged population with 60 years and above was 57 million and in 2000 it was 77 million. In India, system of pension was first introduced when the country was under the colonial rule. It dates back to 1881 when Royal Commission on Civil Establishments was introduced for the government employees – both Indian and British – a pension system. After Independence, for next twenty years in Five Year Plans, provision of pension benefits and other welfare facilities were introduced for all employees under the central government as well as state governments and also employees of large basic industries. Under these schemes, a total of 10 per cent of the elderly population were provided with the benefit. However, 90 per cent are not covered under the present scheme. They are mainly the agricultural workers who have spent almost their entire lives with least job security, low level of wages and hardly without any job protection. About 97 million people fall into these categories, who are temporarily employed or are casual labourers. Other than this support from families, some insurance schemes were there, which were providing support to the elderly and were low in return, the condition which continued till the 1980s. Gradually, pension schemes were developed by each state. The administration also proved to be difficult in some places and implementation of the schemes was also problematic in some instances, with an improper process of application and problematical criteria were chosen regarding eligibility and irregular payments and delays were constant scenes in India (Vijaya Kumar, 2003). Some safety-net programmes were started for the poorest sections of society, where 'Boyoshko Bhatta' was introduced as an allowance for the elderly and 'bidhoba bhatta' was introduced for widowed women (Roy, 2009).

In a study, in Belkuli village the aged people of Santals, are distributed pensions under District Rural Development Project to the elderly on the basis of some criteria, with the amount being ₹ 100 on a monthly basis. Criteria are set to distribute the amount only to a few selected elderly individuals and not every person who reaches this age bar. The first criteria are set by age, where a person must be at least 65 years old or more than that to receive the amount. The elderly person must also fall below the poverty line to claim the pension. The last criteria that makes one eligible for the pension is that the elderly has to give a declaration stating that she is not dependent on any family member to eat. Therefore, the amount is meant to address the need of just a small section of the elderly population, although this was a welcome step for the betterment of the aged population. Today is the time when the traditional form of family structure is getting disturbed and breaking down as a result of which families are compromising the elderly care. In such a scenario, the daily elderly issues that society is confronting cannot be expected to be taken care of and left to the family members only. Hence, besides family, the voluntary organizations and the government must take a step forward in providing help to the elderly people more intensely (Ray et al., 2003).

We asked the elderly people in the slum whether they have any savings or any bank account. Most of them denied of any savings or bank account. It was interesting to note that most of them have heard about it, but had never felt the requirement to open an account with any of the banks. A lady who had heard about the bank and seemed to be aware of its functioning said, '*Ami kokhonoi tamon kichu rojgar korini je akta account khule taate taka jomabo. Jai rojgar kori khoroch hoe jae tokhoni*' ('I have never earned sufficient enough to create an account and save it. Whatever is earned got spent right away'). This was a common reality, seen in the field. A single respondent reported about building her home with her earnings. Consequently, she had meagre savings to survive through her life. Another elderly lady had a bank account about which she is not aware of as she is dependent on her son and is happy about the way he is fulfilling his obligations towards her without any complaint. Most of the respondents either had to take care of themselves or were dependent on their children's income. Some of them were dependent on 'Bardhyokyo Bhatta' (old-age pension). However, all these sources were not seen as a permanent source of income. It will be discussed in detail in the following section of the chapter. However, it is important to mention that the ones who were getting the old-age pension were uncertain whether they will continue getting it or not, as there were several occasions when many of the other elderly people's pension was stopped without any prior notice. For those who were aged and were still working were concerned about their deteriorating health. They were also scared of the ultimate destiny when they will not be able to work anymore. The ones who were dependent on their sons were all the time fearful about their future. They were apprehensive about what will happen if their children turn against them, get them separated and stop providing the necessities of daily life!

When and Why does One Retire from Work?

Growing old and retiring from work was considered a degrading situation full of embarrassing experiences for the old in pre-industrial society. According to Thomas (1976), the arrival of old age was all about shifting from heavier to lighter jobs, but with time it was about a situation where the old had no other option but to lead a life, in complete dependence on others for survival. Old-age pensions were considered to be given at the age of fifty after it was proposed by Defoe and Dowdeswell in 1690s and 1772 respectively (Bond, Coleman and Peace, 1993).

The practice of fixing a particular age for retirement is a new arrival, therefore, initiated to keep pace with the changing labour market to raise concern against the prevalence of health and the social and economic needs of the elderly. For several years old men and women worked for many years. For example, in 1881 in the United Kingdom, there were 75 per cent of men who were more than 65 years old who were very much working. With a fall of their participation for about a few years, there was again rise in their active involvement in the labour market during 1931 with 70 per cent of people in the age group of 65 years to 69 years old and more than 35 per cent of people above 70 years old being economically active. Later on, with the increase in life expectancy and growing ageing population led to a gradual departure of old people from economic sphere. There was a time during the initial years of the nineteenth century when it is believed to be a period where old people were considered the dead woods, being forcefully dragged into poverty for which they had to put their shoulders to the wheel to do tedious jobs for the sake of survival. Later on, during later part of the century, there was so much hatred and disgust breeding in mind against the old that their employment in a flourishing society is a sign of living in squalor. Hence, they were regarded fit for such poor conditions (Harper, 2006).

However, in Beleghata slum, the people never really entered into jobs which would give them pension benefits later, i.e. they were engaged in unorganized sectors. The people, especially the aged women, have worked as maids and a few of them were involved in some business, or had worked as peasants, or were wage earners in glass factories. The pension was a distant dream for these workers, who have struggled with saving their money all their lives. Only a few of them had bank accounts, but unfortunately, they have either closed it or do not access it and hence the accounts have become dormant. People here said that they have worked or will work as long as they can and that work has got no relation to their age. We met many people who were above 70 and one of them even claimed to be in her 80s and still active. The National Council on Aging commissioned Harris Poll in 1974 and asked for the opinions of Americans on the issue of 'mandatory retirement'. Nearly 86% of this national sample of Americans responded that retirement should not be forcefully imposed on people if they are willing to work. Another Harris Poll conducted four years later concluded that both the working and retired professionals supported the idea of complete withdrawal of 'mandatory retirement'.

There are many suggestions which show that quitting from a job can lead to poor health. In many studies carried out in Britain and France, however, it has been seen that poor health is often the reason why one opts for retirement and not vice versa (Parker, 1980; Cribier, 1981). Retirement seemed to be primarily caused because of ill health. In the American literature also it has been shown how people with poor health tend to retire more than the people who have maintained good health (Burtless, 1987).

An American survey found that 25 per cent of people retire forcefully from work because of being unfit (Ozawa and Law, 1992). Even in Canada, the same reason has been cited as retirement for people. General Social Survey of 1994 also showed that 27 per cent of people choose to retire for issues related to poor health. Data collected from Survey of Ageing and Independence shows that 47 per cent retire for health concerns (Schellenberg, 1994; Denton, 2011). However, most of the old women in the slum said that the demand for their work has decreased to a great extent with age and now they hardly have any assurance of work. Sometimes they get seasonal work but during the rest of the days, they sit idle simply frustrated. Many of them said that physical condition does not allow them to move out, but then there is nobody to take care of them, as their children have left them in this despair condition which has made it almost compulsory for them to work. We came across a number of them who had to quit work much before they stepped into the 60s because of health issues. In a survey it was found that in the age group of 55–64 years old, people who had poor health or were fairly healthier retired from work in large numbers compared to the ones who were in good health. The people who were retired reported that it was not compulsory for them to retire at this age and were not subjected to any rigid retirement policy, but had to because their health did not permit them to work any longer. Almost 94 per cent of the unhealthy elderly showed signs of disability in this age group and 75 per cent of the elderly aged 65 years and above showed similar signs (Gaitz, Niederehe and Wilson, 2012).

Sixty four per cent of the elderly population living in rural areas of the country and 55 per cent of elderly from urban areas of India has at least one or more than one type of disability. In rural communities, the concept was to continue working (Govil and Gupta, 2016). A lady Parul (name changed) said she used to work as manual labour along with her husband to repair the road and before she could complete, she went blank and stopped talking. Her husband was sitting right beside her who then narrated the whole story. He said,

> *'Amra dujonei rasta sharatam, ar eta sthayi chakri chilona. Jodio amader chele meye nei kono amader pokkhye ja taka ache shei nie dujonke chalano khub mushkil hoe daracchilo. Hotat kore amar stri marattok matha byatha hocche bole janalo. Amar oto taka chilona je dactar dekhabo. Kintu byatha marattok bere gelo. Akdin o ogyan hoe gelo. Ami khub bhoe peye gelam ar oke pashe akta daktar khanate nie gelam jekhane kono taka nilona amader theke. Janina ora ki pelo, kintu kichu oshudh likhe dilo ar or oshukh ta kokhono thik kore boleni. O besh bhaloi korchilo ak mash moton. Hotat kore shorir er ba dik e oshar moton onubhuti bodh korte laglo. Ami oke abar dactar er kache nie gelam. Amar stri tokhon thik kore cholteo partona. Kintu totodin e o or kaj chereo dieche kanoki sheta chalie jawar moto obsohthae o ar chilona. Oshudh ar kaaj dicchilona ar ami akdomi bujhte parchilamna je ki hocche ar keo chilo o na jar shathe ektu kotha bolte parbo. Or paralysis hoe gel oar bhule jawar rog hote shuru holo. Ami janina eta ki. Ami khali jani o bhalo nei, ar amar kache taka nei akjon bhalo dactar dekhanor. Ami ar rojgar korina karon akhon amar boyish hoeche. Amae ager chakrti ta charte hoechilo amar bhebe rakhashomoer onek agei karoki amar heart er shomoshya chilo. Dui kilometre dur e akta jaega ache jekhane binamulye khawar daebriddhyoder. Shekhane ami amar stri ke roj nie jai ato oshombhob shomonshyar poreo, karon o jane e bhabe chara ar beche thakar kono upae nei'.*

('Both of us used to repair road and it was not permanent employment. Though we do not have any children, it was unbearable to sustain ourselves with the money we got. All of a sudden my wife complained of a severe headache. I did not earn much to visit a doctor then. However, then the pain got severe. One day she fainted. I got terrified and took her to a nearby clinic which took no fees from us. I did not know what they found but gave her some medicines and never explicitly mentioned her disease. She was doing well for about a month. However, gradually she complained of numbness in the left side of her body. I again took her to the doctor. My wife was not even able to walk properly and by that time she had already left her work as it was not possible for her to continue. The medicines were not working and without anybody to talk to I was utterly clueless. She slipped into paralysis and had severe memory issues. I do not know what it is. All I know is she is not well and I have no money to see a good doctor. I do not earn anymore as I am aged now. I had to quit the job earlier than I thought because I have a heart problem. Two km away there is a place which gives food for free to the elderly people. There I take my wife daily, despite immense teething troubles, as that this is the only way we can survive').

Another lady in her late 60s, said,

'Ami aya hishebe onek bochor kaj korechi. Du bochor age ami bujhte parlam je bhishob byatha shuri hoeche pa e ar komor e. Ami haat e pari, kintu akbar boshle uthte khub oshubidhe hoe. Arekta jinish holo, ami ager moto taratri shob kaaj korte parina. Gaate gaate o khub byatha. Chokhe dekhateo shomoshya. Eishob shomoshya amae boddhyo ojogyo kore dieche aya hishebe kaaj korte dite. Jodio ami tarporeo cheshta chalie gechi, karon amar takar khub dorkar, kintu hoe amae or anumoti daena chakri korte nahole charie dae dhokarkichudin pore. Amar sharer shomoshya rojgar take bhishon bhabe probhab koreche'

('I used to work as a nanny for many years. Two years back I realized that I had developed acute pain in my legs and waist. I can walk, but it becomes excruciating for me to get up once I sit down. Also, I am not able to carry out my duties as fast as I used to do it. I have pain in my joints. I cannot even see properly. All these have made me unfit to continue my job as a nanny. I have tried a lot even then, as I needed money. However, either I was not allowed to join or was asked to leave after few days of service. My health has affected my earning excessively').

I met an elderly man who used to work as a plumber and was earning enough for his family when all of a sudden one his sons married a girl without his consent and settled elsewhere. He was unemployed and hence took his father's saving forcefully to settle his new family. After a week when the savings got consumed, he kept demanding for money. According to him he was not able to take the stress anymore and finally had a heart attack. He became so weak that he had to quit his job, which he wanted to continue desperately. Now he is survived by his daughter and her husband. There were some whose physical conditions were deplorable, but still, they had no choice but work. While walking down the slum, I came across a lady aged above 70 years who works even today as a maidservant. She said,

> *'Amar duto meye ache. Akjoner biye hoe geche. Chotojon amar shathe thake kintu okhyom. Amar or dekhbal korte hoe purotai karon tumi dekhtei parcho ami bodhoba. Ami oishob shubidhe gulo paina jegulo amar ainoto paowa uchit shorkar theke jar karon gulo amar jana nei. Amader jibon jodio ekhane theme thakbena. Ami boshe thakte parbona ar asha korte parbona je ei shubidhe gulo boshe boshe peye jabo. Tai ami kaaj kori. Ami dekhte paina. Hatute khubi byatha. Khub beshi blood pressure. Kichu bochor age kaj charte hoe shorir kharap howar jonne and bujhlam jotoi koshto hok ar jai hoe jaak amae kaaj chaie ei jete hobe. Ami akjonma ar amar meye amar daityo. Amar aro rojgar korte hobe karon or bhobishyot amae nishyit korte hobe. Jotokhon jobon ache ami kaaj kore jabo'.*
>
> ('I have two daughters. One of them is married. The younger one lives with me and is a disabled child. I need to take care of her all by myself as you can see I am a widow. I do not get the benefits that I am legally supposed to get from the government for reasons unknown. However, our lives will not stop here. I cannot sit back and hope to get these benefits. Therefore, I am working. I cannot see properly. I have hearing troubles. I cannot stand properly. I have tremendous pain in my knees. I have high blood pressure. A few years back I had to quit my work because of my health but realized no matter what and no matter how difficult it is I have to work. I am a mother and my daughter is my responsibility. I need to earn more because I have to secure her future. As long as this heart beats I will work').

A study found that when a person's health improves, chances of retirement decrease. The overall earnings increase as a result and hence the medical expenses are met in a better way further helping to improve and maintain a healthy life (Sickles and Taubman, 1986).

The people engaged in construction works or labourers in farms or mine workers have a higher risk of impairment compared to others. A mining worker complained of impairment 17.3 per cent more than other men who had similar occupation and salary and level of education. The works which are physically demanding limits physical ability after a period forcing early retirement. It is considered that widows occupy a disadvantaged position in a society there is still less awareness regarding people's knowledge about the difficulties that widows have faced for years until now on a daily basis. They also suffer from poor health and other disadvantages which makes their situation more vulnerable. This makes their position important to be considered in policies concerning health programmes and other issues related to the development of the economy of the country. Widowhood is a highly alarming situation among the old age people. It is related to susceptibility to various other difficulties which has its consequence on health. For example, keeping in mind their situation during widowhood, Indian women often opt for high rates of fertility for they believe their children especially sons to provide them with social support during their old age. However, to secure future during old age, they do not realize they are compromising with the health of not only women but children as well. Children of the widows are vulnerable in two ways. First, they have a high risk of suffering from ill-health because their widowed mothers do not have enough money to meet their necessities. Second, when mothers are in poor economic condition and are widowed, they have no option but to accept help from their children. This will have its negative impact right from forcing children to give up childhood pleasures and leisure time to getting exposed to hazardous health conditions. Getting occupied in some or the other job before widowhood and after that can have a remarkable difference. Rates of self-employment have shown to have decreased among women after they got widowed as they made a shift towards wage employment, though working as domestic servants showed no such change especially in households which had no male adult. Households which had a male adult were the ones where salaried works were seen to be dominant (Chen and Dreze, 1992).

For the ones who could make some earnings were not happy as they could hardly do anything with it, be it proper diet, living or clothing. Barely had they earned ₹ 1,000 a month, with slight variations which went up to ₹ 5,000 for some of them, though very rarely. There is no such thing as retirement for the residents out there, though some of them are aware of the term. A survey was done on 600 old people from south-central part of India and the population was divided into two groups. One was from scheduled caste category and the other group belonged to the general caste, with the former being comparatively poor than the latter. The ones who were poor were wage earners and did not receive any pension when they were forced to quit a job for health reasons (Pati and Jena, 1989).

NSS study reported by Dandekar showed that states like Karnataka and Haryana had half the population who can be regarded as entirely dependent. However, with the efforts of Dandekar, the extremely old people living in poverty would be provided with a pension of ₹ 300 per month (Chatterjee, Patnaik and Chariar, 2008).

Many of them said that working was almost equal to unemployment as neither could they accumulate much money to save it for future nor could they meet their expenses easily. Therefore they were often forced to take loans from others which they are struggling to pay back even today at this age where their sole source of income is the 'Briddha Bhrata' or 'Bidhaba Bhata' and for some their children. Though 'Briddha Bhrata' and 'Bidhaba Bhata' can be legally claimed by old people and widows respectively, our study found that only 5 of them could utilize this benefit. The amount is a meagre one to maintain a family, yet something is better than nothing according to the people there. A very old lady who lived in a rented house had just '*Bidhaba Bhrata*' (widow pension) as her source of income as she had no children who could support her in this age. Out of the total ₹ 500 she earns, ₹ 100 goes to pay off the rent of the house which is devoid of any electricity. Her daily meal comprises of puffed rice and onion with water. She takes this both as her lunch and her dinner.

When we entered her house, we could see nothing. The door had to be kept wide open to let sun rays come in which was hardly sufficient even to see her. While we were talking some insect bit me and I felt a bit of a pain in my leg, to which she said '*eta to ekhane hotei thake, ami eshober shathe manie nite shikhe gechi. Tobe ami amar otithi eshob koshter moddhye die jaak sheta dekhte parbona. Cholun barie giye kotha boli*' (It is a common thing here. I have learnt to deal with it. However, I cannot see my guests go through this pain. Let's move out and talk). I was taken aback by her sweet gesture and continued talking to her in the room as it would have been disrespectful of me to show any negative reaction to the place which is her life. Neither can she see properly nor is she able to move much, but still feels happy that unlike others she gets the needful amount which allows her to have a roof over her head. She was a maid when young and was forced to quit this job because of her ill health a few years back. I met others who were old enough and were physically unfit but continued working though only on a temporary basis.

There was a lady Sabita (name changed) who said that she works as a caretaker out of sheer luck. Once she was attached to a centre, which had compelled her to leave the job, as she was not able to turn up regularly for health issues. She is not able to work during the summer season as working during this period worsens her health. Even during winter she finds moving out of her house quite a headache because during this season she finds difficulty in mobility. Therefore, she gets the time in between to earn her living which is a question of uncertainty as there is no surety of whether she will at all get a call or not from people. There was another lady who also works as a caretaker, but hardly any family shows interest in taking her. Her main problem is that she has severe back pain issues and hence is not able to do any job which requires her to bend. She is unable to stand-up as well and often cannot move. Before taking up this responsibility, she clears her health issues to the families and then gets rejected immediately as most of the jobs require vigourous physical activity. She said,

> '*Jodi kono poribar chae tader chele meye ke othate hobenamate hobe tahole ami raji. Kintu, durbhagyoboshot ei akta kad\jer jonyo amae rakhte keo raji hobena. Amae erom akta kaj onek bochor age akta jaegae diechilo. O akhon boro hoe geche. Tarpor theke amar shorir kharap howa shotteo ai jor kore amon kaaj kori ja amar shorir ke aro kharap kore dae. Janina ar ki korle ami nijeke shahajyo korte parbo. Amar kono dharona nei*'.

('If there is any family who would want me to do child pick up and drop off service I am always ready. However, unfortunately for this single job, nobody would offer me a job. Many years back I have been offered one. She has grown old now. Since then despite my physical condition I forcefully do tasks which deteriorate my health further. I do not know what else I can do to help myself. I am clueless').

Some of them did not apply for either 'Briddha Bhrata' or 'Bidhaba Bhata' because they felt the application would get rejected and moreover they thought they have children who would be their support. Unfortunately, for most of the slum dwellers, children especially sons of widowed people, did not provide any help and had shifted elsewhere as they felt spending on parents is an extra expenditure that must be avoided.

The Basic Necessities of Life Remain a Dream

The Beleghata slum starts with a narrow passage which opens to the houses scattered here and there filled with frail old people looking back at us through their wrinkled and exhausted eyes, weak legs and grey hair. Most of them wore white saris, which were worse for wear and at times stingy. The only ornament they carried with them was a smile which hid all the sorrows deep inside. We asked one of the elderly who was smiling at us as she saw us, that what according to her the definition of being happy is. She said,

'Shukhi howa mane poribarer shathe thaka ar shonirbhor howa. Tumi tokhoni shukhi jokhon tomar kache shob kichu thakbe ja tumi chao ar tumi bonchito onubhob korbena. Shukhi howar onubhob ta bhetor theke ashbe' (Happiness is being with family and being self-sufficient. You are happy when you have everything you need and don't feel deprived. Happiness is a feeling that comes from within). She continued explaining, '*ami bhabi Jodi amar akta shontoshjonok jibon ar amar jibon er iti ta Jodi dhukher hoto tahole kamon hoto, kintu tumi bujhtei parcho amar hasher kono karon nei karon ami akjon bidhoba, gorib, amar cholera amae chere chole geche, sharirik obostha jar khb kharap, jar kono kaj nei ar rojgar nei ar amon bari te thake jekhane alo nei, hawa nei kicchu nei. Amar atto lojja lagche je tomader bhetore daktei lojja korche nijer barite*'.

('I wish I had a satisfactory and happy ending to my life. However, as you can understand I have no reason to smile for I am a widow, a poor one, whose sons have left her, whose health is in the most pitiable condition, who does not have any work and income and lives in a house which has no light, no air ... nothing. I am so ashamed that I am afraid to ask you come with me to my house').

However, we insisted on going and she kept on feeling nervous all along the way and hesitated to ask us to get in. We convinced the lady and got inside just to discover her plight. The house was indeed lying in a miserable condition. She had no source of income and was dependent on

This is the room of an elderly, where there is no proper ventilation, no light or air to pass through

her relatives for everything. There was no light or fan. It was during peak summer and it was quite heart wrenching to witness how she lives in such a small room with not a single window to let in the air or light. The door of her room opened to a shanty passage which was hardly a foot wide. She had just two saris to wear including the one she was wearing at the time. She does not have any breakfast or Tiffin when she is starving. With lots of physical problems about which the elderly lady has very less knowledge as doctors did not convey it accurately, she is living her life. She had problems with the small space of her room, as that is not enough for a person to move freely and therefore she has to stuff in everything below her bed.

Gurumurthy (1998) said a vital area that one must not overlook while studying about the aged people are their living arrangements. The house where elderly live indicates their socio-economic status, their preferences and tastes and also what kind of facilities are they able to afford. It is kind of a property that the elderly can own individually or with others jointly and can be built with one's own hard earned money or can be inherited. House is not only meant to provide safety and comfort to the aged but it is equally essential in providing the aged with security (Gurumurthy, 1998).

In Beleghata slum, elderly people also had similar problems. Water was a fundamental problem for most of them. Access to water was limited and they could get it only after reaching a specific place where water was distributed. However, for the elderly, it was not possible to travel such a distance regularly. Hence, they often remained without water, though many of them acknowledged that relatives and neighbours never said no if they needed it. Most of the houses share toilets which were unclean and unhygienic. Most of them have problems in mobility and at times because of the severity of health problems visiting a doctor becomes necessary, yet challenging. For this reason, they might need a car and somebody's assistance to take them to the clinics. However, for lack of money they fail to afford the car and for lack of time nobody turns up to accompany them. The financial condition was so bad for most of the people that they could not afford even the basic necessities of life. They hardly had enough warm clothes to bear the cold during winter or even enough for an entire year. They did not even have enough food for an entire day, money to skip work for a day. They did not have enough resources to send their children and the later generations to school. They could not afford decent housing, sanitary facilities and fans and lights at home even during hot summer. Also, seeking proper medical attention from a respectable health institute and money to buy medicines when recommended was a big problem.

At times when health troubles were severe, because of lack of money, they often tended to stay back at home and visit a nearby hospital only when they felt that situation is out of control. However, whether their situation is necessary to visit a clinic depends on their children's or their care taker's assessment of their illness. If they find that the elderly needs help they would try to make an arrangement, else they are made to wait until something more serious happens.

The toilets are unclean, having no one to take its care for time unknown. It is not only unclean and unhygienic, but each of them is too dark and ill-ventilated. The people complained that sometimes the unclean and unhygienic toilets create trouble for aged, especially for those who are already distressed with their frail and diseased body. Many times they are not able to see the holes if they have vision problems or when the toilets are dark. Therefore, they sometimes defecate in places other than the hole and also because of lack of water the toilets are left unclean, which in a way is an invitation for diseases like diarrhoea and typhoid. Children of the area use the same toilets and hence, there is a high-risk factor present whereby they can get affected when exposed to such germ-infested conditions. The toilets if situated far away from their houses, creates difficulty for the aged to travel the distance. Health problems made it impractical for the elderly to do the cleaning job of toilets. Neither anyone was willing to take the responsibility of emptying the waste nor were they much aware of the procedures that might be followed to do the job.

A study was carried out in Kigali, to find out whether people in the area have any issues with sanitation facilities or not. 80 per cent of the people interviewed reported to have a minimum of one problem related to sanitation. 58.5 per cent said that the shared usage of sanitation is one of the major troubles that they were facing. The second most important problem for them was smell as 38.7 per cent reported it to be a genuine concern. For 38 per cent of them, difficulty in cleaning the toilets was a big issue. 32.4 per cent had problems with insects in these toilets. Safety concern affected about 30.1 per cent of them. The position of sanitary facilities from the houses of respondents was also a reason for concern creating trouble for 21.2 per cent of them. Last but not the least about 20.2 per cent of the respondents said that toilets were not always available when needed.

The researchers found that most often the latrines had foul smell, many a time uncovered, shallow and full. In these informal settlements, there is an absence of emptier and that is the reason why they are not able to empty their pits which are always full due to its high usage by some users. Also, due to unavailability of space building of new latrines is an impossible solution to this problem. The owners held a different point of view and said the shallowness of pits are responsible for the high water table and because the soil in this area is rocky and also thought that tenants throw solid wastes like tin, plastics and garbage and fill up the pit. The proper sanitary facility has become a constraint for various reasons, out of which about 68.2 per cent was because of lack of money. About 13.8 per cent was because of the area's topographic features. Space issues accounted for 12.3 per cent of the problems. Difficulties in getting a permit to get this done were 3 per cent, lack of proper materials needed for the construction stood at 2.4 per cent and absence of specialized equipment and short of proper information was 0.2 per cent for each. The holes are sometimes too big for kids and hence they defecate beside the hole or somewhere on the ground. For those households where defecation facilities are not available nearby, they practice open defecation. According to respondents, this is done by drunken people, children, young homeless people and outsiders. This is so because of the absence of toilets in one's household and lack of public toilet facilities, or because of shared toilets creating extremely unhygienic conditions. Sometimes it is because of attitudes of people, who choose to defecate in the open. It has also been reported that people often defecate in bags and then select rooftops to throw them. The smell often enters into the kitchen causing the spread of diseases. Some of them could be seen to have become breeding grounds for flies. The floors were of mud, were dirty and this created water drainage difficult. Thus this logged water became the reason for flies to breed. The participants were part of a focus group study where for most of them the dirty toilets were the reasons behind their health issues. They suffered from diarrhoea, typhoid and also sometimes from intestinal worms. Unhygienic conditions prevailed because some households shared one toilet. The people who were disabled or the ones who were ill and of course the aged people felt that the unhygienic condition of the toilets was posing a challenge to them. The shared toilets were mostly unhygienic and these people often required touching the floors or the walls which were extremely dirty to take support. Also, in the traditional styles of toilets, it was necessary to squat. Squatting put an immense amount of pressure on their knees and back, which in turn resulted in undue pain. The study also showed that there was an issue with proper availability of lighting facilities. The tenants of houses reported this to cause a major problem for not being able to see the hole and therefore fail to defecate at a proper place. Sometimes doors are not there in the toilets which often invade the privacy of the user and also are the reasons behind sexual assault of women.

The distance of toilet and one's house is an area of difficulty for people who are disabled and have problems in mobility. Also, sometimes the paths to the toilet are not always paved. Hence, the elderly and

A makeshift structure for defecation

A place for defecation purpose

Shared bathroom space

disabled people find this troublesome. The paths that lead to the toilets are constructed for the non-disabled people and without showing any concern for the disabled people. Sometimes people fear getting injured along the path and therefore find it safe to defecate somewhere nearby their house (Etingoff, 2015). This is very similar to the situation found in Beleghata. There was no proper sanitation facility and none to help the elderly to defecate in a hygienic condition. Therefore, they lived in areas which were germ-infested and this was creating a very unhealthy living condition. A woman in this interview said, that if she remained in the squat position for a long time, it became difficult for her to get up without any support. Therefore she had to touch the dirty floor, which means the disease can get easily contaminated in these situations. The situation is very stressful for the aged apart from health issues, according to the respondent.

The bathroom area is also open and shared by men and women, elderly and children. There is no proper drainage system and the area is extremely slippery.

In Africa, a study was done by Nawi and others who estimated that approximately within 2030, 50 per cent of people of the country would be seen to be affected by chronic and diseases which are non-communicable (Nawi et al., 2010). The developing countries in the world, in fact, have such characteristic features with high levels of poverty and lower levels of sanitation, with widespread prevalence of diseases like diarrhoea, typhoid and AIDS (Robinson et al., 2007).

One of the houses where the elderly keeps her cooked food for days!

A cooking space as well as washing area of an household in the slum.

One such house where the major part is covered with cooked food and utensils.

Most of the households do not have a fridge or proper storage place, as a result of which the cooked foods are supposed to be eaten on the day it is cooked. However, because of the physical problems, they cook as much as possible to not to engage in physical activities like cooking daily and protect them by covering them up with some lid. In some cases, they even push their food under the bed and keep them uncovered. Jayanti (name changed) said, '*jokhon ami ranna kori ami dekhe ni je ami du din er jonne kore rakhchi kanona prottekdin ranna kora amar pokkhye shombhob na. Ami onno bashon die Dhaka die rakhi*' ('When I cook food I make sure I make it for two days, as it is just not possible for me to cook daily. I cover them with another utensil'). The cooking and other unwashed utensils pile up and are then washed in a very dirty area where animals roam around. The people are so much used to this that they do not even bother to drive them away. One such instance got captured during our interview.

When we interviewed, they often invited us for lunch and that is when we saw that everything right from parched rice to cooked food everything was kept under the bed covered with newspapers or other utensils. Clothes are bought only when it is too much necessary for the aged, but this affects their social performances. As mentioned by Hurlock (2001), that with changing fashion often because of lack of money, elderly people especially old women are not able to buy up to date clothes they find that getting social would invite embarrassment because of old-fashioned clothes. At the same time, reduced income leads to shift in their focus from increasing their status in societies to things they want to buy to something which is important for them to survive without anybody's help and independently. For this they often lead a simpler life where they no longer spend much money on clothes, for social gatherings, travel, entertainment, grooming (Hurlock, 2001).

Lavia and Moore (2009) study on elderly people showed how poverty is connected to age. It also brought to light that financial crisis affects the health of the aged about which the young are clueless regarding what solution would improve the situation. Some felt the life of the aged is not significant enough, while others questioned the worth of living such a life. The old were living in such dire poverty that they were not able to buy clothes even when they wanted to, no money to make plans and buy a better house which is needed at this age. Because of this crisis, they are not able to treat their ailments, or buy medicines or even avail the free medical treatment if available and the worst part is that there is nobody to help them in this condition. Moreover, medicines which are recommended to be taken after meals go waste as the elderly are not able to have any food. They feel so helpless about their condition that they consider death to be a better solution than to live such a painful life. Many accepted their impoverished life was responsible for their poor economic condition which disabled them to afford the basic necessities of life. Families where females are the heads or where many generations live together or even the households where a single elderly person lives are the ones which are the poorest of all types. Survival is possible only when one has enough food to eat, but these poor families are so economically deprived that they are not able to afford this minimum need especially when the cost of living is high. Through the interview, Lavia and Moore found that there were job-related issues which gave rise to the present state of poverty, as there were some households where none of the adults was employed. Some were engaged in odd jobs, some were lowly skilled and were into jobs which were of low status and therefore wages earned were also less in amount. This was not sufficient to fulfil their basic necessities of life. Therefore, there were specific strategies implemented by these old men to survive. They chose to rely on their relatives and friends for money, but the dependency although was very much necessary to sustain in these hard circumstances, it often turned out to be small and irregular. Also, dependency as the primary means of livelihood often meant inability in standing on one's dignity. Also, people were poor and therefore they lived in communities which were poor and were deprived of proper facilities like library, good roads and amenities for recreation, far away from medical centres, poor quality of medical, etc. (Lavia and Moore, 2009).

According to Arber and Ginn (2003) often, old people who are otherwise considered as a burden in society can actually make a positive contribution in the economic and social sphere of society. Aged people's work often goes unpaid while they provide informal care to those people in families who are less able including their own partners. This means that because of their assistance the cost of health and personal care services is reduced to a great extent. Also, elderly people play a very significant role in providing care and love to their grandchildren. Shouldering this responsibility helps the daughter or daughter-in-law of the house join the labour market.

According to them, these elderly people can help the children of the house with financial support. They can help them with loans, buying gifts, paying of fees. They can also be the source of their emotional support during traumatic times in life (Arber and Ginn, 2003).

However, there is also a view that more than 150 countries are providing public assistance to the aged, disabled people and their survivors who would get aid after the death of the people, they are serving. The health care provided to the aged is quite expensive, the cost incurred by the governments can often be more than their budget. Therefore, different countries plan different ways to deal with this stressful situation. For example in Japan emphasis is laid on activity, where people as long as possible irrespective of their age. Also, in this country there are laws on a national level which is in favour of employment. They provide training to workers who have become old. Private business houses also extend their support to the idea of retraining workers. In United Kingdom, people depend on both state pension and

National Health Service to meet the needs related to health and finance (Giddens and Griffiths, 2006).

To learn about the lifestyle of the aged, a survey was conducted in Britain on about 1,317 people who discovered the existence of two different 'worlds', where one world consisted of people who have just retired and were in the early years of their retired lives. They were living in households that they were sharing with others and were receiving a pension. Therefore their lives were pretty much comfortable in terms of their lifestyle. On the other hand, the second world consisted of people who were more than eighty years old, living all alone with fewer savings. In this second world, people were in dire poverty as a result of which they were always anxious about money and were suffering from health problems (Milne and Harding, 1999).

In Kerala, aged people falling in the age group of 60 to 69 years old are 3.48 million and for the range 70–79 years the number of the aged population is 1.57 million. When joint family structure existed, aged people had a position of respect, held power and had security. However, joint family structure faced erosion with the advent of modern developments that shook the very basic arrangement of living and at the same time the value system that so long existed got affected. This impacted the lives of the elderly. Nowadays, young people attain education and both males and females participate in the labour force. Hence, the time and amount they need to devote to the elderly family members get reduced. There is also an increase in unwillingness among the young people to adjust to the needs of the aged people (Sain, 2008). In Kerala both matriarchal and patriarchal family form exist (Kapadia, 1966). In the existence of the matriarchal form of a family system, women were in a position of power and influence. They had property rights and they enjoyed the position of dominance. No longer is this family system is in prevalence as gradually it has been replaced by a patriarchal family system, which means the position that women held in these societies will degrade in all respects which at times will lead them to be in a situation of acute poverty (Sain, 2008).

Conclusion

In Beleghata, the situation of the elderly irrespective of the genders was very poor. According to most of the respondents, the situation was worse when under such circumstances their children were not able to understand their plight and made sure to foment trouble for them. In most cases, the children have a separate household and the elderly live in a condition of acute crisis. As a result of their physical difficulties, the poor living arrangement makes their daily lives more troublesome. Majority of the aged people in the slum are having mobility issues, therefore need to travel which created extra burden. However, their dependency on their children for money and other supports is a reason for their humiliation, which forces them into the workforce even at this age. Sometimes, they have dependent family members and therefore whatever earned becomes challenging to save for emergency. For some aged people, the money which is earned is extremely less and is not enough to meet their daily needs. As a result, they remain dependent on neighbours and others. The dependency of the elderly people may sound to be a natural affair because of their age but this dependency of the elderly population on their families, society and per capita income as a whole act as an unwanted liability. Through various behavioural attributes they are often treated as burden. With reference to the field, it can be seen that here we are exploring the plight of elderly quality of life in coherence to socio-economic dimension, where unfulfilled needs, wants as well as money shortages are quite common, here one can clearly imagine the plight of elderly population inherently the aforesaid not only affect their physical aspects of life where they are compelled to sustain themselves in spite of acute problems. These also serve as consequences of mental breakdown and depression, which with reference to the field can be perceived yet the respondents as well as their family members may find it difficult to conceive.

The field gives a grim description of health and sanitation facilities, which will be discussed in detail in the following chapters. The sanitary facilities are so poor that it becomes difficult for them to carry out their sanitary activities with ease. The basic necessities of life such as proper food, a proper shelter and proper clothes are often hard to afford under acute economic distress and they continue living in this situation till death unless helped or taken care of by someone. To cope with this condition when they enter into job market they are forced to work with the immense amount of physical problems, thus further worsening their health. Aged people who get the old-age pension are in a vulnerable situation for the amount received which is too less to sustain themselves and their family members when necessary and also because of the criteria of selection and uncertainty of its continuation the elderly people are always in fear of economic insecurity.

Therefore, one of the main issues affecting the elderly is the financing of medical care especially the ones on a long-term basis and both government and other officials from health care sectors must be severe in dealing with it. One way this can be managed is through the implementation of specific insurance policies which can help in meeting the requirement of finance for those people who are disabled functionally and also the ones who are senescent. Disabled people can also be helped through subsidies in lowering the prices of the appliances that the disabled use, to decrease the cost of the support devices which they require and also to minimize the cost of the gadgets they need. To take care of the different initiatives in the spheres of health issues, the hazardous ventures in the health domains must be taxed (Alam, 2013).

Under National Social Assistance Programme (NSAP), Indira Gandhi National Widow Pension Scheme (IGNWPS) was introduced in 2009. Under this scheme, the criterion is, if the applicant is a widow, then she will get ₹ 300 on a monthly basis. After attaining 80 years old or after 80 years old if a woman is widowed, then the pension amount is increased to ₹ 500 per month (NSAP, 1995).

There is another scheme known as the Annapurna Scheme. Under this scheme per beneficiary would get 10 kilograms of food grains – rice or wheat every month. This scheme aims to cover all those aged people who are eligible but did not get the benefit under Indira Gandhi National Old Age Pension Scheme (NSAP, 1995).

8

Health Concerns and Senile Population

The World Health Organization describes health as 'a state of complete physical, mental and social well-being and not merely the absence of disease or infirmity' (WHO, 1971). On the other hand, National Opinion Research Committee opines illness as 'any condition, i.e. any disease, impairment, symptom or a group of related symptoms, which was reported by the aged as having bothered them' (Soodan, 1975).

Health is very important for aged people because they stand at a high risk to suffer from health related problems because of their age. A long life is not worth living if the years spent are not satisfactory, where health often becomes a major obstruction in the path as the ability to resist diseases decreases with age and at times complete cure is just not possible (Sahu, 1998). With advancement of age, physiological condition also deteriorates, as a result of which body is not able to resist illness. The illness which a elderly face are mostly chronic and they are affected by a number of diseases. The fact that, illness or any kind of physical problems and infirmities that accompany old age, is deeply ingrained in the minds of Indian elderly. This is regarded as an inevitable destiny of every aged person and therefore it is accepted and considered natural, even when some of these diseases are curable (Raju, 2002).

In India, older adults in the year of 2010 were approximately 100 million (Department of Economic and Social Affairs Population Division, 2010) and because of this, the health and welfare of the aged people is very important in influencing the planning of government in the present as well as in future times to come (Alam, 2013). It is also revealed that feminization of the population of the elderly is taking place, as number of elderly women is on rise, with the most rapid rate of this growth has been observed to be in the section which is beyond 75 years old. It has brought along with it another reality which says that there will be large number of widows among elderly women. This increase in number of women can be attributed to the development of the health care sector and also to the developments taking place in the socio-economic aspects of the world (Kinsella, 2000).

However, in order to face any kind of challenge that comes in the way proper measures are to be taken that can provide security and enhance the well-being of the elderly. Intra-country studies conducted with the help of cross-sectional information has shown the vulnerability of the aged section of the population who can fall prey easily to some serious ailments and it has also been seen that with age people suffer from increasing levels of functional disability. A considerable improvement has been observed in the different parameters of health in India and the other countries residing around it. Life expectancy has improved and also people living more than 60 years old have also been on rise. In 2010, where in India the population was about 92.7 million, it is expected that there will be 3.5 times increase in this population by 2050, when this population of the aged people will be more than 320 millions. With this high growth of elderly population and particularly of elderly women and those who are older among old, there is going to be undoubtedly a huge pressure on the country, on its government and various institutions, and issues related to health care of the aged and disability. A household survey conducted in Delhi, mainly aimed at finding out diseases that have been medically diagnosed. It tried to incorporate the elderly views about their own health and also a paramedical team was there who would assess their health and determine their capabilities at this age along with their strengths. The study showed that women were suffering from multiple forms of disabilities and also their strength in physical tests was quite low. Conditions of widows were worst who were seen to be suffering from a number of functional impairments. It was found that during widowhood women face the problem of gradually losing their functional autonomy and in case of India and other countries of South Asia, women are alive more in number than men and this will soon become the central issue regarding the aged in the country that will also have an effect on all those who are the caregivers of the elderly people. Since with age, people become more susceptible to health issues, policies must be framed accordingly which would take into consideration the various aspects and heterogeneity of old age (Alam, 2013).

There has been too many works which have focused its attention on the funeral rites of the Hindus. What has been left ignored for a long period is an elderly person's feelings and concerns regarding death and encountering it. Lamb's study in Mangaldihi village, planning for death is a very important part of a person's life when he/she grows old. In the village it was found that people wanted the elderly people to show willingness both emotional and spiritual in order to die and also to engage themselves in praying for death and embracing it when it comes, for there, it is considered that death is not only natural for an elderly, but is equally desirable. This would smoothen and make the process of death easier and cut short the prolonged years of life which is not necessary as one has already reached his/her most suitable ending year of life (Lamb, 2000).

It is seen that in various societies, it has its own 'right' time which it considers fit for a person to die, which is usually the old age. It is thought that the fear which is associated with death lessens with age and is not present during old age. Man is mortal is an acceptable fact: by the time they reach this age they have had enough time to accept the inevitability of death. With advancement in medical field and technology span of life has increased to a great extent, people now hope to live longer. Therefore, nowadays even 85 years of age seems to be inappropriate for death. In a study on old people, Howarth found that even if a person crosses 75 years of age, acceptance of death is not seen, which contrasts with what the young people believe it to be (Howarth, 2007).

The longevity that has become a characteristic phenomenon of the modern world is again a phase which brings with it lots of negativity that adversely affects the elderly. These negative aspects can be poor health, poor financial condition, declining levels of control that they can hold, conditions of disability and last but not the least stigmatization. Old age is stereotypically connected with such pessimistic attributes, that has created fear among young people about this phase of life, for which they try to avoid and maintain a distance from them. This is a kind of negative representation that leads to stigmatization on the basis of age (Bytheway, 1995). Any discrimination based on age is a reflection of ageism, which means disliking an elderly person. United Nations gave a report on ageing and defined ageism as a process which 'reinforces a negative image of older persons as dependent people with declines in intellect, cognitive and physical performance. Older people are often perceived as a burden, a drain on resources and persons in need of care' (United Nations, 2009).

Ageism has been properly explained by a specific theory called Terror Management Theory (Pyszczynski et al., 1997). In United States, young people attach negative meaning to old age, because it reminds the young that this age and its bad effects and eventually death are all unavoidable and are bound to be everyone's ultimate future. Therefore, they try to evade the sight of aged individuals to escape the plight because otherwise it might unveil their hidden terror of getting older. When they realize they are growing old the only trick that they can adopt is to blame them so that they themselves can live with a feeling that neither old age nor death is the reality of their lives. This kind of a attitude increases the prejudices against the elderly. The more this negativity exists, the more weak the presentation and perceptions of older people turn out to be. This increases the rate of anxiety about death of younger generations, which in turn strengthens the ageist attitude (Martens et al., 2005).

In Beleghata, ageist attitude existed among people and there the old people are consistently being avoided by the young ones. A very senior woman, aged 85 years, who was so upset with the negative attributes imposed upon her by the young people that she once said to a young boy, '*Tomaro boyish hobe. Tumi amar jaegae esho, tokhon boyish howar koshtota bujhbe. Amar pokkhye eta ato khoshtokor kore tulona*' ('You will grow old too. Be in my shoes and you will realize the pain of old age. Don't make it so difficult for me'). However, instead of understanding her plight, the individual was aggravated for being reminded of his ultimate fate and treated her more badly by calling her names and by humiliating her whenever possible, even cursing her to die. When a person continues to live longer and if an untimely death happens of a young one, the elderly people are blamed for living long years. In Mangaldihi similar instances are seen where elderly people especially elderly women are often a victim of the blame game. Here, it can be aptly remarked that gender trajectories while mapping elderly discourses needs to be penetrated across classes with special attention to the lower stratum.

Lamb's study in Mangaldihi also reveals that a person, does not have the will to die, since one is attached to various things and this attachment will not let them die. Desire to live might include anything from one's wish to eat, to wants, craving to be with children, or it may include other things which are believed to be acting as constraints to death. The desire to live is often not socially acceptable and has been received with anger as found by Sarah Lamb during her stay at Mangaldihi. Also, fear of death was seen in these people, who were quite scared about their reasons of death, whether they will be able to face it with courage or will they try to run away, whether it will be painful or will just be fine. When Sarah Lamb, tried to console the elderly people who themselves were accepting death as their destiny were interrupted with a willingness among the people there which showed their readiness to die. Mostly, the aged people wished death when their body is still able to function without being completely dependent on others. They felt that children stop taking care of their elderly parents when they grow old and become dependent, therefore it is better to die before such a condition arrives. For some, if all responsibilities in life are met, which means if marriage of sons have taken place and if their grand-children are also married, then death is acceptable (Lamb, 2000).

In Beleghata, elderly people also wished to die. Their reasons were just like Sarah Lamb found in Mangaldihi, that they wanted to live as long as they are physically active. They feared the consequences of dependence which has overshadowed the other elderly people's value in society and self respect. They felt dying is necessary when one grows old because this phase according to most of the elderly is full of humiliation and sadness. The ones who are willing to live even after lots of physical problems are mostly those who have the responsibility of other family members on their shoulders, like seeing their children settled with a job and family. An elderly woman said,

> *'Amar akta ektrish bochor er meye ache jar biye hoeni. Se protibondi tai taake keo biye korte raaji noe. Amae meye shob korte pare taar protibondokota shotteo, tao keo egiye eshe oke mene nite chaena. Etai Jodi hoe tahole ami kibhabe mori. Or daityo ke nebe ami more gele? Ami chae keo khub bhalo oke biye koruk. Nahole ami moreo shanty pabona'*
>
> ('I have a daughter who is 31 years old and unmarried. The reason is she is a disabled child and therefore no one is willing to marry her. My daughter is able to do everything despite her disability, but sill no one comes forward to accept her. If this is the case, then how can I die? Who will take her responsibility after my death? I really wish someone really nice marries her. Else, I won't be able to rest in peace even after death').

This is true to many elderly women who still have dependent children or spouses to be taken care of. They not only are unwilling to die but are also extremely scared of becoming completely dysfunctional after being burdened with various diseases. However, good health can be maintained if certain things like addiction of tobacco, consuming alcohol, or smoking can be avoided. These are not only costly, but also have other adverse consequences as well. When one is young the side effects of these diseases are easy to dodge, but when old age arrives because of weaker immune power it is no longer easy to resist its side effects.

Raju (2011) in his study on addiction habits among the elderly population in Mumbai concludes that more than 60 per cent of the aged people had no addiction. However, 18 per cent of the population was found to be addict to Paan chewing. It was also seen that 13.3 per cent of them were addicted to smoking. In case of low income group people 40 per cent of people have no kinds of addiction, which means addictive habits were present in 60 per cent of the people from this group and this group is addictive far more than any other group. Amongst the elderly from lower income groups smoking or tobacco chewing was quite common. The reasons for such a high percentage of people among the lower socio-economic strata who are addictive are that such habits are common in their community and among other members in the different households and less number of other ways to divert themselves to some other activities. Females were less addictive than males as maximum number of them had no addiction and about half of the male population practiced no such habits. In lower socio-economic groups, a considerable number of elderly people have consequently reduced their food intake significantly, which can be a consequence of less availability of food or family attitude which eventually affects their health. Nearly 80 per cent of people from lower social and economic groups had irregular sleep and the reason for this is mainly because of work pressures that continues till old age and also because of inadequate facilities in households which prevents them from taking sufficient amount of rest. In order to have a nutritious and balanced diet the food items one must consume are vegetables, rice, eggs, milk, wheat, curd, dal, fish, butter or ghee, etc.

However, 70 per cent of the poor elderly people could have only rice or wheat, dal and vegetables (Raju, 2002).

Good health can be maintained only when proper diet is maintained and this can be done through consumption of good and nutritious food. In many cases poor economic condition becomes the barrier to let them have access to such healthy food. Poverty can never be seen as exclusive restraint, cultural barriers are also another way which obstructs elderly widowed women from having animal protein in their daily diet. Therefore, even if they suffer from malnutrition, their plight is hugely ignored. It was found in the study that there was not a single widowed elderly from non-slum area who consumed non-vegetarian item like fish or flesh, but from slum areas there were about 42 per cent of the elderly women who consumed fish and almost 19 per cent who consumed flesh. The reason why elderly widows from slum areas consumed non-vegetarian items was that they otherwise will not be able to carry out the tasks that they normally do both inside and outside their house. However, elderly widows from non-slum areas although did not consume non-vegetarian products they consumed milk and fruits. These products are high in cost and are not affordable by the people of the slum areas. Despite the fact that dal, rice, roti, sabji, etc. are very important as parts of the main diet elderly women are not able to have that because of their work pressure (Ray et al., 2003). And a person who suffers from physical ailments like eyesight issues, hearing problems gets confined to the four corners of the house. For him, there is not anything abnormal with old age. The pathological problems that old age brings are similar to the problems an individual faces at other ages, but the only problem is that it gets more intense because of several factors along with illness, like disorganization in family, absence of jobs which in turn affects the income level and at times leads to dependency of elderly people on others (Sahu, 1998).

In order to lead a quality life there must be a balance maintained among the various social, emotional, economic and physical aspects. Old age however, finds maintenance of such a stability immensely challenging when health starts to deteriorate, social supports decline and housing facilities become inadequate, economic resources get reduced, along with the insufficient and inefficient public services. For such high rates of inadequacies, elderly people start depending on others. For this reason the social status is often on the wane during old age (Gurumurthy, 1998).

In the village of Belkuli, health practices are still at primitive stage where an ill person is treated by an Ojha (Healer). Their medication is spiritual care and herbal medicines. These people also pray to deities who they believe would be able to heal them. In this village the serious health issues like Tuberculosis or Paralysis have affected about 31.50 per cent of people with approximately 18 per cent aged males and almost 14 per cent of aged females as its victims. Thus, males suffered more than females as per the data. The study also showed that increase in age, increases health problems. Just 2 per cent of the population as noted by the authors have received proper treatment for their ailments and 15.06 per cent of male elderly and 13.69 per cent of female elderly are deprived of proper medical care. The primary reason for such an inadequacy is found to be poverty. Lack of economic resource means a person would not be able to have access to medical care when necessary, get nutritious food and take sufficient amount of rest during periods of bad health. As noted by Sahu (1998) and in Belkuli village also, people after the age of 50 starts to suffer from hearing problems. 12.32 per cent in case of elderly males and about 34.24 per cent of elderly females are suffering from hearing difficulties in the village (Ray et al., 2003). If a person ages productively and retains the capacity to have a continuous level of growth and development, he or she cannot be assured to not to confront losses (Orr, 1998). Such losses are loss both of vision and hearing abilities. These problems are the most common issues among the aged people who are 65 years and above and women are more vulnerable to suffer from this loss (Fallcreek and Mettler, 1984). Even according to National Center for Health Statistics this problem is the most frequent issue reported by people who have crossed 65 years of age (National Center for Health Statistics, 1995).

Old age people who have difficulty in hearing with problems ranging from mild to moderate levels said that they face issues when they try to communicate with others in different social situations and since they are not able to hear properly it affects people's reaction towards them (Mulrow et al., 1990). Old age women seems to suffer more for loss of hearing in terms of difficulty in communication with others and therefore take the help of non-verbal methods to convey their messages. However, it has been noted that the way one adjusts to this problem differs from old men to women, with women showing signs of frustration, getting upset and stressed out more than their male counterparts (Birren and Schaie, 2001).

Beleghata slum consisted of many such elderly people, especially women who are facing this difficulty on a daily basis. Since, in this slum elderly men are less in number, sex difference in terms of hearing ability could not be considered. We found just one male elderly to suffer from hearing difficulties. A considerable number of Beleghata slum elderly people have hearing difficulties and they said this had a negative effect on their daily lives, including issues in doing daily chores. Here, we see that majority of these people are dependent on their children, where the latter consider them as burden and when elderly people have hearing difficulties it makes their situation more problematic, as they are not able to communicate at one go and react to others in a prompting manner. Frequent interruptions and constantly asking to repeat what has already been said, invites negative remarks for most of them. They thought it gets more frustrating for them when they are not able to understand what they are being told. Durga (name changed) said,

> *'Amar shunte oshubidhe hoe. Tai jokhon manushe kichu bole ami tader abar bolte boli. Nischoi tader birokto korata amar uddyeshyo noe., kintu tader akdom thik bhabe shone. Kintu durbhagyochrome ora sheta bojhena. Muloto nijera ei jaegae na asha porjonto burora ki jalae bhoge sheta era bujhbena. Eta khali bishonnyo kore amoni na, eta amader arekta jinish o mone korie dae je amader boyesh hoeche ar amader sharirik shomoshya din din aro kome jabe. Ora jamon bhabe byabohar kore mone bhoe dhore jae. Oder shathe kotha bolte bhoe lage. Bacchara much bhengae, nanan naam e daake ar amader ghrinhito bodh hoe. Bridhyo boyesh ta besh kothin'.*
>
> ('I have difficulty in hearing. Therefore, when people tell me something, I usually ask them to repeat. Of course, my intention is not to irritate them, but to distinctly understand them. Unfortunately, they don't seem to get that. Basically, unless they are in the same situation they won't ever feel the problem we the aged people go through. It not only is depressing for us, but at the time is a reminder of the fact that we have grown old and slowly our physical abilities will go on decreasing. The way they behave creates a fear. I get scared to talk to them. Children make faces, call us names and we feel hated. Old age is tough').

Another lady shared a similar instance where she expressed her dissatisfaction on costly medical facilities and therefore she could not use hearing aids. For her it was extremely shocking initially to even think that her hearing abilities are diminishing. She said,

> *'Ami jantam ashche din gulote amar bhagye ki lekha ache, ar sheta khub chap srishti korchilo. Bacchara apnar kheyal ekarone rakhena karon apnar akhon boyesh hoeche, kajei apni akhon tader opore bojha hoe gechen. Tar shathe jokkhon eshob shubidhe thake tokhon ghurte jawa aro mushkil hoe jae. Apni oder shomane proshno korte thaken. Ora shobshomoe kotha bolte chaena apnar shathe, ar jokhon oder abar bolte bola hoe ora aro rege jae. Ar, amar boyesh akhon jodio shatshotti, ami charte barite thike kaaj kori. Orao amar shathe kotha bolte birokto bodh kore. Kokhono kokhono ato bhoe kore je oder abar bolte bhoe lage, ar tai ami oder ager kothar opore darie i kaaj kori. Ami kebol anuman kori. Eta to oenk shomoe onek bhulbojhabojhi hoeche, tai amae kaaj charte onekbari bola hoechilo. Amake 'kaala', 'paagli' eshob name daake. Amae eshob shune khub kharap lage, ar kokhono khokhono ami tulkalam machie di. Ami bhabi ato boyoshko akjoner shathe oder shahosh kibhabe hoe oshobhyotomi korar. Amra er jonne dayi na, tao amar bhugte hoe'.*
>
> ('I knew what I had in store for future and it was stressful. Children don't take care of you because you are old now and hence a burden. When along with that you start having these issues it makes this phase more difficult to travel. You keep asking them questions. They are anyways not interested in talking to you and when you ask them to repeat they get angrier. Although, I am 67 now, I work as a maid in four houses. Those people find it irritating to communicate with me. At

times I am so scared to ask them to repeat, that I work on the basis of what I thought they told to me. I simply assume. This of course often leads to serious misunderstanding and for this particular reason I have been many a time asked to leave. People call me by names like 'deaf', 'insane', etc. I feel really bad and at times I create a mess out of it. I feel how they dare misbehave with someone so old! We are not responsible for this, yet we have to face its consequence!').

For Rosow, accepting old age is difficult for aged people, especially when their age is connecting to any kind of negative evaluation by the society (Rosow, 1974). It might be so that they wish to be considered middle aged, or to be called a 'retired person' or even be referred to as 'senior citizen' and not to be called by tags such as 'aged' or even 'elderly'. Aged people are not necessarily interested to mix only with people who belong to their own age group, but may also wish to connect with people of different ages (Menachem, 1982). Believing in the fact that one has become aged is not a simple process, as for an athlete it is tough to believe that by the time he reaches the end of his thirties he would not be able to retain his physical ability (Getzel and Mellor, 1985).

Alongwith hearing impairment, loss of vision is also a major problem for old people. As it includes the problem of perceiving depth, adjusting to light, or even a slowdown of the activities of eyes, etc. Coping with these several changes needs more time than before and aged people find driving and walking difficult and dangerous during this phase. Cataract makes vision a problem and when it develops it makes the lenses get clouded and in old age cataract becomes senile. In people aged 65 years and above, about 75 per cent of people develop cataract and 95 people out of hundred suffer from cataract problems by the time he reaches 85 years old. Visual impairment caused because of cataract affects 15 per cent of people and the people who require surgery because of this is 5 per cent (Tovée, 1996).

About one-sixth of those falling in the range between 55–64 years of age, who develop cataract become blind, 25.7 per cent of them aged 65 years of age or more than that face the trouble. Because of poor eyesight, people suffer from a number of difficulties, like they get socially isolated, suffer from low morale and also experience decreased self-esteem and diminished cognitive abilities, difficulty in dealing with road traffic, etc. Despite so many difficulties, aged people feel that vision problems are bound to happen during old age and once this problem has seeped in, it can not be altered anymore (Keegan et al., 1975).

However, it does play a major role and hampers normal functioning of life (Cullinan, 1977). Old people often consider loss of vision as unavoidable part of ageing (Keegan et al., 1975). Vision problems have affected about 30.13 per cent of males and 35.61 per cent of females in Belkuli, but only four of them have undergone eye operation despite this high percentage of people suffering from vision issues. The reason why the disparity could be seen is again because of poverty. As they do not have enough money they are neither able to buy spectacles nor able to get operated. The people here are dependent upon camps which will offer them free eye operation facility. They are not much connected with people other than their own village, hence are not aware of the government's initiative of free eye operation and the free camps which are planned by voluntary organizations (Ray et al., 2003).

Raju (2002) found that in Mumbai 68 per cent of male elderly people and 62 per cent of female elderly had eyesight issues and despite such problems, old people in large from poor economic backgrounds are not using any kind of aids (Raju, 2002).

In Beleghata slum, most of the aged people were suffering from eye problems and only some of them had cataract operation and a considerable number of elderly people of the slum amount to considerable per cent who did not undergo any such surgeries and are using spectacles. Vision problem was seen to affect large number of elderly in Beleghata and have hugely affected their daily dealings. For some, inability to see the minute detailing of the various things in front of them was a reason to get offended, while for some the seriousness was so severe that they could not see anything unless it was within the range of their sight. We met elderly people who could not even see us till we made our presence felt by placing ourselves at a close proximity. They seemed to find walking in their own neighbourhood difficult and at times movements inside their house was dangerous for some of them. Usha (name changed) 79 years old said,

> *'Amar chokh nie oshubidhe toiri hoe jokhn ami panchash er kothar shesher dike. Ami kaajer lok hishebe kaaj kortam, kintu ami jehetu dekhtei paina motamoti tai ora amar kaaj oponchodo o korto. Ami jai kortam tai ohompurno thakto. Ami jokhon muchtamo tokhono ora bolto mejhe oporishkar ache, ami kapor kachleo ora bolto moela jaeni. Prottekta bari nalish korto ami jai kortam tai niyei. Ami choshma pora shuru kori, kintu taate kaaj ditona, ar ami konobhbe chalie nitam jotokkhon amar aatshotti bochor boyesh holo, ebari theke oibari korte korte, kokhono kokhono ora charie ditto, ar kokhono kokhono am ii chere ditam'.*

> ('I started having problem with my eyes when I was just in my late 50s. I used to work as a maid servant, but since I could barely see, they disliked my work. Whatever I did, was incomplete. Even when I swept they complained that the floors are not clean, when I washed clothes they said the dirt did not go, when I cleaned the dishes they said that the muck is still there. Every house grumbled about whatever I did. I started using spectacles, but that did not work and I somehow managed till I was 68 years old, switching from one house to other, sometimes after they asked to leave and sometimes after I decided to discontinue working').

There were people who not only found working difficult during old age, but also felt that it was equally problematic to do one's own work inside the familiar surroundings. Pushpo (name changed) said,

> *'Amar akhon bahattor bochor boyesh, ar ami chokhe praye dekhtei parina. Amar ghore kono aloi nei, ar jai alo ashe shobtai chader fatol theke ba din er belae baere theke. Ami shob kaaj i ei aloe tei kori, ar manushe bole ei karonei amar chokh er aro khoti hoeche, tobe amar kichu korar nei. Amar taka nei alo kenar. Amar drishtishokti ato kharap je ami manush dekhte parina jotokkhon ora amar khub kache na ashche. Ami bujhtei partam na tomra eshecho jodina tomader uposthitir bayapre na jantam. Manush amar oshubidher shujog nae, churi kore nie jae eta ota bari theke, ar baccader moja lage dekhte ami edik odik jhujchi oder bhul jaegae rekhe dewa jinish gulo. Manush ato nishthur je ora iccha kore mejher majhkhane jinish rekhe dae jaate ami hochot kheye pore jai. Oder bokamir jonne ami khub kharap bhabe onek bar pore gechi, ar pore bhishon byathar moddhye die gechi. Ora oder chelemanushi kajer fol er kotha bojhena, ar eta khubi dukkhyojonok. Onek manush ache jara rastae haatte bhoe pae jokhon dorkar tokhono ar bina kono karone bhoge'.*
>
> ('I am 72 years old and now can hardly see. I have no light in my house and whatever light that comes in is from the crack of the roof top or during day from outside. I do everything with this light and people say that has affected my vision further, but I can't help. I have no money to afford light. My eyesight is so weak, that it is difficult to see people if they don't come very close to me. I would have not known whether you all have come in had I been unaware of your presence. People take advantage of my problem, by stealing something or the other from my house daily and children find it funny when they misplace things and see me searching for them aimlessly. People are so heartless at times that they put objects in the middle of the floors so that when I walk I stumble over them. I had bad falls because of their silly behaviours and later on have suffered from severe pains. They don't understand the consequences of their childish act and this is really disappointing. There are people who are scared to walk on road alone even when it is essential and end up suffering unnecessarily').

There were people who said eating, drinking, sleeping, getting up and down the bed, all become difficult with age when eyesight becomes an issue. The edge of bed also becomes blur which increases risks of fall. The ones who are dependent on their children are not able to see, do not even realize what they are eating. There were some elderly people who live all alone and therefore cook their own food. Out of them, there was a lady named Jayanti (name changed), who said,

> *'Ami nijer ranna nijei kori amar chelemeyera amae chere chole jawar por. Jehetu ami dekhte paina tai prayi thik beej ba moshla dite bhul kori. Nun er jaegae ami chini die dite pari, moedar jaegae shuji diye dite pari. Tumi noshchoi bujhte parcho ki jinish toiri hoe sheshe giye'.*

> ('I cook my own food after my children left me. Since, I can't see properly I often make a mistake in selecting the right seeds and spice. In place of salt I might add sugar in place of flour I might add semolina. You can surely understand what kind of a product is eventually created').

Some said that problem in eyesight creates trouble in sewing clothes as well, as that needs tremendous amount of pressure on eye and requires a good vision.

Locomotor problem is another issue which is quite common among the aged people. In Beleghata also people generally wait for such free camps to get their checkups done, but hardly get the information when such camps are held. For very old people, or physically frail ones information is not sufficient to access such camps, as they need aids and people who would accompany them to the place, which again is a difficult help to ask for. In a study by Liebig and Rajan found that in a district in Tamil Nadu, that 40 per cent of people in total were suffering from locomotor troubles (Liebig and Rajan, 2003)

In another study which was carried out by Sharma (1999) found that disability because of locomotor issues and loss of memory was quite common among old people. Raju (2002) found that locomotor problem affects the elderly men more than the elderly women.

In Beleghata, locomotor problem affected most of the elderly people. It disturbs the proper ability to move painlessly. It disables free movement to such an extent that for some of them sitting down, getting up and walking even a slight distance becomes troublesome. Many of them reported that they had to quit jobs because they felt mobility is not possible with such a condition where legs become painful and weak and disrupts movements. Many women said that if they are required to work while sitting, they gather everything that is needed to carry it out in order to avoid getting up to gather them later on. Also, if there are several tasks that are to be done in a seated position, then they try to do all the tasks together, so that later on they are not required to bend their knees and put pressure on their joints. Many of them are so traumatized with their pain that they prefer death as an alternative to it. According to some, doing things which require one to stand and walk is not a problem, but anything where knee bending is required, is a problem, hence they avoided the tasks. An elderly couple living here, get their food from a nearby Christian Church which donates food for free to poor people. He and his wife go there daily on foot despite having serious joint pains. This couple had no other choice but to go as otherwise they would die of starvation. They claimed that regular travels are exhausting for them and are deteriorating their condition. The couple was so frail and weak that they could not sit for long in one position and constantly kept on pressing their waist and legs.

Almost every house we visited, had such elderly people who have pain in their bodies and were suffering from some or the other form of locomotor problem. Shushila (name changed) said,

> *'Apni amae haatte ar darate bolun sharadin, ami khushi mone kore debo Kintu amae boshe uthte bolben na kono karone. Balti tola ar ghor mocha amar pokkhye shombhob na, ar jokhon dorkar por ami kauke deke ni. Shadharonoto amar protibeshira ba bacchara joler balti bhorte shahajyo kore, ar ami batar, rannar, ar mochar kaaj ak taane kori. Kintu eta dui theke tin ghonta lage shesh korte ar tarpor jokhon ami uthte jai tokhon khub koshto hoe. Ami ashepasher shob kichur shahajyo ni othar jonne, jokhon ogulo chara ar parina. Jehetu amar ei oshubidhe ta hocche, ami akbar Campbell er daktar ke dekhiechilam ar uni bolechilam amar Osteoarthritis ache'.*
>
> ('You ask me to walk and stand for an entire day, I would gladly do that. But, don't ask me to sit down and get up for any reason. Lifting up of buckets and sweeping the floors are not possible for me and when it is required I call someone. Generally, my neighbours including children help me in filling up the water buckets and I do the grinding tasks, cooking, sweeping, etc. at a stretch. But, it takes at least two to three hours to finish and after that when I try to get up it becomes so painful. I take the help of everything possible present nearby to help me get up, when I just can't do it without them. It did happen that I had called someone to assist me stand. Since, I am facing this difficulty, I once visited the doctor in Campbell and he said I have Osteoarthritis').

Osteoarthritis is one of those diseases that make locomotion difficult of many aged people and this tends to create obstruction in performance of various tasks. However, if crutches or canes are used then relying on others including family members will get reduced and one can be self sufficient in performing those activities which so long was difficult for them (Blazer and Palmore, 1976).

A study found that one of the main problems that elderly face are injuries and 15 per cent of aged people who have crossed 85 years of age are admitted to hospital because of injuries. The rate of death caused because of injuries among old people of 65 years of age and beyond were seen to be higher in comparison to young ones and therefore it is a serious issue among the aged, especially because home is the main place where such injuries occur. Falling down and getting injured are the most common occurrence among elderly aged 75 years and above, which often end in fractures and it has been found that 90 per cent of the hip fractures are responsible for such falls. One of the most common forms of disability among elderly people related to locomotor is a consequence of osteoarthritis, limiting a person's movement. Another form of arthritis which can cause disability and inflict pain is rheumatoid arthritis that can also disable a person. In aged people amputation and problems in legs are other troubles that can disable an elderly. It is suggested that such sufferings can be controlled if certain steps are taken. If osteoarthritis can be detected at an early stage and treatment can be given to avoid further problems. A person suffering from diabetes, if controls it then chances of osteoarthritis can be limited and if anybody is suffering from any kind of vascular trouble then proper treatment must be carried out. Also, like the other sections of the population who can make use of hip replacement facilities, the elderly must also be able to assess surgical facilities (Kumar and Kumar, 2009).

In a study among aged women, various diseases that are present among them was assessed. It was found that about 52 per cent of them were suffering from problems related to locomotor disability across various income groups aged more than 60 years old (Dave and Mehta, 2008). A study was conducted by Sharma (1999), where they found locomotor problem to be one of the major difficulties faced by them along with amnesia.

Another study carried out in Kolkata, highlights two main issues that affected the elderly in their early years of old age. One problem was related to locomotor abilities and the other one was related to visual problems where both males and females get affected. The study also showed marginal difference between the elderly irrespective of gender suffering from locomotor and visual disabilities (Ghosh, 2007).

In another study, in Netherlands, a longitudinal research was carried out where cohort survey was done where problems related to ageing was examined among people who were not mentally fit. A 4 years study was carried out on about 1600 people, from two provinces of this place. During the age group, from 50 to 59 years old, increasing problems in locomotor abilities was observed (McLellan, 1997). Joint pain and swelling was also prevalent among the people of Mumbai as found in the study conducted by Raju (2002), with 52 per cent of elderly women suffering from it and male sufferers were much less in number. It is said that out of the various medical issues which an elderly suffers, pain can be said to be one of those problems that constitutes most of the visits to doctor (Ferrell, 1991). Also, pain affects the elderly more than it affects the young people (Brattberg et al., 1989). Some population based studies were carried out which have expressed that the elderly people from communities from 25–50 per cent suffer from pain (Ferrell, 1991). Pain sensitivity varies among people aged 80 years and above and with further increase in age tolerance of pain decreases (Farrell, 2000).

Elderly suffering from pain, have a number of other consequences that affects them further. These include, impairment of activities that are needed to be carried out daily, ambulation, disturbances in sleep and eventually in order to cure these problems the cost gets increased to a great extent (Ferrell, 1991). Other health issues that may result because of pain are dysfunctional cognitive abilities, deconditioning, falls (Weiner,

2001). Different patterns of pain were noticed among elderly people in a study which was conducted on those aged people who visited clinics. There, complains associated with joint pains and fractures were seen to be reported more frequently compared to other pains like backache and headache (Harkins et al., 1984).

Another epidemiological study on patients suffering from osteoarthritis found that different forms of arthritis have made 80 per cent of the elderly undergo this pain (Davis, 1988). A report by National Health and Nutrition Survey 1987, mentioned that elderly people who are suffering from pain are going through depression and also, are experiencing impairment in their daily activities (National Health and Nutrition Survey, 1987). Therefore, it can be said that when an elderly suffers from pain, his/her regular activities get restricted (Harkins and Price, 1992).

Shortness of breath or pain in the chest were quite common among poor people as found such as in the study by Raju in the district of Mumbai, along with other problems such as long periods of cough and asthma (Raju, 2002). In a study by Martin and others it was found that asthma is increasingly becoming a global problem among elderly population. The prevalence of asthma in this population ranges from about 6 per cent to 17 per cent. The reason for such an increase is the existence of allergies, the level of smoking, the heightened level of pollution to which this population is exposed to and many such other factors. The patients with asthma in the late age can be divided into two groups. One group is the one whose exposure to the disease is since their association to it from childhood and the other group has its association with it from 60 or 65 years old (Martin and Preedy, 2012).

Blood pressure test conducted in Mumbai by medical experts found that high blood pressure was found more in the lower economic group which was about 22.5 per cent of them, as compared to the people from other status and males had higher pressure compared to that of females. Nearly 47.5 per cent of the elderly from the lower economic group were reported anaemic, which was quite high compared to the other groups. Female anaemic patients were more affected by it than the males, which shows that the females had less intake of iron and healthy foods than the males (Raju, 2002). It has been seen that cases of hypertension among elderly is large. Most of the cases are found among aged individuals who are more than 75 years and older. It has been found that out of every 100 elderly women 65 women suffer from high blood pressure and out of every 100 elderly men 75 men suffer from high levels of blood pressure (Rubin, 2009).

During times of illness, various studies have shown that when a male elderly is ill then he is mostly taken care of by his wife. In Belkhuli, 75 per cent of elderly males were provided the needed care by their wives.

Unmarried daughters were seen to be very much concerned about their illness and about 14.28 per cent of them were recorded to take the responsibility of playing the role of caretakers of their fathers. 7.14 per cent were looked after by their daughters-in-law. Brothers, grandson, etc. constituted 3.57 per cent of the caretakers. Here, the elderly people who live alone are mostly dependent on their married daughters and neighbours who attend their health issues when necessary. For female, just 2.22 per cent of husbands take care of their wives when they are ill. 6.66 per cent of aged women are taken care of by their sons. A good percentage of about 42.22 per cent constitutes of daughters-in-law who take care of their mothers-in-law. Unmarried daughters, about 31.11 per cent of them take care of their mothers during illness and other family members of about 17.77 per cent are fulfil this responsibility of elderly women in Belkhuli. However, whoever takes care of these elderly people, 25 per cent of elderly males showed dissatisfaction about the care they have received. As many as 64.44 per cent of elderly women showed dissatisfaction with the way they were treated during their periods of illness. The reasons understood were many, system of patriarchy seemed to be one of them, because under such a system men in a society are given extra care and importance by others, while females are always treated with neglect. As most care takers of women are daughters-in-law conflicts are bound to arise between them. However, the reasons can be more specifically defined under two different heads – economic and social. Social causes consist of reasons ranging from neglect of aged people to conflict between aged parents and the children. Under economic causes, falls the poor financial condition of the people in Belkhuli. The result is that they are not able to avail adequate medical facilities, have healthy food which in turn affects their health. In this village economic causes have bothered about 88 per cent of elderly people who are not taken care of properly by the members of their families. The people here, therefore, lives in acute economic crisis along with long periods of neglect which hurts their self-respect. This has negative consequence on their psychological well-being which again affects their health and destabilized their relationship with their near and dear ones (Ray et al., 2003).

> *'Akbar amar khub jor hoechilo ar sheta onek din obdiyei chilo, ar khali bomi korchilam. Khub gurutoro byatha hocchilo shorire, ar tai ghumateo parchilamna. Du din er pore jokhon amar bondhura kheyal korlo, tokhonora amar chelemeyeder janalo amae daktarkhanae niye jete ar sposhto bhabe jene nite je eta Dengue, Malaria ba Chikungunya na jeta oi shomoe puro deshe probhab felchilo. Ora pattao dilona. Amar chele amae akta jorer oshudh dilo, ar o tokhoni amae daktarkhane niye gelo jokhon oshudh ta kaaje dilona, ar amar shorir aro kharap hoe gelo, ar amar kichu bondhura oke bollo nie jete jarpor jana gelo je eta dengue. Amar amar ei oshushthotar shomoe ja opoman shojjhyo korechi tokhoni jibon nie bhoe hoe gechilo atota okamyo ar mulyohin bodh korar jonne'.*

(‘Once I was having high fever that lasted for days and was vomiting constantly. I had some serious body aches and could not sleep because of this. After two days when my friend noticed me, she informed my children to take me to the clinic and get checked to ascertain it’s not Dengue, Malaria or Chikungunya which was affecting the entire country at that point of time. They hardly cared. My son gave me a medicine for fever and it was only when it didn’t work and my health worsened and some my friends insisted that he took me to the clinic just to know it was Dengue. The extreme humiliation that I had to face during my illness was the time when it was the most disgraceful experience of my life for feeling so much unwanted and valueless’).

In a study in Central Africa’s Democratic Republic of Congo, it was found the miserable health condition affects a quarter of old men and women owing to extremely poor financial situation. At health care centres old people were not treated without money and therefore they stayed back at home to get recovered by themselves as money stood as the main obstruction between their health and utilization of proper health care. Several respondents showed their disappointment for not being able to treat themselves for lack of enough financial resources. The aged people who could afford went to seek medication from the pharmacies, while the ones who could not remained dependent upon the traditional healers when their health worsened and in return often paid the healers in kind and not in cash, like they got medicines in exchange of a chicken, or a bag of cassava, etc. (Maharaj, 2012).

Among the major resources for managing chronic illnesses are time, energy, money, presence of social support, access to a proper housing, knowledge and also information and availability of such facilities which would enhance the independence of person and not the dependence. Psychological support is also essential in order to deal with such diseases. All these resources and the degree to which one can avail them or the range of facilities that one is surrounded with and the coping mechanisms that patients and their family members can avail all play an influential role in managing the chronic conditions of the patients. The handicap situation that is created by some of the chronic illnesses can be solved with the help of these resources, for example to give money to someone to help in activities such as to do shopping, or do the job of house cleaning. When one is chronically ill, a number of resources start decreasing with time, for example money starts deceasing when the person leaves his/her job, or when a working spouse decides to quit his/her job and take up the role of caretaking on a full time basis. Social support gets disconnected for the tensions that the chronic illness cause. The entire life starts revolving around the ways to treat disease and control it (Scambler, 2008).

Inaccessibility of resources inherently epitomises the plight of the miserable situation, viz. the deprivation existing and the disadvantage which some people are experiencing. It also brings us to the power dynamics including the question of accessibility binaries viability versus inability situation of society and the unequal distribution of resources among people belonging to various socio-economic groups. The personal matter of sickness and disease gets connected to the issues of wider social and political context. Certain sections of society are in a more disadvantageous position than others, like women, working-class people or people from the urban communities who are deprived of the required benefits.

According to Bury (1988), two meanings can be associated with sickness and disease. One is the case of deprivation and disadvantage and second is the implication that diseases have in a particular cultural context, whereby he/she is considered incompetent in performing the daily and ordinary jobs in a socially acceptable and approved manner. The level of devaluing a person is also associated to the cultural context in which one is suffering from a particular disease, where culture plays a determining factor of perception of the disease. This can be explained with an example. If someone is suffering from as AIDS, the society treats him in a stigmatized manner and is devalued just as a homosexual, or someone who has drug addiction. Of these, AIDS is considered more as a stigma and as a revelation of one's identity in society and of his/her lifestyle and that cornering a person and handicapping him/her is often related to values embedded deep social and cultural environment (Bury, 1988).

According to Estes (1981), one of the most important thing is reaction of the people towards elderly populace which has a long lasting impact. In a social context which comprises of various institutions, different organizations and a number of people, aged people get involved in interaction with all of them and through these interactions the meaning and understanding are shaped. Other than these, social context also has structural constraints which can play an influential role in controlling interactions and in limiting the levels of understanding which encourages certain actions and discourages some others (Estes, 1981). There can be uncertainty in case of some diseases. A disease can start with showing some unclear signs and be slow during its onset and continue to be so till it is diagnosed with clarity and this diagnosis can take quite a few years at times. A patient may understand that something is wrong with him/her and may complain about this to his family members and even medical experts, but then these complaints might not receive the amount of seriousness and importance they deserve and can be ignored as mere carping about one's own health, or malingering or even can be thought to be hypochondria. However, since this is an ongoing conflict between what the patient feels and what the physician thinks, it leads to a very stressful situation for both the individual concerned and his family members. With a proper diagnosis this disagreement over the issue of validity of the symptoms is resolved, which of course is a sigh of relief for everyone involved, thus leading to legitimization of the patient's complaints (Robinson, 1988). According to Talcott Parsons, when a person is sick, he is exempted from performing the social roles which he was responsible to perform. This exemption varies in degrees depending upon the seriousness of the illness and for Talcott Parsons, the patients have the right to be exempted from such responsibilities, however for him in order to avoid malingering, legitimization of the rights are equally crucial so that people do not take its undue advantage. The physician is the person who is bestowed upon with the right to act as the legitimizing agent. He is also the 'court of appeal' who might be reluctant in granting legitimacy to those people who assumed the sick role by exempting oneself from performance of the normal social roles for a long period of time without visiting the doctor and getting the medical legitimization. Such people are considered 'hysterics' by physicians and also 'crocks' whose complaints are no more evaluated with importance even when it has reasons to be investigated. This legitimization of sick role also means that people were legitimately depended on others for being sick and must get back to their normal life as soon as they are cured (Parsons, 1951).

Charmaz has explained that people who are chronically ill face difficulty in leading a positive life and a life which is valued and worthwhile. The cultural definitions of a particular illness can be so negative that it can have an unfavourable affect on the sufferer thus causing a diminished sense of self-worth (Charmaz, 1987). Uncertainty related to diseases can be a problem even after diagnosis. This can be about what course is to be followed and what will be its consequences, in short it is the uncertainty about the trajectory, which often occurs with symptomatic uncertainty which means changeability of symptoms. And all of these can be quite stressful in maintaining a proper family environment, which makes planning difficult and constant modification of the living arrangements. Rheumatoid arthritis can fill in to the aforesaid classification. It has no specific symptom and have no fixed level of pain, is extremely distressing for the sufferer (Locker, 1983).

Through a study in Kolkata in Ward 87 where both the slum as well as the non-slum areas were covered, the health status of the widowed elderly women were studied. Arthritis was common in both the areas, along with occurrence of multiple ailments (Ray et al., 2003). Sometimes arthritis can be chronic. For example rheumatoid arthritis which is not only chronic but is also a progressive disease, that is responsible for causing good amount of pain, destroying the condition of the joint of the person in which it occurs and also at time causes disability (Kvien, 2004). The study that was conducted by Ranjana and others in 2003 in Kolkata. They found that occurrence of chronic illness was more prevalent in elderly women of the non-slum areas than those of the slum areas. Cough and joint problems seemed to affect them more than anything else with 73.3 per cent of elderly widows from non-slum areas suffering from chronic cough problems and 86.1 per cent suffering from problem in limbs or joints. There are two other issues which seemed most important problems included blood pressure with 68.3 per cent suffering from it and heart problem with 61.4 per cent suffering from it (Ray et al., 2003).

Chronic illnesses often disrupt family life, because of long term suffering, the amount of care and love that is needed from family members, relationships can face challenges along with changes in the roles, the members play. There are families which are extremely cooperative and willing to provide all sorts of help and care that is needed, but because the sufferer in certain situations dismiss any kind of help being offered for perceiving oneself as a burden. Some people might withdraw oneself from family life and in certain cases, the sufferers along with their families get detached from others and sometimes breakdown of marital bonds can also occur as a consequence. The consequence that chronic illness might have on marital relationship has been properly explained by MacDonald (1988). She has assessed those people who have been or have suffered from rectal cancer and are living with its sequel. Irrespective of whatever treatment they have received, a majority of them have reported to have suffered from loss of capacity in sexual activities and as a result a drop in the quality of marital relationships. Young men were especially concerned about their surgeries and its following consequences which may affect relationship with their wives (MacDonald, 1988).

It is not only about marital relationships, but all kinds of relationship bring them similar embarrassing feelings for they feel that the smell coming out of stoma or because of the noise from it can give rise to disgust within people against them. All these worries control the people undergoing such surgeries from mixing with others. Therefore, out of such fears they tend to lead a life which is more restricted in its form (Scambler, 2008).

Rosow (1974) through his role theory says that the position of old people has changed and unlike the traditional societies where the youth respected the presence and wisdom of elderly, modern societies have changed its outlook in such a way that has degraded the status of the elderly. Earlier gerontocracy was an accepted aspect of various societies, however with changes in value structure, inter relationships across generation also had a transformation where in the present times, respect for the elderly has been altered with the notion of liability, which on the other hand is a consequence of utility notion. For Rosow, modern society has failed to maintain such a cordial relationship between the generations and feels that today's time is the time of the young. He explained this in the form of five phases, which according to him is essential to understand how slowly the aged people have moved into a position of disadvantage (Bianchi, 2011).

In Beleghata, few people already had heart attacks. Several people developed disabilities much before they were in their fifties. Some, at the time of interviews, said irrespective of their age right now, they were thrown out of their jobs at early ages because of their disabilities. In this place, while interacting we also find an elderly man with whom we could not talk. He could not understand what was going on. His son said he is in his late seventies and is suffering from dementia for the last two months. Therefore, we decided not to stay there any long, for it might bother him and moved out of the room. In spite of that, this particular observation helps us in delving with the issue of dementia which has been quite common among elderly across the world.

In Asia, the rate of dementia increases with age. This prevalence rate is similar to the rate found in the western countries (Shah and Guh, 2001). Other than this male elderly we met a female elderly person who was 84 years old suffering from dementia. She was taken care of by her neighbours. Her own son left her few months back on the ground that she was tough to handle and was very disobedient. When we went inside her room she gave us a blank look, with one neighbour rushing inside followed by two others and then few others following her, with others trying to make their place in the small space as fast as possible. We asked the elderly about her problem but unfortunately could not find any concrete reply from her end and what she said was very vague and was related mostly to something of her own village and family and unrelated to our questions.

We saw a very strange peculiarity in her activities and found her relentlessly trying to get up and down from her bed. She also had a feeling like there is something on her pillow or above her eyes and therefore in order to get rid of it she tries to shoo it off. She is unable to go to the toilet by herself and needs somebody's assistance. The room was extremely pungent and when we asked about her care givers who are liable to take care of her, the present members of the room (six to seven) kept on passing the buck to others. Another elderly lady who was her friend said that, since her children left her, neighbours try to take care of her. We observe that her faeces is not cleared at the time when the interview was carried. The elderly women who was her friend, was complaining about it. She said, '*Protibeshira or dekhashona kore kintu shobshomoe sheta shombhob hoena, oder onno kaaj o thake. Protibeshira oderke nijeder moton kore shamlae, tomar bhalo laguk kin a laguk, sheta kono byapar na*' (The neighbours do take her care, but it is not always possible. They have other works to do as well. The neighbours manage it the way they want to, whether you like it or not, does not matter. They thought you are from some party and you will do something dangerous. Therefore, they rushed in and tried to manage as much as possible. See, they are not her children, still they do something, but I wonder where her own children are!). The following narrative can inherently be comprehended from the discourse of macrophysics of power as explained by Michel Foucault, whereby neighbours with the help of their superior position tried to keep the aged under their control (Foucault, 1977).

We find several cases of heart patients in Beleghata and had interacted with a patient who had a pacemaker installed. Heart problem has been featured as one of the main health problem, affecting the elderly population. National Heart, Lung and Blood Institute says that in America about 2 million people have heart attacks. Heart failure is such a problem that can attack a person at any age, but it is particularly life threatening and rampant among elderly population (Rich and Nease, 1999). Here, we met another elderly man in his late sixties. He said that he used to work in a coalmine, but got this job when he was approximately 40 years old. It was not possible for him to continue it for more than 7 years as he started suffering from breathing troubles. He later on developed hearing problems. From this, we can conclude that physical problems of various types affect elderly people which inherently make them dependent as well as a liability for the family members since provision of care in coherence to present cultural context is often a product of service industry.

Mental Health

Issues related to mental health of the elderly is a subject which has been viewed with utmost negligence. Age and mental health problems might not be related, but certain problems related to mental troubles such as depression and dementia are associated with old age people (Levernson and Jackson, 2006). People aged more than 65 years are the ones who are prone to mental problems. In United Kingdom, 10.5 millions of people belonged to 65 years or more, wherein about 3 per cent of this population is suffering from severe depressions. Nearly 15 per cent of them are suffering from mental problems which are quite common such as depressions, panic attacks, nervousness and neurosis (RCPsych, 2006). Elderly people are often in charge of taking care of other people who are old and therefore there are chances that these care taking responsibilities often make them susceptible to mental health troubles (Singleton et al., 2002).

Depression is common amongst elderly. It is affecting the self-worth of a person, the feelings that a person has about his/her surroundings. It gives rise to a sense of worthlessness and hopelessness within a person. Consequences of depression can affect a person's sleep and everything that is related to a person's daily life starting from loss of appetite and participation in the various activities. Concentration gets disturbed and activities which previously interested them no longer attract them and they do not enjoy doing it any longer because of depression during later life. It does not stop here as it extends all the way to affect the overall functioning of the person and affects his morbidity and eventually his chances of survival as well (Lopez and Murray, 1997).

The main risk factors for which depression is caused are found to be economic, events in life that might have caused stressful situations, loss of close ones, detachment from social activities which might have led to social isolation and this eventually have ended up in making the person feel lonely (Hall and Scragg, 2012).

But what is being lonely? It is an emotional state where a person's empty feelings and isolated conditions are very powerful and it is more than just a willingness to want to have somebody's company to be with for participation in some or the other activity. It is a state where disconnection from others happens and feelings that one is alienated or cut off from society at large is very strong. Attachment of any kind helps a person to integrate to larger society which in the long run helps in reducing isolation among people and finally reduces mental problems (Chakraborty, 2009).

Aged people have hardly any access to resources which can alter their situations to improve their relationships with society at large. Therefore, isolation as well as exposure to various lifestyle pressures followed by degrading economic status results in constant decline of the physical health, which can snatch away their ability to remain active for long and take part in social activities and be regarded as valueless member in their communities (Hall and Scragg, 2012). A person who so long survived around certain number of people, some of whom probably meant the life to them slowly starts to meet their end, one by one. Thus, the amount of grief gradually gets accumulated within the person because of the loss of family members, spouses, relatives, friends, etc. Problems in financial condition can also lead to depression among elderly people (Rogers and Pilgrim, 2014).

Murphy in his study found out that people who are poor and have faced issues with housing facilities and economic stability are the ones who have become more depressed compared to the ones who were financially stable and had better housing accommodations (Murphy, 1988). Blaxter in his study revealed that among older people psychological health and social well-being is proportional to their respective social class. The study further states that in case of old people, if they find that they have someone to confide in their families or if they realize that the relationships around them are not unstable and fleeting in nature then chances of depression will be less (Blaxter, 1990). Murphy (1982) conducted a community survey. In this study it was found that 30 per cent of the people who could not find any confiding relationship suffered from depression.

Lowenthal found that depression is found mostly among those people who tried to create relationship with others but could not do so, on the contrary it is less among those who could sail through all by themselves without the need of being in a company of others (Lowenthal, 1965).

Another factor that is responsible for depression in elderly abuse as observed by Eastman (1993). It was found that in United States of America the elderly abuse varied from 6 lakh to about 1 million. Some abuse of elderly people include abuses from improper skin care, inability to control infection, timely diagnosis of physical problems, neglecting the weak elderly people in situation where they can have chances to fall, providing insufficient diet, etc. The consequences of these abuses on the psychology of the elderly are difficult to determine in terms of its long or short-term effect. Any kind of abuse on the elderly, be it psychological or physical or even sexual will not have any positive effect on an elderly individual, in fact the effect would be outrightly negative, sometimes being life threatening. Dementia patients often are prone to violence and because they are mostly at the mercy of their care takers who often resort to various means of violence as a way of reaction towards the elderly people. Hence, it is seen that aged people pass through a series of obstacles in the forms of discriminations, age being the sole reason. They are also excluded from their society because of the same reason (Beeston, 2006).

What Beeston found was found in Beleghata as well. Aged people struggled to find peace and craved to be valued by the people in the slum. They feared to talk, to ask for help, to sit and even in some cases to smile at them. We met an old lady Gouri (name changed), who said, that when she was in her 50s one of her three sons married when he was just 17 years old without her permission. Within a span of two years her middle son married in the same manner. Initially since she was not in favour of their marriages according to her the sons' wives hated her. She felt they instigated her sons against her. She said,

> *'Amar chhelera kom boyeshe biye korechilo ar oder kono chakri chilna tokhon. Amar tokhon boyesh hoe i gechilo ar kaaj charte chaichilam. Oder biye howa mane chilo amae akhono kaaj chalie jete hobe karon akhon dujon noun lok er dekhashona korte hobe. Ami oder dayityogyanhinota dekhe rege gechilam. Ami oder karon ta bojhalam, kintu janina kothae bhul hoe gelo, kintu ora amar biruddhye chole gel oar amar apotti thaka shottei biye kore nilo. Eta oder hoeto koshto diechilo, ami janina. Oder biyer por theke galagali ar bachbichar ja ami shojhyo korchi sheta shesh i hoena. Oder boura amae bole, 'ei buri kheyene', 'ei buri shorto', 'ei buri chup kor', ar eta choltei thakto. Ora eibhabe kibhabe kotha bole. Ei barite jai kharap hoe puro dosh ta amar ghare eshe chap e. Ora jai shidhantyo nae amae baad diye nae. Akbar amar natir iskul e bhorti howa nie alochona hocchilo ar ami bhablam pushpar nati jekhane pore shekhane bhorti korale bhalo karon ami oi iskul ta bhaloshunechi. Ora bollo ami nakgolar cheshta kano korlam, bishesh kore porashonar byapare. Ora amon bhyabohar korlo jano amar kono kotahi cholbena ei shongshare. Amar boro bouma amon akta much korlo ami bhoe peye gelamar bhablam hoeto amar eder shathe ektu durotyo bojae rakhte hobe. Ami onek briddha hoe gechi ar tai ar ami jogyo noi nijer mon er kotha bhag korar jonne ba kono rokom paribarik alochonae bhag newar jonne'.*
>
> ('My sons married at an early age when they had no jobs. I was old already and wanted to quit my work. When they married, it meant that

I have to continue working as there were two more members to be taken care of. I was really angry by their acts of irresponsibility. I explained them why am I against it but they thought I am against the girls and I don't know where did I go wrong, but they went against me and got married despite my objection. I feel this had hurt them or something I don't know. Ever since their marriage the amount of abuse and discrimination I have faced from their end is endless. Their wives have all the time said, 'Hey oldie eat!', 'Hey oldie, move', 'Hey oldie, keep quiet' and this goes on and on. How can they talk to me like this? Whatever wrong happens in this house the blame is always on me. Whatever decision they take I will always be excluded. Once a discussion about my grandchild's school admission was going on and I thought of saying that admitting him to the school where Pushpa's grandson is studying will be good as I have heard the school is nice. They said why I tried to interfere in their matters, especially in matters which are related to education. They behaved as if I have no say in this family. My eldest daughter-in-law made such a face that I got scared and thought I should probably maintain a distance from them. I have become old and no longer deserve to share my feelings with them or participate in any kind of family discussions').

The first phase is *Devaluation*. According to it the elderly people are not considered important, they are treated indifferently, with no compassion, with their knowledge and experience considered out dated and least needed being sometimes rejected openly by people and forced to go through a negative environment where people would treat them with pessimism (Bianchi, 2011).

In United States of America, there is a negative value underlying in the society about the aged people, where the self worth of an individual is connected to one's productive abilities in economic spheres. As a person starts to grow old, his ability to remain economically productive starts to decrease. Therefore, it is quite uncommon for a person who has reached the late-life stage to be a part of the society's work force. Now, the aged people for having experienced a number of losses already, like losing of someone too close to them, including the loss of a spouse, they are under deep depression. To add to it when the society devalues them their level of depressive symptomatology increases (Loue and Sajatovic, 2008).

Beleghata is a place where most of the elderly people, we met have lost their spouses and since the majority of them were women, widows were more common and in fact, elderly men who lost their wives could not be found here. Having lost their partners and in some cases, their children, parents, siblings, relatives and friends, the elderly population of the slum were suffering from high level of depression and anxiety. Most of them said that losing people in their lives was already stressful and when devaluation was added to that, their level of pain become acuter.

Making elderly people feel 'less worthy', compared to younger people can lead to several negative consequences leading to social rejection, separation from society or even exclusion. Things that we take for granted and things that we value are therefore made inaccessible to the elderly through such forms of denial. Less allowance to receive these goods in life means they get less opportunity to get them. This, in turn, makes the elderly participate less. Less participation in different activities means that there will be more withdrawal. With greater level of withdrawals, there will be higher chances of isolation. The relationships which were once treasured by the elderly are lost, the respect which they once had in society disappears, the autonomous role that they could play in their lives are of no value anymore and finally, participation in different spheres of lives are obstructed. All these losses lead to nothing but a sense of hopelessness and depression, the reason why aged people often commit suicide. Devaluing elderly people and discriminating them because of their age and rejecting them as part of this society would make them feel that they are a burden and cause of trouble in other's life (Hall and Scragg, 2012).

It has been found that people who are widows or are widowers or those who have become very aged suffer from loneliness more than other people (Excell, 2010). The fact that one is lonely or the fact that one is suffering from lack of anybody's company or unhappy with his or her present situation then it is more likely that he will feel alone. This takes a dangerous turn if the person is not able to have any control over his/her life. Thus depression becomes obvious in the aforesaid situations where an individual is incapable of bringing a change to it (Hall and Scragg, 2012).

The second phase is *Stereotyping*. Stereotyping has been explained by Rosow (1974) as a harsh reality of the life of the elderly who are forced to be attached with negative tagging by people on the basis of their age (Rosow, 1974). Old people are often regarded unwell, senile, worthless, lonely, impotent and stuck in acute economic deprivation. They are therefore, often associated with terms like 'touchy', 'cranky' and many such negative titles (Palmore, 1999). A study was conducted to understand the reaction of common mass to facial expressions of young and old people as a symbol of non-verbal communication. The study mainly discussed the neutral and stress free expression of people of counter generation. It was found that the perception of common was that they expect old people's expression to be inclined to sadness and depression compared to the young ones (Fredrickson et al., 1989).

The aged people in Beleghata were the victims of stereotyping more often than expected. Name calling was frequently practised and old people often complained that their children and their spouses engaged in it more than others. They find it incredibly depressing as a result and mental peace is often out of the question in extreme cases.

Exclusion is the third phase. This is the time when the value of elderly will be so less and so insignificant, that they will not be allowed to take part in social activities of any sort (Basford and Thorpe, 2004). In Beleghata, any important decision-making is seen to be mainly taken by the children of the aged people. The ageds are cornered and are forced to live an isolated life. In a study it was found that loneliness can affect the health status of an elderly. Deterioration of health was seen among those people who live an idle life. The study finds that in male population the ratio is quite high in comparison to the female counterparts. Therefore, it can be concluded that idleness among elderly population leads to dangerous consequences related to their health. It is important that elderly population and its ever increasing percentage be confronted with compassion and steps should be taken to include them to the larger society. Hence, in case of elderly scenario, good health is directly proportional to active physical life and social attachments (Raju, 2002).

The next phase is *Role Loss and Role Ambiguity*. People when young are occupied with several roles and while managing these multiple roles they often face role conflict. However, being always within the environment of role performances they do not realize what it is to be to live a life where there would not be any role to play. When a person ages, slowly he loses the roles he once used to play and ends up where there is not any specific thing to do. There is no recognized activity in which they can take part. We met several elderly people who helped us understand the prevalence of role loss and role ambiguity. Out of them, Biba (name changed) said,

> *'Jobber theke ami bari te thaka shuru korechi, amar opore ghorer kacj chape dewa hoe. Amar kaaj charar karon amar sharirik shashthyo. Akhon amar tin te jinish korte iccha kore, prothom ta puja kora, ditiyota nati ke niye khela kora, ar tritiyota holo bondhuder shathe barate adda mara. Kintu ami baere giye boshe thakai pochondo kori karon amar bouma amae hingshe kore. Oo chae amar moto aram korte eta na bujhe je amar ar or boyesher moddhye tofat ache. Jodi ami barite thaki tahole o amae kichu na kichu kortei bole, jamon joler balti bhore din, kapor dhuye din, ba oder mele din baere, ba cheler ba natir jonno akta pod ranna kore din, ityadi. Talika ta choltei thakbe'.*

> ('From the time when I started to be at home I had constantly been loaded with household works. The reason why I left working was my physical health. Right now there are three things I like doing. The first one is worshipping, the second one is playing with my grandchild and the third one is talking to my friends in the neighbourhood. However, I choose to go out and sit all the time, as my daughter-in-law is jealous of my leisure pursuits. She also wants to relax like me without realizing that we have an age difference. If I am at home, she makes it a point to ask me to do something or the other, like fill-up the buckets, wash the clothes, or hang them outside, or cook an item for your son or grandchild, etc. The list would go on and on. I have nothing specific to do, so she thinks she can ask me to do whatever she wants').

The fifth phase for Rosow (1974) is *Youthful Self-Image*. He thinks at this phase, old image is often believed by the elderly to be an invitation to negative stereotypical comments by other people. Therefore, to evade such negativity, aged people often reject the old image and try to look more youthful to create an enduring sense of self. This kind of an image at times is seen with criticism by both the young and old generation themselves where the old who wanted to refute the old image is mocked and ridiculed for their actions, eventually leading to a difficult relationship (Bianchi, 2011). During our study, we met a lady who had a tattoo in her hand and wore a half-sleeved blouse. She had cut short her hair and wore her sari in a way which according to her neighbours was not the right style. For all these reasons she was a subject of ridicule for her age groups as well as the young generations. When we approached her, she said due to sweltering weather and because of her lack of enough financial resources she can not afford fan. That is why she wears half sleeve blouse and most of the time she pulls her sari above her knees not to show off her skin but to allow the flow of air. The same is for her short length of hair. She has high blood pressure for which she has cut her hair short as the long length of hair increases her body temperature especially during summer. She said,

> *'Ami eta amar shorir er jonne korechilam, kintu ora eta onno kichur shathe jure dilo, jano ami iccha kore alpoboyeshi shajte chaichi. Jodi ami alpoboyeshi shate chai o, oder odhubidhe ta kothae? Ami arekta mohila k echini je nijer haate thakur er chobir ulki koreche, kintu bostir lokera shei karon ta janena ar or oi ulka koranota ke dosh dae jano o alpoboyeshi shajte chaiche. Jodi kichu hoe tahole ora bole nijera jamon acho oitake bodlao tarpor shahajyo asha koro. Mane ki bodlabo boloto?*
>
> ('I did it for my health, but I found them linking it with something else as if I am trying to look young deliberately. Even if I try to look young, what is their problem? I know another lady who has tattooed a goddess's picture on her hand, but the slum people are not aware of this reason and are after her accusing her of tattooing and blaming that she wants to look young. If anything happens to us they would say first change the way you think, then expect help! I mean, tell me, what to change?').

Old Age and Suicide

History of suicide is old. Suicide was variously interpreted throughout various times at various phases. Sometimes it was hyped, sometimes it was romanticized. It was sometimes complained about and sometimes it was strongly opposed. Whether we talk about Cato or Demosthenes, or about other Greek heroes like Aegeus, Socrates or the Roman heroes such as Mark Anthony, Brutus, or the Egyptian princess, Cleopatra; or from the Old Testament the Abimelech, Achitophel, Saul, we find interpretation of suicide everywhere even if we look at the suicide bombers of today's world, we will find that occurrence of suicide all over the world goes much beyond religion and culture (Evans and Farberow, 2003).

Ancient Indian textbooks have portrayed suicide in ways that have glorified the act in ways in which people have used it as ways to avoid shameful events and then have become part of courageous stories. Even the great epic stories of *Ramayana* and *Mahabharata* have not missed episodes of suicides. The death of Lord Sri Ram also contained stories of suicide, in fact, stories of epidemic suicides in the kingdom of Ayodhya. We can also hear the sacrificing story of Dadhichi sage, who gave away his life so that Gods can use his bones in the war against the Demons. However, suicide is condemned as an act in *Bhagavad Gita* and according to *Gita*, suicide is considered to be a selfish act on the part of the doer. When a person dies after committing suicide *'shraddha'* ritual cannot be performed, 184 Health Concerns and Senile Population which is considered to be essential funeral rite and it is believed that from the Brahmanical point of view that those who commit suicide, fast can be done for a stipulated number of days. Even *Upanishads* and other Holy scriptures as well are against suicides and say, 'he who takes his own life will enter the sunless areas covered by impenetrable darkness after death'. *Vedas* permitted suicide for reasons related to religion and considered sacrificing one's own life to be the best sacrifice. Suicide through starvation was associated with attaining *'moksha'* and is known as *'sallekhana'*, which means one escapes from the cycle of birth and death is a practice that is carried out even today (Braun, 2008).

Sati is another practice, where women would immolate themselves instead of living a life like a widow. Another practice is *Johar* where Rajput women would kill themselves to save themselves from getting humiliated from the invasions of the Muslim armies and some stray cases can be found even today (Bhugra, 2005; Vijayakumar, 2004).

Durkheim's treatise on suicide in 1897 had a major impact on the ones who wished to both study suicide and prevent the same. Suicide among elderly population has been a subject of enquiry in various books of gerontology. Intervening, elderly suicide through Durkhemian discourse of suicide seems to be quite appropriate, since he searched for the roots of suicide beyond individual to the social and external factors which are conducive for suicides in respective societies across ages, classes, castes, etc. According to him, regulation and integration levels affected suicide rates. A society functions well and guides its fellow citizens with its specific norms, laws, values and traditions. However, this 'regulative force' and balance loosens in coherence to various social factors. The situation becomes chaotic, leading to normlessness, which Durkheim addresses as a situation of anomie. He said, 'In anomic suicide, society's influence is lacking in the basically individual passions, thus leaving them without a checkrein'. Whereas, if there is too much of regulation then it gives rise to fatalism and also increases desperation. He said, '... the suicide deriving from excessive regulation, that of persons with futures pitilessly blocked and passions violently chocked by excessive discipline... we might call it fatalistic suicide'. Too much or too less of integration into society thus causes suicide. When social integration is too less, people tend to be self-focused and their attention is cut off from other people, resulting in feeling as though one's existence does not matter to others at all. When integration is too high, then, however, one might not hesitate to give away one's life thinking that if one does so, then this can benefit others. For this same reason, Protestant countries are modern with modern forms of economies and lower rates of integration in society with decreased levels of social regulation giving rise to high rates of suicides. The opposite is the trend in Roman Catholicism countries. There the economies are not developed and levels of social integration and regulation are under control. Therefore, suicide rates are also under control (Durkheim, 1897).

In Beleghata, people have spent almost more than half their lives working. In the previous chapters, it has been mentioned, that even in 80s people, work for survival. However, in some instances, when due to particular problems mainly because of physical troubles, they lose their jobs they do not understand what to do.

In our study, Jyoti Rani, aged 74 years, has been working as a maidservant since she was 28 years old. Her husband died when she was 30 years old. She had to take responsibilities of 3 sons and one daughter at the age of 30 itself with no one to help and all of a sudden at the age of 55, faced with acute joint issues had to quit all her work and sit back at home. Before this phase, she had a hectic life. After her work, she used to cook for herself and children and manage her household work, wash clothes, did *pujas*. However, after losing the job, she slipped into a situation of anomie and what according to McInnis-Dittrich model as mentioned above is 'reactive depression'. The treatment protocol maintained can be a mild antidepressant, however, according to Durkheim through this, depression cannot be treated as structural problems cannot be solved through this. For him, the rapid change in the structure has pushed the lady into such a troublesome position and something must be done so that the condition can be restored and level of regulation can be maintained. If some alternative yet economically productive activity can be provided to her, then she might feel normal and regulate her day (Marson and Powell, 2011).

Durkheim maintains that there are various forms of suicide where he was the one who felt that social factors are the driving force in pushing a person to commit suicide, not because of issues present in the person. Depending upon the level of social integration and one's social environment for which the various social factors make the occurrence of suicide possible. Durkheim classified it into few forms – anomic suicide, altruistic suicide, fatalistic suicide and egoistic suicide. Out of these suicides, egoistic suicide occurs among the old section of the population. This kind of suicide is prevalent among those individuals who find such a step is to be the best solution when he or she feels to be detached from society. This explains why the United States of America the suicide rate amongst elderly is one of the highest in between the age group of 75 to 84 years old (Coren and Hewitt, 1999).

In general, during young age, people are well integrated into society because of their works and because of the other personal bonds they have with their families and communities and society as a whole. Gradually with time, there appears to be a weakening of these very bonds and therefore rates of increase in chances of egoistic suicide are more. Elderly people because of their age have already been through such a phase where they have higher tendency to get depressed and commit egoistic suicide (Berkman et al., 2000; Nisbet, 1997). However, while discussing this concept of suicide, it should be known that it is an act which not every elderly would indulge in by just one reason and AMA, i.e. the American Medical Association formulated a typology for this. From this typology, in 2003 the reasons for suicide among the elderly were to some extent known. Some of the prevailing ideas related to the fact that elderly people commit suicide are thought to be that they are depressed and lonely, or because they feel less important, or because of their declining health abilities according to AMA might be mostly related just to these reasons only.

Different Typologies

1. *Not Distinctively Elderly Suicides:* AMA found most of the suicide among elderly was not related to age issues at all. Therefore, we cannot say, that once people age, they commit suicide because of depression, decrease of physical health or anomie. In fact, interview conducted among people aged between 30 to 50 years showed that their reasons for committing suicide are not any different from elderly suicides. It was found that nothing instigated them intrinsically to push them to take such a step exclusively at such an age.
2. *Protest Suicides:* every individual faces ageing differently and the way the challenges that old age carries with it are different. The demands that every aged person has during this ageing process are also different. In the research that was carried out during AMA, it was found that some of the aged people were not able to adjust to their ageing processes. They were not flexible enough to be able to deal with the physical changes that ageing was bringing about and were very much irritated and frustrated when ageing caused physical immobility and forgetfulness. Such changes are so hard to accept for aged people as normal. The entire experience becomes so painful and disturbing that they go to the extent of committing suicide.

3. *Preemptive Suicides:* this kind of suicide is committed by those people who have lost a very close person in one's life and the death has been a distressing one, one which the elderly person would not like to experience at all. This Preemptive 'strike' can be set off if the aged person gets sick and falls ill and fears that now he might undergo a similar experience. It is similar to what Durkheim described as the fatalistic suicide (Holmes and Holmes, 2005).

McInnis-Dittrich's cites another four typologies of depression among people that might lead to suicidal acts. These are as follows:

1. *Reactive depression:* this depression occurs when there is a mild depression because of a loss or when a range of loss gets accumulated and piles up and adds up to increase depression.
2. *Clinical depression:* this kind of depression is severe and happens when symptoms last for more than a reasonable period and disturb the normal functioning of a person.
3. *Endogenous depression:* it is such a state of mind when a person is down in the dumps without any specific cause that may turn out to become stronger and severe as they age.
4. *Involutional depression:* this kind of depression is related to problems related to lifespan related issues. It occurs when during middle years there is a biological deterioration. This biological decline might be reactive when one steps in old age (McInnis-Dittrich, 2009).

According to Sourcebook of Criminal Justice Statistics Online, there are few statistics – less than 15 per cent of the population consists of the aged population, yet 25 per cent of them accounts for the total suicide rate and 75 per cent of those elderly who took this step visited their primary physician a month before committing suicide. Females commit more suicide than males and according to this Statistics, males commit six times more suicide than females and males aged 85 years have a high risk of committing suicide. In case of women, after the age of 65 years, the rate of suicide did not increase (Holmes and Holmes, 2005).

Since, 1987, it was found that there was a decline in the suicide rate among elderly people in the United States of America (American Association of Suicidology, 2011). However, it cannot be ignored that it is still a severe problem in the country (Hooyman and Kiyak, 1999) and since more than hundreds of years, this issue has been brought into our attention by Lorand (1912). National Institute of Mental Health says that more than any other age group elderly people are more likely to die by committing suicide. In 2011, American Association of Suicidology stated that in the year 2005, at every 100th minute an aged person committed suicide and in the year 2007, at every 97th a person committed suicide in the United States. It is also claimed that white males who are more than 85 years old are a higher risk of committing suicides and have a higher risk of committing such acts than others with chances four times higher than the general population (NIMH, n.d.). Almost 92 per cent of males commit suicide using firearms and women use it in a much lower percentage with just 8 per cent of them using it while committing suicide showing the disparity in differences in the fact that there is a difference in males and females in suicide (American Association of Suicidology, 2011).

Suicide among elderly people is not confined to them only. It extends beyond that. A data as provided by DeLeo and Spathonis showed that aged people across the globe has high suicide rates compared to all age groups (DeLeo et al., 2004). It is said that active suicide occurs when people kill themselves deliberately through their actions. Passive suicide is just the opposite of active suicide. Here, individuals do not cooperate to remain alive and take necessary steps that are required to do so. Examples can be they refuse to take medical treatment or refuse to have food and water (Marson and Powell, 2011). As Durkheim mentioned in 1897, 'Though suicide is commonly conceived as a positive, violent action involving some muscular energy, it may happen that a purely negative attitude or the mere abstention will have the same consequence. Refusal to take food is as suicidal as self-destruction by a dagger or fire-arm' (Durkheim, 1897). The figures of suicide we have are an underestimation of suicide rates as they are not the correct portrayal of actual suicide rates and both active and passive suicides are equally alarming in getting identified or prevented (Marson and Powell, 2011).

In 1997, Koenig and his colleagues found that issues of blood pressure rate can be reduced if religious activities are performed and C–reactive protein also decreases along with interleukin–6 and cortisol. They also claimed that there would also be a drop in levels of white blood cells with religious observances (Koenig, Cohen, George, Hays, Larson and Blazer, 1997; Koenig, George, Hays, Larson, Cohen and Blazer, 1998). There is wide availability of religious institutions to the elderly (Tobin et al., 1986). For older adults it has turned out to be a very important support source (Mechanic, 1974). There are severe difficulties because of disabilities caused by physical infirmities for advancing old age and for issues found by the elderly people regarding the unavailability of transportation and communication facilities to the elderly people. On a weekly basis, in America, religious services are attended by more than 50 per cent of aged American people. It was established through a Gallup Poll in 1982 and through the same poll, it was found that within the last month was carried out 80 per cent attended the services (The Gallup Poll, 1992).

Aged people are expected to be engaged in religious associations more than in any other groups (Payne et al., 1972). Nevertheless, this case dates long back in the time of 1970s (Lindenthal et al., 1970). Since then, things have changed quite a lot. Clark writes in 1992, that there has been a slight change in perception about elderly where it is witnessed that in the popular seminaries instruction on mental health were set up for the elderly population. Amongst elderly people who are suicidal, arrangements were made where they can seek help from clergy men who often counsel them through the help of religious factors (The Gallup Poll, 1992).

Religion was considered to be a very appropriate coping mechanism for both males and female sufferers irrespective of any form of disease. It has been seen that in gay patients who are suffering from this disease and take the help of religion to deal with it were seen to have decreased levels of depressive symptoms as they started to increase their belief in religious phenomenon. In case of women, the way to deal with their disease with the help of religion was praying and a gradual re-recognition of oneself (Kaplan et al., 1997). Losing of life partners and then associating oneself with one or the other congregation shows decreased signs of depressions (Siegel and Kuykendall, 1990).

Intrinsic religious practices are some of the ways through which depression can be reduced. Positive religious appraisals and various mechanisms of religious engagements might be effective in reducing the consequences that depression might bring about on people who have lost their near ones or on people who have slipped into depression for years of care-giving service or on people who are suffering terminally. It has been found that if a holistic approach is taken where religious practices and spiritual practices are integrated into therapy, then it can produce positive results and reduce depression in people (Plante and Sherman, 2001).

It has been seen by a study that involvement in religious and spiritual activities for people who are undergoing stressful life events, experience decreased amount of anxiety (Holtz, 1998). Substance users who had high faith in religion were seen to have low levels of anxiety (Plante et al., 1999). Richard and Folkman (1997) explained it with an example of people whose close ones were suffering from HIV, although, we have not got any case in our field, similar to this. People who were experiencing the death of their partners because of this disease saw that through the performance of religious rites, helped them to deal with the bereavement with much ease (Richards and Folkman, 1997).

Pargament and his colleagues did a study on aged people who were medically ill and also on students who were studying in college and were dealing with some forms of stress. They found that in all there were 17 different coping religious mechanisms. This highlighted the complication of such coping practices and the range of existing mechanisms (Pargament et al., 2000). The coping mechanism is a way in which the stress individual's face is reframed where both religion and spiritualism, guides people in solving a problem through its religious path, teaches the method of forgiveness. The different coping strategies adopted could be categorized as positive coping mechanisms as analysed by higher-order factor analysis that can establish a much-secured relationship of God and communities that support religious activities and a negative interrelationship in between these two aspects (Pargament et al., 1998).

According to Pargament, religion is a way through which people adapt to their lives and its challenges. The coping mechanism they adopt is often effective that help them make easy the process. That is the reason why Bible of the Christians and Torah for the Jews are full of guidance on matters on how should one deal with situations which are not in their favour and are challenging to handle (Pargament, 2001).

On, 11 September 2001 the attacks in the United States, by a terrorist group led to a loss of several lives. A study was done to see how clergy dealt with people and their traumatized experience. About 814 Presbyterian ministers were chosen for the surveys and were seen how they could handle the post-traumatic shock of such a terrorist attack (Meisenhelder and Marcum, 2004). It was seen that out of all the coping strategies both religious and secular ones, the strategies which have proven to be the most frequently reported ones were religious coping strategies such as seeking blessing from God for all strength and deriving support and the second most reported strategy of coping these trauma was prayers.

A crucial point noticed in this study, was that 75 per cent of these cases had shown signs of post-traumatic stress and they have used religion as a means to cope with such levels of stress. Although one's involvement with religion did not protect him or her from the impact of psychological impact that such a disturbing tragedy could bring about. Religion as a coping mechanism was considered a way to deal with the stressful life events (Vredeveld, 2009).

About 400 psychologists were also surveyed to find out how they deal with stress which is related to their workplace. It was found that spiritual practice was most commonly practised by the participants who were religious. These practices included praying or meditating. Religion did not protect against any distress but of course, it was a coping mechanism adopted by psychologists who were religious (Case and McMinn, 2001).

Mentally sick or those who are elderly not only chose to select to cope but also at the same time support the strategy of religious coping. An example can illustrate this. From the Caucasian population, a total sample size of 100 elderly people was selected. This was done to know the happiest and the unpleasant experience of their lives and the best and the worst that had happened in the last ten years and lastly the greatest and the most terrible memories about the present times of their lives. It was seen that the way they cope with them indicates that religion plays a very important role throughout their lives. About 17 per cent of the people used religion to cope with the traumatic experiences for all these three experiences and 45 per cent of people used religion in two of three of the experiences they have faced in their lives (Koenig et al., 1988).

In another study where patients were mentally sick with Schizophrenia, Schizoaffective Disorder, disorders due to major depressions and lastly bipolar disorders were made a part of a study. Nearly 406 of them were selected. The researchers found that more than 80 per cent of them used religion as a coping mechanism or held some or the other form of belief in religion to deal with daily stress which might include constant worry from mental illness. The most common form of religious coping adopted was prayer, 50 per cent of them adopted it. Another 30 per cent of the mentally ill chose to attend church service, offered worship to God and read out the scriptures. Another 30 per cent of them considered religion to be the only way of helping them to cope with their illness and function continuously despite their issues (Tepper et al., 2001).

The Brief RCOPE is a 14 item based Short Measure of Religious Coping it was first developed by Pargament and his colleagues and was validated by them. They formulated a measure of both positive religious and negative religious coping and defined positive one 'as an expression of a sense of spirituality, a secure relationship with God, a belief that there is meaning to be found in life and a sense of spiritual connectedness with others'. Negative religious coping, on the other hand, would be explained as 'an expression of less secure relationship with God, a tenuous and ominous view of the world and a religious struggle in the search for significance'. Three samples were tested. The first sample was selected from Oklahoma City bombing incident, where the people were struggling hard to deal with the frightening event that they had lived. The second sample was from the college students who had faced some sad incidents in their life and were in a way trying to manage. The third sample was of the elderly population who were suffering from severe medical issues and therefore were admitted to hospitals. They were asked that how did they cope with the most stressful negative event that had taken place in their lives so far in the last three years. It was seen that religion turned out to be the most optimistically associated with the overall psychological growth and spiritual well-being of the people concerning the stressful life events they have faced. Negative forms of religious coping affected the psychological well-being of the individuals causing emotional stress, causing depression, bringing down the quality of life, health (Pargament et al., 1998).

State Initiatives

The Government of India is concentrating on health scenario of the country. Every health need of the elderly needs immediate attention and cannot be ignored. In fact, a separate geriatric ward needs to be created for its attendance where geriatric professionals need to be kept at its disposal. There is also a need to keep mobile geriatric care centres so that more number of elderly people can be reached, especially the ones who live in the rural areas. The elderly people who reside in rural areas do not have financial resources to afford the high cost of taking care of the elderly on a long-term basis. Subsidized care can also be another way to reduce the financial burden of the elderly to a great extent (Venkateswarlu, 2008).

Health discourses are an important subject of enquiry in coherence to varying community. In this regard, there is a need to have an interdisciplinary outlook towards the issue. In case of elderly population, geriatric health cannot be kept restricted to medical professionals, there is a need for social scientists to join hands with medical professionals to have a macro level study on elderly health and more importantly elderly quality of life (Gurumurthy, 1998). In the contemporary world, inequality is a severe problem that is affecting varying aspects of the society and its respective people. It is a well known fact that economic disparities lead to unequal life style standards and consumption patterns. As a consequence of the aforesaid, slums keep increasing, the gap between the rich and the poor and the wealthy nations keep broadening. King (1966) asks why such an inequality persist and what steps can be taken to improve the conditions of society concerning alleviating disparity.

In Third World countries there is a gap as to who would enjoy the affluent health status and the majority who would suffer from mortality and morbidity. The minority would be the affluent one who would be healthy and enjoy the health status and behave like the ones found in developed nations of the world. The health services are also served to the urban people and the rural majority are left out. The slogan of WHO 'Health for All by 2000' could not be achieved for sure that is true but has been taken seriously by people as its impact has been felt and its consequences have been understood and realized (Halfdan, 1981).

In 1999, the NPOP, the National Policy on Older Persons was announced in which the older person's well-being was reassured with regard to the provision of shelter to them as well to their spouses. Providing food, health, developmental equality, protection against exploitation, improvement in the quality of their lives were some of the other listed provisions. Few others involved such as encouraging the members of the families to take up the responsibility of the elderly, encouraging both voluntary and non-voluntary organizations to support their initiatives in supporting the elderly. There were further provisions also to improve and facilitate training of geriatric caretakers and increase awareness of aged people for leading a life which is more self-sufficient and independent whereby they no longer need to be reliant on others for the fulfilment of their daily purposes (Laxmikanth, 2011).

Indira Gandhi National Disability Pension Scheme is another component of National Social Assistance Programme. The eligibility age of the pensioner is quite low, which is 18 and beyond. However, the level of disability of the person has to be 80 per cent. The pension allotted under this scheme to the pensioner is ₹ 300 every month and once he or she attains the age of 80, the amount would rise to ₹ 500 every month. Under this disability criterion, Dwarfs have also been included in it. Under National Family Benefit Scheme or NFBS if a person who was the bread-winner of a family, dies, then an amount of ₹ 20,000 will be given to his or her family as a compensation amount. The death of the family member can be both natural and otherwise, in either case, the entire family is eligible to claim for the assistance as they are eligible for it. It must be noted that in this case the term 'breadwinner' is not considered for men alone, as women who are homemaker are also breadwinners. The benefit will be given to the breadwinner's spouse, the ones who were dependent on him/her, the minor children if any, minor brothers or sisters, dependent parents, unmarried daughters (NSAP, 1995). However, there seems to be an issue with optimization of resource value of policy making. Several reforms and assistance policies are formulated, but a gap still remains in its effective utilization.

NPHCE which is National Programme for Health Care of Elderly was launched in 2010–2011 by Government of India for the elderly people of the country to address their health-related issues. It was during the 11th plan period that 21 states were identified and within those, 100 different districts were selected under the scheme. There were eight regional medical institutions covered under the programme. Through this programme the aim was to provide health benefits to the aged people in a specialized manner, providing comprehensive care to the aged people, managing their illness, rehabilitating them, providing them with therapeutic intervention. Certain accomplishments to improve the lives of the elderly that could be met so far have been listed below (Gupta and Amita, 2006):

1. MOU was signed with 19 states,
2. Implementation guidelines were made operational, at AIIMS in New Delhi,
3. A geriatric OPD was inaugurated,
4. A workshop was organized for the training of specialists from both medical and surgical backgrounds from 21 different districts (Gupta and Amita, 2006).

A National Council for Older Persons was formulated to assist people regarding the policies for the aged. The council also tried to evaluate various old age policies by taking feedback from people who are facilitated by various policies. Under this scheme, up to 90 per cent of the project cost is provided to the NGOs, to build the day care centres, or the old-age homes, or to avail non-institutional services for the aged people. Under this scheme, a promise of 30 lakh was made to the institutions which are eligible enough to construct old-age homes or build up multi-service centres for aged people (Pathy et al., 2006).

Another policy is Integrated Programme for Older Persons. This programme has been initiated to facilitate the old age people who are 60 years and above, particularly the ones who are widowed and are destitute. This policy aims to take care of diverse list of interests of the aged people. Here broad-based interventions are targeted, where families and communities are focused upon so that the overall well-being of the aged is taken care of (Goel, 2004).

This Ministry of Social Justice and Empowerment has also launched another scheme, which is Scheme of Assistance to Panchayati Raj Institutions. This means that there will be the provision of one-time construction grant for elderly housing and provision of a multi-service centre for aged people. In 2007, Parents and Senior Citizens Bill was passed by the Government of India which stated that it is mandatory to take care of elderly people. There is a legal obligation for descendants of people to make sure that they take care of their old parents. Under this Bill, economic assistance is given to respective state governments to construct old-age homes. The aim of the bill is to provide economic security to elderly people who are otherwise financially unstable. The Code of Criminal Procedure of 1973, Hindu Adoption, Maintenance Act of 1956 had made it compulsory for the children to take the responsibility of their patents if their parents are not able to take their care (Parker, 2007).

Several Indian states like Goa, Maharashtra and Himachal Pradesh have taken a fantastic initiative to protect parents of neglected children and therefore have launched maintenance bills for parents, therefore safeguarding parents of children who are left unattended. It has been reported that sometimes there is a lethargic attitude among officials to implement solutions and dispose of the matter fast. So, there is a need to check on the execution of various bills and policies since the policies can then be accessed by a larger proportion of the citizens (Purohit, 2014). Community education can help enhance the levels of awareness about the different problems elderly face and can augment their position.

Old-age pension is allotted under the programme of IGNOAPS (Indira Gandhi Old Age Pension Scheme) which is directed by the Ministry of Rural Development. Herein, every person falling in the age group of 60–79 years old would receive the central financial assistance of ₹ 200 on a monthly basis. If a person is more than 80 years old, then he becomes eligible to receive ₹ 500 again on a monthly basis, provided he or she is below the poverty line, i.e. BPL of the country. The same amount has been requested to be contributed by the State or UTs of the country as well (Ministry of Social Justice and Empowerment, 2015).

Some incentives have been covered under the Department of Revenue, Ministry of Finance, under Income Tax Act, 1961, to all those senior citizens who are residents of India and are or have crossed the age of 60 years at least the previous year of the time when it was needed.

Some of the incentives are that if the total income of the senior citizen is below 3 lakh, then he will be exempted from income tax. In case of senior citizens aged 80 years or more, the total income can be up to 5 lakh per year to be free from income tax (Details of Welfare Schemes for the Aged Persons, 2015).

OASIS – Old Age Social and Income Security scheme was launched by the social defence bureau for the welfare of the elderly people and to make them economically sound. This was to encourage young people in unorganized sectors while young to save as much as possible during their working years so that when they retire, they have enough to sustain themselves, which would in a way reduced the load from the government. An expert committee with OASIS has recommended improving the coverage, customer service and enhancing the rate of return. Under this programme, a pension account was incorporated for every person, which was known as individual retirement account (IRA). This account was created so that people start saving from their early careers where per contribution has to be at least ₹ 100 and annually it has to be ₹ 500 (Sadhak, 2009).

The Department of Pension and Pensioners formulated a welfare policy whereby beyond policy coverage other benefits are given to the policy holders. The department also hosts a grievance redressal cell which takes care of the issues related to retirement. Minimum pension or family pension every month has been fixed at ₹ 1,275 provided the person does not get more than 50 per cent or 30 per cent respectively from the post from which he has retired. The ceiling of the gratuity can be allowed up to ₹ 3.5 lakh. Definition of the family has been made wider where parents have also been included to make them eligible for a family pension that has been effective from 1 January 1998 (Gupta and Amita, 2006).

Role of Civil Society

Every social challenge can be effectively handled with the parallel contribution of the state as well as the civil society. The latter plays an important role in micro level interventions to the issue whereupon elderly care is often provided by them along with exposing the grim reality which in the long run allows the policy makers to understand the situation and its varying degrees. Here, we shall discuss a number of civic bodies which have been working in the field of gerontology.

There is a service in Kolkata, West Bengal known as Deep Probeen Porisheba where the elderly people are taken for morning and evening walks and are assisted for yoga and with other technological gadgets like Skype, iPad, iPod, tablet and email. They are also provided with psychological counselling and a facility of social gatherings, organization of picnics once a year, paying a visit to religious places twice a year to enhance their moods. The aged people who are enrolled with Deep

Probeen Porisheba for more than six months are eligible to avail the facility under specific terms and conditions to go for long distance travel with their assistance. Specifically, for medical facilities, it is affiliated with the top nursing homes, diagnostic centres for conducting diagnostic tests, medical hospitals of Kolkata for emergency facilities and Ambulance services. The diagnostic centres also arrange for collection of home samples. They arrange a monthly visit of doctors. For female elderly, Deep Probeen Porisheba makes special arrangement for quarterly visits by well known geriatric specialists. Physiotherapists also visit Deep Probeen Porisheba. Blood pressure monitoring or glucose tests are regularly conducted to check the health status of the individual elderly people. After an operation, post-operative care is provided and the members of this organization consider the idea of rehabilitation. They also advise on nutrition. In case of any doubt with medical reports or even prescriptions, or policies related to health insurance. The medical services are held for 30 minutes and they charge ₹ 500 per session. In case of non-medical services, their charges are just ₹ 50 less which is ₹ 450. For physiotherapy, they charge ₹ 500 per session and psychological counselling are charged ₹ 950 per session and the session is held for 1 hour. General Physician's visit is ₹ 1,150 and General Specialist's visit is ₹ 1,875, where their visit is for 30–45 mins (http://dppindia.com/ services/).

HelpAge India has extended its support to the elderly, who because of changing nature of families are left aside or neglected by their children, or are alone, has health issues or are depressed. All over the country HelpAge India has provided financial support for improvement in infrastructure of about 90 institutions. In South Kolkata it is located at Chetla. It is a two-storey building so that it can take care of the aged women. It takes care of about ten elderly women. The amenities provided are age-friendly and are of essential nature. Hence, the aged do not find it difficult to use them at all. HelpAge India provides the elderly women with the facility of physiotherapy and other health care services in a brilliant manner. It also caters its service to the aged people who reside in Kolkata and other nearby places of the city through some of its exclusive measures of reaching out to the elderly people through physiotherapy, excellent medical services and provision of toll-free helpline numbers (http://www.helpageindia.org/programs/old-age-homes.html).

In Beleghata, people are not aware of such opportunities. Free camps are hardly held nearby their area. However, one effort was shown by students of Presidency University, where they came forward to help the aged people of the Beleghata slum people. The University has undertaken as a part of its NSS activity, the task to provide service to the economically disadvantaged sections of this slum. A camp was organized from 6–12 June 2015. About 50 students from this University who participated in this camp tried to solve the problems that the elderly people had. Through this National Service Scheme, Presidency University has been trying to solve their problem for the past one year and trying to raise awareness among the people. This time, however, unlike the other earlier camp health was not the only target as elderly health was also taken into account. Along with that, they were advised on the legal matter and on matters about family pension, widow pension (Ei Samae, 2015).

Calcutta Metropolitan Institute of Gerontology, in the year of 1988, serves to assist all those people who are aged above 60 years old. The institute has a mobile medical care unit and in slums, it has medical centres where food, clothes and in case of adverse weather conditions blankets are also provided to the aged people. There are also recreational facilities for them and shelter is for the ones who are abandoned. Library facilities are made available, adult literacy programmes and computer training programmes are organized. Also, many other job opportunities are there which aged people can opt for after retirement. Indrani Chakravarty, a renowned gerontologist and chief functionary of Calcutta Metropolitan Institute of Gerontology feels that the problem which prevails in the country is the fact that aged people who are bound to retire after a certain age are not always willing to retire. They still want to continue working. She felt that retirement is related to many issues which can affect health both psychologically and physically, leading a person to an increasing level of boredom to an increased amount of loneliness and also, it makes him feel incredibly lonely when he is out of work. All these contribute to illness and of course, health care is compromised to a great extent. She said, 'Even when we have medical camps for the elderly, we find people bringing their children instead of their aged parents' (http://india.ashoka.org/fellow/ indrani-chakravarty).

Concluding Remarks

Health issues of elderly people are taken for granted and young people are given more importance. If an aged person falls sick, it is considered as if it is obvious to happen. Unless his condition is not too serious, his family does not pay much heed. For example, deafness and a decrease in vision are always thought to accompany old age. It is taken for granted, an assumed change in the body of an aged person. Not only the young, the aged people themselves feel that complaining about these health conditions is not important as ageing and health problems such as these are too trivial at this phase of life. They feel like concentrating on other matters such as helping their young ones to manage themselves in their lives and not to create any disturbances should be their goal, they also feel as they have grown old they are becoming frail and weak. So a majority of them said that before they become completely disabled, they must die and in the meantime be able to involve in religious and other activities they love to do and spend time with their loved ones.

9

Elderly Interactions in the World of 'Sacred'

There are varied definitions on the discourse of religion. It is thought to be an experience which is distinct from everyday experience, where interaction takes place with God, intangible entity who is above humans. It can be defined as a belief in the existence of God, practicing of religious ritual which includes attending church or temple and other religious institutions and observations related to one's own religious faith, etc. religion according to some can be defined as a very private practice. However, for sociologists, 'religion is an institutionalized system of symbols, beliefs, values and practices by which a group of people interprets and responds to what they feel is sacred and provides answers to questions of ultimate meaning' (Glock and Stark, 1965).

Religion and Depression

Religion has been included in research activities and its recent position has revived the interest of the social as well as the behavioural sciences. According to Koenig and others, involvement in religious activities improves mental health (Koenig et al., 2001). Also, lot of work is being done on gerontology journals (Idler and Kasl, 1997). Religion has an age-old tradition in gerontological research as well as in various issues related to engaging in social roles, the overall mental, physical and psychological well-being of an individual and helping a person facing the daily challenges of stress, sufferings and losses (Koenig et al., 2012).

It is believed that the main problem faced by aged people includes their ignorance of how to behave as old. There are number of losses that the aged people face when he or she becomes old and it is difficult to deal with all these losses. Along with it, ageds are vulnerable to various forms of humiliation. About 90 per cent of aged people face disabling troubles of severe forms when they reach old age. Post industrialization, massive transformation of values-consequently eroded the traditional role or status of the elderly people in society. In the field of social science, the theory of disengagement is seen as connected with loss of role and their nearness to death for the inevitable stepping into the last phase of life. Emotional confusion and turmoil, and isolation because of one's location are sometimes not within the control of aged people and therefore the relation between the personal and social levels of integration are deeply connected. The decision-making choice and the selection in deciding upon what to believe is very important to bring about the overall development of an aged person. In gerontological works, one of the weaknesses is that biological variables are given more importance and social aspects are paid no such attention which it deserves and is seen to be a result of heredity and not of the environment. Life satisfaction has often been assumed to be linked with one's association with one's family members which improves their lives. Elderly people are expected to live with their kiths and kins and therefore their lives usually revolve around relatives and the meanings formed and developed. Hence, we find these relations play an important role in the lives of elderly. Aloofness from family members gives rise to alienation which in turn harms and hurts the dignity of the aged, more than how medical or biological issues cause the loss of dignity. At this point, religion comes as a saviour to the aged, which through its spiritual support provides independence to the elderly which helps them with proper adjustment in coping with the difficulties in life. Religion can guide the elderly people and provide them with an ideal bond of social relationships that might be of high value to the elderly. The moral virtue of the older people and overall spiritual development of the elderly people makes their life more satisfying and improves their quality of life.

In *Religion and Aging* by C. Margaret Hall, history of 500 families was taken. In social science research, in general, has shown that with old age compared to the young ones people participate less in religious activities because of their increasing disabilities and along with that their inabilities in travelling to offer worship to places to different religious places also increases (Hall, 1985). In classical research, religion has often, received less significance with reference to its role in the daily lives of the old people, however, if we refer to elderly life histories or narratives, we can show how their connection to religious communities and their re-examination of religious beliefs can help in breaking of social isolation with which they were living for so long (Pierik, 1982).

In life history research, there is a finding that experience of the aged can be transformed through religious beliefs. Involvement in religious act tends to decrease stress and anxiety. Religion tends to shift their focus from negative resources. Religion also helps to curb out depression as well anxieties among the aged (Hall, 1985). Devaluing elderly, once they grow old is common in Western cultures, whereas the opposite holds true for the Eastern culture where social honour and ageing are connected with each other. US values are mainly rooted in Protestant Ethics which supports an independent lifestyle and independent way of life and these are the causes of some of the problems in Western countries. In the East, for the aged, it is a necessity to be integrated to others in society through the connection of one's self to the ethical beliefs and elements of religion (McKenzie, 1980). Durkheim also analysed the suicide rates among Catholic and Protestant countries. He found that suicide rate was lower in Catholic countries because they stressed less on individualism and have stressed more on the ethos of communitarian aspects. However, we find just the opposite feature in most Protestant countries. In Catholic countries, the relationship with God has always been established with an emphasis on one being a member of the community, while in Protestant countries the relationship with God is based on one's relationship as an individual member (Greeley, 1997). As a result, protestant people commit egoistic suicide compared to that of Catholic people because Protestantism is 'a less strongly integrated church than the Catholic church' (Krieken et al., 2013).

Family associations are based on the Confucian ethics, which plays a significant role in determining the survival ability of the aged people (Lewis, 1982). Decent and healthy living must be recognized. To view from a more general point of view, religion was a way to wipe out the influence of disconcerting sentiments of culture. These were believed to be destructive in nature. The other general trends are harmful and negative, such as the various ways in which media portrays elderly people, or how the old are represented in a cartoon, or how birthday cards mock about their age. At this point, religion can help to increase their awareness whereby their position can move to a position of advantage from a position of less advantage (The United States Congress House Select Committee on Aging, 1980). Religion can be beneficial in connecting personally the self-estranged, isolated and alienated people and gradually transform into the ones who believe in the purpose of life (Hall, 1985).

One method can be beneficial in meeting the needs of the elderly people. It is a therapy which can be regarded as a secular religion and thought to be very supportive. During times of crisis, religion can be a strong source of support for connecting with as it is elderly people's primary activity. Also, through it, they can identify with and attach themselves with the values of the long-established and institutional aspects that help in normalizing the feelings of isolation that the aged people are facing (Hall, 1985).

According to surveys carried out by National Opinion Research Centre, The University of Chicago with the help of data collected from International Social Survey Programme, from 30 countries of the world, revealed that people who are 68 years old and above were found to be more certain about the existence of God. Their percentage is as high as 43 per cent and just 23 per cent of people aged 27 years and less believe in His existence as per the same report. Tom Smith, a researcher, remarks 'Looking at differences among age groups, the largest increases in belief in God most often occur among those 58 years of age and older. This suggests that belief in God is especially likely to increase among the older groups, perhaps in response to the increasing anticipation of mortality' (Mail Online, 2012). According to Posner, on an average level compared to young people, the elderly are more religious. Their religiosity did not differ according to Posner, on practices, but on the beliefs. Increasing incapacities accompanied by ageing limited their attendance to church (Kart, 1990).

Several people in Beleghata were devotees of Loknatha Baba and some believed that number of ailments is under control because of their offerings to him. One of them has been abandoned by her son at 65 years of age and has never been asked to get back or paid visit by her son. Still, she feels praying to God is her responsibility towards her son, as he is the only person around whom her life revolves at the moment. When asked who her biggest strength or support is, she said,

> *'Jodio amar chele amae chere geche, amar tao asha ache je o akdin amar kache fire ashbe. O akhon baba hoe geche, ar ami jani o khub shiggiri bujhbe kotota kothin eta mene newa jokhon nijer chele tomar opore chechae. Ami khali asha kori o eta bujhbe. Ami Loknath Babar kache prarthona kori oke ektu bddhi dao ar gyan dao jaate o bujhte pare ami ki koshter moddhye die gechi ao gulo bochor. Amar akhon atattyor bochor boyesh, ar akta din o jaena jokhon or bhalo cheye thakur er kache prarthona kroina. Kintu oke jigyasha korun, o thik ulta tar jonne prarthona kore. O amar barita chae, o khub shombhoboto bhabe amar kichu baki taka ache jeta ami or shathe bhag korte chaina, ba kothao kono gopon shompotti ache jetar kotha oke bolchina. Amar kono dharona nei, kintu o amae onekbar ingit dieche eta bole –'amae shob die dao ja ache, nahole ami tomae charbona', 'baba ja taka dieche dao, nahole konodin o ferod ashbona'. Ami Loknath ke puja di roj ar uni amae shob koshto theke bachan. Onar shimahin korunar shathe uni shobaike koshto theke bachan, uni amar icchao puron korben'.*
>
> ('Although, my son has left me, I still have the hope that he would come back one day. He has become a father now and I am sure soon he will realize how tough it is to bear when your own child shouts at you. I just hope he realizes it. When I pray to Loknath Baba, I keep praying Him, please give him intelligence and knowledge so that he can understand what pain I went through all these years. Right now I am 78 and not a single day passes when I do not pray to God for his well-being. Whereas ask him, probably he prays for just the opposite. He wants my house and he probably thinks I have some leftover money which I am not willing to share with him or some hidden property somewhere which I am deliberately not willing to disclose to him. I have no idea, but he has given me hints several times by saying – 'give me all that you have, else

> I will not leave you!' 'Give me the money which father gave you else I will not come back ever'! I offer Puja to Loknath daily and He saves me from all sufferings. With his unlimited mercy He fulfils everyone's wishes and just like He has saved me from many sufferings, He will fulfil my wishes too').

People from Beleghata also in large numbers visit Chakla Dham Lokenath Baba Shevashram. Chakla is believed to be the birthplace of Lokenath Baba. The affordability of *bhog* at a less price of just ₹ 10 contains *khichuri* and vegetables along with a reasonable amount of *payesh*. This has also attracted some aged to say '*eta bhalo je kom takae apni baba ke dekhte paben ar pet bhore bhalo bhabe kheteo parben*' ('It is good that at a less price you will get to see baba and have some food to satisfy your unfed stomach'). The aged people preferred to visit the temple on special occasion days such as the birthday of Lokenath Baba which is on 31st of August, or on Lokenath Baba Tirodhan Day or on other religious days where special arrangements are made for thousands of Lokenath devotees to join the Sevasram for some dining purpose (http://www.kolkatabengalinfo.com/2010/08/chakla-dham-lokenath-mandir-temple.html).

Influence of religion varies depending upon the structure of organization and system of belief (Bainbridge and Hatch, 1982). Participation in religious activities helps the aged to influence each other. Religion reorients aged by motivating them through involving them in action and engaging them in the processes of interactions by pushing people out of isolated zones with the help of its supportive function. It provides a rationale and consistent belief system which guides individuals with its distinct view of the world that provide a particular meaning of action to people (Hall, 1985). Ageing is not about a social movement. However, with increasing number of aged people in the industrialized societies or in the ones where the phase of industrialization has started will eventually attract the attention of policymakers and social planners. Religion often helps to improve the overall quality of the life of the aged people so that they can manage spirituality with much ease (Paul II, 1982).

Frameworks of religion and spirituality ask what is the underlying purpose of living a life and what is the meaning of living it, especially when one is amidst huge losses both at the societal and personal level as one starts to age gradually. Concerns about religion become important for people when they become old and for people who belong to minority groups. These people compared to the younger generations or the non-Hispanic Whites are seen to have religious traditions and have distinguishable behaviours which are religiously oriented and also have religious sentiment (Levin, Taylor and Chatters, 1994; Krause, 2010; Taylor, Chatters, Jayakody and Levin, 1996).

Old people are deprived and are in need of more support than anyone else because of their illness and level of disabilities that occupy their lives. For many, chronic pain makes life a daily struggle. It is said that at this phase the role played by religion becomes very significant where it can be defined as 'the belief in a power of to be obeyed and worshipped as a creator, often involving rituals and a code of ethics'. A single belief does not exist in religion which can be universally applicable. The concept is completely individualistic and as human nature varies the shape it gets by them varies as well. An elderly person who is sick, who is aware of his terminal condition finds peace in professing religion because then it becomes a significant source of proving him the needed comfort and warmth that is required in this experience which he will be forced to go through. It can often turn out to provide a healing experience to those elderly people who are made to feel dejected and unwanted and where the fact of being old is a subject of ridicule and rejection. Religion in all these places can often turn out to replace victory over such negative values. Some people who have been entirely against religion has chosen to follow the path of religion believing that religion can be meaningful and add a new direction for the new times to come in their lives (Davis, 2001).

Religion is considered to be associated with practices which are healthy and which in return are predictors of good health and long life. Also, since, involvement with religion is associated with healthy behaviours it is associated more with lifestyles which are healthy (Hill et al., 2007).

Research findings show that connections with religion enhance mental health across. It controls anger, decreases depression, manages anxiety and other non-psychological concerns, improves satisfaction in life and also develops cognitive functioning in life (Levin et al., 1996). If people are more into religious performances, then chances are more that there will be an increase in the number of activities that will encourage their cognitive abilities. Religious activities include singing, meditation, praying, engaging in the study of scripts and discussions of philosophical levels. It also enhances social get together with other people who assemble in these religious places. The social bindings they have formed and the activities they are involved in can enhance the cognitive functioning of individuals and at the same time, the time taken for failures of such functioning during old age presumably can also be delayed because then the firing potential of the synapses of the brain remains coordinated. Healthy lifestyles for example reduced substance use can be beneficial regarding improving mental health (Van and Kasl, 2003). The social ties that are formed through church are significant in helping develop an excellent level of health. This means there will be a development of both physical and mental capacity. Studies have proven this benefit, which shows that absence of such social bindings does no such good (Berkman and Glass, 2000).

Social support acts to be fruitful, if religious involvements help in connecting one person with another. Studies which are based on religion and depression show that religious social support is positive and is recognized as a beneficial way to get out of depression, including its harsh form and its duration of occurrence (Parappully, 2002). In a study, it was found that private religion did not help much in alleviating depression so much as did public religion which showed the role of social support is influential in alleviating depression to a great extent through which person's mental peace is protected (Bosworth et al., 2003). Private religion can be helpful for those aged people who are not able to take part in community worship because of physical problems, who through this means can feel integrated socially and neutralization of feelings of isolation can be done through providing them with a motive and purposeful action (Hall, 1985). If the signs of depression are major among older adults, then the health problems can be severe. With depression present among the adults who are old there are two times higher chances of a cardiac attack and the second risk is of eventual death arising because of problems caused by some other forms of illness. The other risk after suffering from a severe illness is a reduced chance of the ability to restore oneself from that point. Death caused because of heart attack is more common among people who are suffering from depression just like any death which are caused because of diseases such as cancer or illness caused by failures in immune system (Bremmer et al., 2006).

Studies show that Asian Americans are more religious than any other section of the population. Signs of depression have been reported to be lower in these people. This can be measured by one's way of coping with the help of religious mechanisms or organizational or religious activities which are non-organizational. Organizational religious activities may include Church attendance. Non-organizational religious activities may include praying privately in houses. They feel that religion is a psychological resource which helps in coping and adds meaning to life. It helps in dealing with stressful life events and adds purpose to an otherwise useless life by reframing the adverse experiences in a positive light (Diwan et al., 2004). Asian Americans also believe that religion is connected with feelings of well-being (Iwamasa and Iwasaki, 2011). Elderly Japanese American feel that what brings about inner peace and contentment and something which gives them satisfaction is religion and faith in God. In Thailand, elderly people believe that visiting temple gives them meaning in life. It provides them with comfort and security, brings peace and happiness, accepts them and helps to maintain harmony in life which eventually is important to remain healthy in late life (Pincharoen and Congdon, 2003).

Religion and Life Satisfaction

Elderly people who are more religious according to some scholars are more satisfied in life than the ones who are less religious. Of course, the health of the elderly plays a crucial role here. For example, those elderly who have good health will be able to attend the church services, but the ones who are physically inactive would not be able to attend because of their poor health conditions (Blazer and Palmore, 1976).

Elderly respondents in a study were asked that what were the different ways in which they felt religion benefitted them. The respondents in the study said everything that is good is because of God and therefore they all are grateful to Him. They thank God, for what they have and they feel. He would help them sail through the hard times and material deficiencies and other such crisis (Barusch, 1999). A few scholars found in 1999 that satisfaction in life correlates to connection with religion (Ayele et al., 1999).

Church, according to some researchers became an institution for the elderly that gradually replaced family and started playing its role and provided all that it once played, i.e. Church started to play the role of providing the emotional care and started to provide financial care to its members. Also, it is such a place which calms down the fear of people who are a part of it. There are shreds of evidence which reflect upon the fact that African Americans derive life's satisfaction if they are engaged in activities of the church. A study was conducted in 1992 by Coke where African American people aged 65 years to 88 years old were taken and a total of 166 of them were chosen to see how personal religiosity influences levels of life satisfaction. In this study, 87 males as well as 79 female were interviewed. The samples were asked about their involvement as well as their attendance in church per week. There were other covariates as well, like sufficiency in earnings, education level of respondents, self-rated yearly income and health. The study showed that among the female respondent's religiosity was self-rated and very important as a predictor of life satisfaction (Coke, 1992).

Good amount of empirical work has been done which shows that visiting church and religiosity which is self-rated have a positive influence on the life satisfaction levels of aged black people. Studies have also mentioned the significant role played by the black church, which provided social welfare to the people from black community, finally enabling members of the church to do a large number of social welfare services. Elderly members of the church find such activities to be particularly important as such kind of engagements paved the path of involving the elderly population in constructive activities (Taylor et al., 1987).

Church members also play an important as well as an integral part in the lives of its members, as found in a study of Walls and Zarit (1991). They researched aged black people regarding how much support so black people receive from church members and also what kind of support do they receive from them. Black members aged 98 years old were interviewed who were from church and were residing in central Pennsylvania. Every kind of social support that these people used to receive were measured, including church as well as family. Other aspects like one's health, overall well-being, one's self-rated religiosity, one's overall ability to function all and one's total network of social relations were taken into consideration.

Walls and Zarit (1991) in their study measures social network through a scale named Social Support Resources (SS-R) which is a technique of asking the respondents by choosing up to 15 people whom they consider close. The ones they chose indicated what kind of relationship they share with them, how many times they interact with them and about their membership of the church. Through the study, it was found that the respondents who were interviewed named those people as close associate, who were members of the church to which the respondent belonged to. The study further concluded that here the members/respondents were found to be participating in a large number of religious activities related to the church. They were also involved in some spiritual activities which involved worshipping, paying visits to pastoral members and participating in Bible classes. The other activities were not spiritual as they ranged from going from trips to doctor visits, to health checkups to shopping. It showed that the support people received from the members of the church enhanced their overall well-being. It was seen that although social support received from the family members was more than the social support received from members of the church, the support of church members was associated with increasing their well-being. The respondents included in the study were all members of the church and results might have been different if aged people who are not members of the church were also made part of the study (Walls and Zarit, 1991).

However, in 1991, irrespective of whether one is a member of the church or not it was shown how elderly people engage privately in certain activities that are not connected to church but are indicators to how important religion is. The sample used here was from NSBA, i.e. National Survey of Black Americans from where people aged 18 years and above accounted for 2107 numbers in total and people aged 55 years and more than that consisted of about 581 people. In this sub-sample, the researchers found that approximately 44 per cent of the population enjoyed reading books having religious content regularly and an approximate 24 per cent of the population reported to have read them on a weekly basis. The aged reported that 33.33 per cent of them took pleasure in watching television or listening to radio programmes was telecast religious shows every day and about half of them would do that weekly. This means that frequent watching of religious programmes was with more than 83 per cent of them, whereas 94 per cent of them prayed every day and another 80 per cent said that they requested other people to pray for them (Taylor and Chatters, 1991).

Krause (2002) saw that when older adults who are regular visitors of the church they feel that their congregations are more interconnected and organized in nature and when such organized congregations are there the parishioners provided better care to the elderly people regarding spiritual and emotional aspects. Also, when there is Church support for the aged people, congregational support will be well received by the elderly, they believe in forming a very personal bonding with the almighty. This connection with God gives them a very positive feeling, which in return enhances their overall health (Krause, 2002). In 1993, he studied over 709 people who were aged over 55 years and above. Also, they were a part of World Values Survey, where data were included from the United States and Canada only. It showed that when respondents followed subjective religiosity that is a commitment to the intrinsic aspects of the religious aspects, there is a positive relationship between subjective religiosity and life satisfaction (Krause, 1993). Park in 2011 also said that one's religiosity has a positive influence on one's satisfaction in life as found amongst the immigrants of elderly population of Korea (Park et al., 2011).

Beleghata people were also very religious. About 84 per cent of their houses had separate space for their deities. They worshipped them either occasionally or regularly, during their needs or on a daily basis. Beleghata slum people were immersed in poverty and the elderly people suffered the most serious consequences. They had faced the most dramatic changes and losses regarding physical disabilities, loss of close ones including spouses, loss of jobs and degradation of self-esteem in the eyes of not only the society but also one's children. Despite all these, they made it a choice not to give up and to make the most of whatever they have in life. The failures and then the repeated zeal and spirit to fight again are ushered upon them by their faith in God. They feel that He is the one who would set everything straight. At times of difficulty they felt praying to God, gives them mental peace and satisfaction and this builds up inner strength. God for them is a source of encouragement and from there they derive hope. Some have built a separate structure where they have put the idols they believe in and visit the place almost on a regular basis to offer their prayers. There are families who with mutual understanding and cooperation have established small constructions and established the God in which they have faith. They then have regular or occasional festivals or rituals, which again is a source of solidarity. In the following paragraph, we would like to depict the life of some aged ladies of Beleghata slum area, for whom religion played a vital role and is part and parcel of their lives. Through these, we will be able to understand how the aged and in most of the cases, widowed elderly women related life satisfaction with the practice of religious rituals amidst family pains and sufferings.

Shadhana, aged 60 years became a widow at a young age of 27. As a result of this, she had to struggle throughout her life to bring up her sons and daughter. Later on, she was thrown out of her house by her sons, resulting in making her life completely miserable. She was there upon forced to seek help from her daughter who was then married to an impoverished family, but fortunately, her daughters family helped her during that difficult times. She said,

> *'Ami bari ferod jete parlam amar jamai r meyer shahajye ar amar choto chele bostir baere chilo chakrir khoje. O jantona ki ghoteche. Ami khub obak hoechilam eta dekhe je amar dui boro chele ato udgrib amae barir bere dekhar jonne, amar boyesh howa shotteo ar ami oder ma howa shotteo. Ami jani amar boumara ei shob jinisher pechone jara hoeto amae bojha bhabto, ba hoeto amar cholera bhabe ami oder koshto kore rojgar kore ana takar opore otirikto chap shristi korchi. Jaihok, ami amar jamai er shahajye jehetu barita amar name e chilo oder chele jete bollam ar bollam nijeder byabostha kore nite Jodi amar shathe thakte oshubidhye hoe, ar Jodi thik thake ora tahole thakte pare. Ora chole gelo, kintu buro boyeshe ke aka thakte chae, tai ami shukhi noi. Sharirik koshto amae durbol kore dicche ar amae bhenge dicche. Amar takao nei. Ami onek shomoe na kheye thaki. Amar kotha bolero keo nei. Ebhabe keo kibhabe thakte pare?'*

> ('I managed to get back to my house with the help of my son-in-law and daughter and my youngest son was out of this slum seeking for a job. He was not aware of what was going on. I was shocked to see both my elder sons so keen to see me out of my own house, despite my old age and despite the fact that I am their mother. I know that my daughters-in-law are behind this entire thing who might have felt I am a burden for them, or maybe the sons think I am creating extra pressure on their hard earned income. However, with the help of my son-in-law since this house is in my name I asked them to leave and make an arrangement for themselves if they have so much of problem with me and stay with me only if they are fine. They did go away, but in old age who wants to be alone and therefore I am not happy. Physical troubles are weakening me and breaking me down. I have no money. I often starve. I have no one to talk to. How can someone live such a life?')

When she went on narrating such a sad phase of her life and paused. I said while she looked me,

> *'hmm, bujhte parchi eta khub koshtokor, kintu apni nishchoi khub shokto manush je ato kothin poristhiti ke ato shundor bhabe shamlacchen. Er pechone chalok shokti ta ki? Apnake chalae ke ba apnake ki utshaho kore je apni roj othen ar ato protikulator shotteo ato shomotkar akta hashi nie rakhen?'*

> ('Hmm, I can understand this must be tough and you must be strong to deal with such tough circumstances so beautifully. What is the driving force? What drives you or what encourages you that you get up every day and despite all that adverse situations and wear those lovely smile on your face?')

Shadhana said,

> *'Thakur jane ami kotota shojhyo korte parbo ar kibhabe ar koto pore onar amar chele ar oder bouder ke shashti dewa uchit hobe. Ami apatoto*

> *bolte chai ami oishob porikkhae pash korte chai jeshob porikkhae uni amae pash hote dekhte chan, ar jodi amar mone hoe amar shanty shob bhenegchure churmar hoe gelo tahole thakur i sheta firiye ante parbe, ar amae shob cheye bhalo upodesh dite parben. Amar shob shomoe mone hoe jinish gulo aro kharap hote parto. Ami amar bari fire petam na, amae amar jamai shedin raat e nao thakte dite parto, kintu orom kichui hoeni. Kano? Thakur ar onar ashirbaad er jonne*'.
>
> ('God, knows how much I can tolerate and how and after that how much he should punish my sons and their wives. I want to say for the time being that I have to pass in every test He wants to see me pass and if I feel my peace as being shattered I feel God is the only one who can reinstate that, guide me in the best possible way. I always feel things could have been worse. I might not have got back my house, I might not have been allowed by my son-in-law to stay with them that night, but nothing like that happened. Why? This is because of God and his blessings').

Next lady we spoke to was Shuvra, aged 71. She was praying when we visited her. Shuvra is a big devotee of Loknath Baba and wears an amulet of Loknath and offers prayer to him in the morning after having a bath. She has arthritis and eyesight issues. She also suffers from hearing issues and diabetes. She has no children and lives on the old-age pension. She said,

> '*ami jibone ato bhugechi je ami bhabi ar amar moddhye ki baaki ache jeta keo nie jete pare. Manush, taka, chakri, shukh, shachondyo, kicchu nei, amar kicchu nei! Tao amar mone hoe amar bhetore je shahosh jogae sheta hocche thakur. Jeta ami onno shomoe hole korte partam na ami korte pari jokhn uni amar prarthona r chintae thaken. Amar mone hoe amar jibon ta khub kharap hote parto kintu jehetu ami onar opore biswas kori ami nirapod achi*'.
>
> ('I have suffered so much in life that I wonder what is left in me, which someone might wish to take away. People, money, job, happiness, luxury, comfort, nothing, I do not have anything! However, still, I think someone who instils courage in me is God. What I cannot do otherwise is something I can when he is in my thoughts and prayers. I think my life could have been really bad, but because I believe in Him, I am safe').

Putul Mandal, aged 63 years, said that being a widow, after her only son's marriage, the only way she spends her time is with god. She has never worked anywhere and lives on her old-age pension. She said that because of her lonely life, inclination to God is the sole route, through which, she finds her peace and comfort. She twisted the strings of beads softly with her wrinkled, feeble and trembling hand, with a voice mumbling the prayers hardly audible to the ears. The lady is a great devotee of Narayana. She keeps on taking all 108 names of Narayana. She expressed that she wanted us to know about the universal nature of the

Lord. She recited a hymn, *'Om sahasra sreesam devam vishwakhyam Vishwa sambhubam, viswam Narayana devam aksharam paramam padam'* in a very feeble voice, but we could hear her clear voice. We could understand what she meant. She also explained that Narayana has thousands of features like heads, hands. However, no one can destroy his seed and that the ultimate shelter is his feet as in the end we all must know that his feet are the peace-heaven for all of us.

Keya Saha, another lady of Beleghata who was a complete atheist before marriage, slowly after marriage became a great devotee of Shitola Devi. Her husband has expired, but her in-law's house has a huge temple constructed in Bangladesh from where she belongs originally. Seeing her in-laws pray religiously everyday she also became an ardent follower of Shitala Ma she keeps fast for the well-being of her children. She strictly worships her after Holi puja and she thinks along with many others that if this worship is done during Sheetala Ashtami, then people can be saved from the eruption of diseases.

Another case was of a lady whose husband had a heart attack and had survived it. She said,

> *'Amar mone dactar er cheyo beshi, thakur oi opore boshe amae ar amar poribar ke ashirbaad dicche bhalo kaaj er jonno ja amra amader jibone korechi. Apni dekhben beshirbhaag mohilarai bidhoba amader bosti te. Kintu ami oneker moddhye akjon je akhono shodhoba. Kano? Karon ta ki? Karon ta holo thakur amader ashirbaad korte cha ear amader prarthonar shathe khushi. Ami beleghatar Loknath babar mondir eo gechilam puja dewar jonne, ar okhane fol, ful die manoshik korlam'.*
>
> ('I think more than the doctors, God is sitting up there and blessing my family and me for the good things we have done in our lives. You see most of the aged women are widowed in the slum, but I am one among the very few who is still married. Why? What can be the reason? The reason is, God wants to bless us and is happy with our prayers. I also, went to the Beleghata Loknath Temple to offer my prayers and gave fruits, flowers to Baba as part of votive offerings').

So, elderly people are trying to find solace in an imaginary fact that life could have been messier but with God's grace things are in proper place and everything is sorted.

Theoretical Underpinnings

Religion appears to provide health advantages by reducing the adversities of stress and by becoming the protective layer. There is a model known as buffering model. According to this model, religion helps to decrease stress when stress is severe and consequence of stress is less on the participants who are active. This, however, does not mean that religion's role in letting people held with traumatic experiences will also help them deal with the everyday stress. One strategy that goes with this model is that increase in pain or any trouble increases the rate of prayer, which helps in coping with the problems. Although prayer is not directly connected with physical health, it improves the mental health of a person (Ellison, 1991; Plante, Saucedo and Rice, 2001).

Several models were thought of and identified by Krause and Van Tran. These are Suppressor Model, Distress-Deterrent Model and Moderator Model. These models of religion were used interchangeably to see which can produce the best possible result to reduce stress. The first that is the Suppressor Model means that with an increase in stress amount of religious practice also increases so that stress can be eased or at least reduced. The Moderator Model religion helps in reducing stress at times only when the stressful factor has become very acute, for example, some serious illness, some form of disability. The Distress-Deterrent Model although does not depend on any stress factor, but according to such a factor religion is advantageous for all those who follow such a model (Krause and Van, 1989).

Another model as used by Levin is prevention model. According to this model, religious practices encourage adoption of those practices that prevent individuals from falling prey to such habits and behaviours that are stress inducing like smoking, unsafe sex, divorce, getting addicted to alcohol and instead adopt practices that are stress-reducing (Levin, 1994).

Idler in 1987 in his theory says that if one is connected with religion, then his propensity to get involved in risky behaviours can be reduced to a great extent. His social cohesiveness can be increased, with an increased rate of coherence and rationality. It also would provide an unswerving faith and a belief which is consistent with regards to how to how to cope with life and share the experience with others (Idler, 1987).

Beleghata slum dwellers also have witnessed two such cases where getting inclined towards religious activities could sever ties with addictive habits. A lady had the alcohol addiction and was subject to the ridicule of her entire neighbourhood. She was abandoned by her children and got widowed at an early age. To live a healthy life she thought of surrendering alcohol consumption and started praying to Ramthakur. Gradually she found a subtle change in her, where from an alcoholic she turned into a religious person who refrained from alcohol and right now she is alcohol-free for about seven years. The same change seemed to occur in a woman's husband when the woman started believing in Loknath Baba. Such faith according to her let her husband slowly quit liquor and other addictions including drugs. She described us how brutally he used to beat her and her children every night after drinking and then how her faith in God slowly changed everything. Many slum dwellers believe that if specially designed amulets and charms are worn by the ones who are addicted then by God's grace their addictive habits would go away and life would come back to normalcy.

Few scholars also suggest that faith in religiosity and one's preference of religion can have an influential role on the overall health of a person, whether it is mental or physical. During old age since the aged feel they lose control over their lives, connection with religion can have a positive connection in bringing about a positive change in enriching and of course protect the lost control they once had during their young age (Kaplan et al., 1994).

There is another theory on the aged. It is the Deprivation Theory which is based on the studies of aged African Americans. According to it, poorer ones scored more on life satisfaction scale than the wealthy aged whites who are not only economically better but healthier (Chatters and Taylor, 1989; Taylor and Chatters, 1986; Tate, 1980).

According to the theory, the traditional way of committing oneself to religion is a significant way of compensating for the deprivation that one faces in life in the form of economic and forms of crisis. The deprivation that one confronts in life becomes more tolerable to put up with when religion intervenes. With religion, life gets a meaning and purpose and the suffering that one faces is also compensated. One's affiliations to particular religious groups also means that these particular groups would send the members moral messages. Every group to which one is connected to then becomes the group's yardstick of comparison (Tate, 1980; Chatters and Taylor, 1989; Taylor and Chatters, 1986).

Concluding Remarks

Beleghata is a place where a majority of people were Hindus and most of them believed in Mahapurush like Loknath Baba, or the Indian mystics like Ramthakur, or believe in Kali Ma, Durga Ma, or do Kartik Puja, Sitala Puja. Through their belonging to such groups they feel good. When we asked them what is the main reason of being a part of a religious group, almost more than 85 per cent of them said: '*Thakur updesh dae jokhon shob kichu haar mene jae*' ('God guides you when everything else fails').

10

Conclusion

The invincibility of ever increasing elderly population is one of the universal truth throughout the world, and it is high time that the world needs to move beyond the demographic discourse on elderly practice. How do we imagine an elderly person? We often visualize them as someone characterized by physical deformities, mental problems, frailty, homely, religious and most importantly as someone who lives in home and awaits death by reminiscing bygone days. The elderly paradox is hidden within this mental imagery of the social structure as a whole, which had consciously provoked and distributed an elderly construction which is inherently cultural. Quite appropriately it can be remarked that the idea of being elderly is indeed a social construction which often can be metaphorically compared with the notion of 'jacket' which has been put on the people who are above 60 years of age by an intangible determined force. Our study in Beleghata slum was indeed an eye opener for us which inherently reflected us the condition of the elderly populace within lower social strata wherein the aged population often opted to work till death in return of money which was essential for their survival. The aforesaid observation is indeed a stark contrast to the established notion of elderly population as the dependent entities or liabilities. In our study which delve into the life of those aged population who belonged to lower income households, elderly population was not completely dependent whereupon they often did 'odd jobs' for their survival. Now the question arises is that whether the elderly populace is acknowledged as completely dependent entities or there is a need to revisit the definitional contents of the elderly discourse.

The present day society is characterized by increasing rates of nuclear family household with dual earning members. Rapid industrialization, migration, urbanization, inclination for betterment as well as hike in 'conspicuous consumption' acted as major reasons behind the aforesaid. As a result of this, members of households/family leave their native place and opt to move out with their spouses. Hence, the reality depicts two separate households, one consisting of the present generation and the other consisting of elderly household. At the same time changing value structures and urge for privacy and acute individualism result in decline of extended families too. Hence the present reality includes elderly people taking care of themselves. In this regard, United Nations (2013) report on ageing stated that most of the elderly population in industrialized countries lives alone and the proportion are highest among the oldest age groups.

The study carried out in Beleghata slum showed up the vulnerable position of the elderly, which was especially distressful for residing on the wrong side of the track. The lamentable state of existence with acute crisis of basic necessities reflected the necessity to revise policies for betterment of these people. Health crisis and economic issues were well-evident difficulties that these elderly dwellers face. The fact that policies are in place, yet are failing to show fruitful results is because of the family members tussling over churning out profits. Underlying this profit making motives lays an eroded apathetic parent-child relationship. With increasing age and decreasing or no flow of income, parents are deserted to plough a lone furrow. Begging on bended knees for mere support from sons and daughters, during old age is the harsh reality of Beleghata slum. Across the slum, there are quite a large number of elderly widows, and their condition is more contemptible. Besides, having to face infinite challenges during old-age, they are often the victims of ageism. Merely able to sustain themselves, they often complained about being mocked and ridiculed by the young generation. This book has tried to substantiate them with relevant theories, and brought into light how in order to escape death as a preordained truth, young people put on a brave face, thus hiding their fears with utmost adeptness.

Health and economic issues seemed to be interwoven. Where hardly any money goes into creation of a hygienic environment or disinfected sanitary facilities, there diseases are inevitable. The ramshackle housing built and inhabited are beyond repairable damage, and are shabby, infected, broken and murky. The book has tried to provide enough visuals to highlight these grave issues with utmost sincerity. The diseases ensuing from such wrecked living conditions or eruption of any other health-related issues usually entails some basic medical attention. Lack of parent-child relationships, and health-care centres situated at far-off places with nobody to accompany or even pay, leaves hardly any avenue opened to go beyond the free facilities, which too are accessed after surmounting obstacles. It is quite evident that the bonds between the members of the family are consequently degrading. Presently it has become essential that the elderly population needs to be self sufficient not only in economic terms, but also in social terms too. Nowadays they are compelled to look after themselves and not get dependent on their children. Lack of time and work commitments may often be regarded as probable reasons in favor of their successors for not helping their parents. Now the question arise is why the elderly populace's plight be like this? Why are they treated as old? Or whom do we regard as old?

In India the concept of elderly is associated with dependency. Elderly people of Belaghata slums feel similar, regardless of gender, they feel that they should take a break now and that their children need to take care of their parents. The old men here said that they are old, their eyes are weak, their bodies are dry, their legs are heavy and painful, their hair is white, and their faces were brittle, and they were wrinkled. They felt that they were mentally ageing because they were reluctant to participate in work when their interest in work outside the house diminished. Children are an integral part in understanding of ageing. For many of them, people's behaviour changes as they get older, and old people are perceived as a burden by their closest relatives, especially their own children. In the study many elderly women implicitly complained that some children have left their parents in the most needed hours of life and have even thrown them out. The ladies who have faced such humiliating situations were not much old and also were physically capable according to the residents. However, for most of them the very fact that they are in-laws and therefore 'old', creates such fears among the young that they feel getting rid of this responsibility right at the beginning, would help them lead a peaceful life without much burden. Accepting ageing, death, dependency, and the ephemerality of life are principles typically held up as appropriate for older people (Lamb 1997, 2000, 2009, 2014). The human body, for example, is compared to rice plants, which grow, shed their seeds, and then wither away in Hindu philosophy. Both Hindus and Muslims in India believe that just as children require assistance when they are young, so do elderly parents. Rather than encouraging autonomous ageing, India's 2007 Maintenance and Welfare of Parents and Senior Citizens Act mandates that children to provide care for their parents and grandparents. This governmental policy might be described as family-oriented neoliberalism, based on long-held Indian cultural ideas that family care is the best and most natural method to care for children. For instance, that elders in India were often encouraged instead to strive to accept the natural transience of the body (Lamb 2014). At the same time, while life-prolonging and individual-centered successful ageing ideology has not yet hugely taken off in India, some among cosmopolitan circles are picking it up.While scholars have pointed out the ethnocentrism and elitism of successful-ageing models emanating from the United States, few empirical studies take seriously the experiences of ageing across diverse social and cultural contexts. Theoretical critiques of successful ageing have wistfully wished for the 'missing voices' of diverse elders themselves or imagine that social inequalities must shape opportunities for and constraints upon successful ageing.

Our study further likes to extend the work to understand how global ideas of 'healthy ageing' are taking root (or not) among the rising middle classes. For those adopting healthy ageing culture – taking morning walks, attending yoga gatherings in public parks, purchasing Fitbit health monitors, joining activity-oriented 'senior citizens' clubs – what motivates them? How do new, cosmopolitan pursuits of health and activity in ageing intersect with more conventional visions of ageing well, such as the ideal of being served in later life (which can allow prestigious immobility) and acceptance of the natural transience of the human condition? The study opens avenues for further empirical research, exploring the experiences of elders in diverse social circumstances and cultural contexts, in order to access the variety of ways, older people envision and reimagine, embrace and resist, the prevailing public health and popular cultural paradigm of successful ageing.

Finally our argument rests on the very question is age be solely restricted to demographic connotation? Durkheim had stated that 'society is over and above individual'. Thus we as members of the very society share similar 'social consciousness', 'beliefs', 'ethos' and 'values'. Deducing these idioms on the basis of utilitarian perspective, it can be aptly remarked that the present time is dominated by the values of capitalist ethos wherein the basic or the exclusive aim of every institution as well as the actor is to opt for the process of profit maximization. Individuals are thereby judged on the basis of their contribution or utility to the whole of society. On the basis of this preconceived capitalist ethos, wherein the idea of utility is also predetermined, the position of the elderly population is indeed a matter of concern. Older population being regarded as a probable 'risk', which is coterminous with the discourse of 'social production of risk'. Thus elderly population is itself regarded as an irrelevant expenditure; hence they need to be kept in isolation. In our journey in Beleghata slum, we have found notable reflections in this regard.

It is quite an interesting fact that the elderly population, which had been often projected as entities to be respected, loved and cared are often been given a negative treatment. Indian society believes in the notion of gerontocracy which is based on 'respecting elders ethos'. However beyond the realm of moral ethos, it is clearly seen that in practice elderly populace is ignored, subjected to abuse as well as their behavioural structure is constructed as well as given and they need to survive within it. Elderly population can often be regarded as marginalized section of the society whereupon their needs and rights are often manipulated and governed by the civil society.

While exploring the field of gerontology, it was vivid that ageing literature has consistently addressed problems of the elderly population in a universal way, irrespective of class, religion or caste. However, ageing as a universal variable is inherently related with various modes of stratification. In the present study, which has been centered in Beleghata slum of Kolkata, gives a distinct image of elderly situation in a society based on economic relations of production. Hence, a pondering question which we confront involves, can elderly discourse be studied through a subaltern lens?

The study helped us to reflect on the complexities associated with the gerontological discourse, where age should not be treated as an exclusive category. The category of age needs to be amalgamated with evolving stratification systems like gender, class, caste as well as disability. The inclusion of elderly rights needs to be focused upon, where, policy level programmes needs to be evaluated. Regarding policy-making, improving the existing or formulating new policies for the elderly poor, it must be kept in mind that its implementation would fail to yield results if the above-mentioned factors are not duly considered. Elderly people are in no position to raise a stink; therefore proper plans need to be made to address such issues which would keep in mind the conditions under which they are sustaining themselves. Also, monthly visits should be carried out in such slums, and the beneficiaries should be separately asked to ensure a smooth execution.

Through field narratives and collective reflection as researchers, ageing in slum and age-friendly slums are two key concepts that emerged through organically. Ageing in slum emphasizes on the specificities of growing old in the slum, at the same time looking at the lifecourse of individuals that sheds light on the present stage of ageing. Slums in the global south pose serious constraint to effective urban planning and design of the city. The main characteristics of a slum is overcrowding, sharing a common public toilet and crunch of space. Despite these visible problems, slums provide an affordable living option to the teeming million who are in hand-to-mouth existence. The image and presence of slums juxtaposed to the development of megalopolis may pose hindrance in the establishment of a 'smart city'. People living within the slums reside in these settlements in perpetual fear as they may be usurped and made homeless at any time. This dialectical relationship between the slum and megalopolis vis-à-vis the state, impinges people across the lifecourse. The older people are no exception to this. Their aspiration for a better living condition and their peripherality in urban development are harsh realities that they have to live with. The 'underdevelopment' of the slums are due to its 'anomalous' status in the development of a megalopolis. Urban and rural areas are divided by the resource distribution, and the slums are the peripheral among peripheral in relation to resource accumulation. Ageing in the slum for the older people refers to the experiences of ageing across the lifecourse for people with the features in a slum shaping their experiences of ageing. Conflict in the slum residential settlements emerges from the spatial distribution, poverty and aspirations being stunted. Living and surviving in slums require resilience, and the ageing population within it continue to make their lives livable through acts of resilience and intergenerational ties. While there are skirmishes with family members across the generations yet families are important support networks for the elders for building of resource and well-being.

Instead of viewing slums as juxtaposed to megalopolis, 'smart city' and urbanism, we propose that slums can co-exist with these symbols of modernity and yet promise to become an emancipatory space for older persons. We recommend the conceptualization of age-friendly slums that emphasizes on well-being of older people through incorporation of certain facilities. Slums can be improved to aim for the best possible ageing infrastructure for the older population. For example, in the slum neighbourhoods people are exposed to poor ventilation, lower sanitation, prevalence of diseases due to environmental conditions, disposal of litter and lack of access to cutting-edge medical facilities can affect the well-being of older people. Older person's attachment to the place where they have grown underlines the importance of their enduring relationship with these urban slums. Health hazards in these slum residential settings are an outcome of water-logging issues, sub-standard living and prevailing widespread poverty. As identified by noted scholars, such conditions of overcrowding and declining living condition results in cultural alienation and disease burden among the slum dwelling residents. Their close location to the industrial units and the roads expose them to pollution and greater health problems. Slum residents report of suffering from musculoskeletal (MSK) issues that remains untreated. Apart from musculoskeletal disease, depression due to unfulfilled aspirations, limited opportunities for work and acute stress are some of the issues that characterizes old age.

Older people in continuation with South Asian culture provide care to their younger generation and are not solely the recipients of care. Experts have termed this as 'generative anxiety' . The stigma of widowhood for older women is another issue that has recurrently being discussed in the study. With old-age being characterized by isolation, widowhood is not just about isolation but the stigma that accompanies it. All these problems leads to an unprecedented turn with the existent ageism in the society. Older people in the study are affected about their life condition and bodily image due to ageing, and do wish to be reminded of their 'signs of ageing'. The inevitability of death and growing old can disrupt healthy ageing experience. While older people have reported mixed feelings about death, yet many of them wished to live. Life is valued and this indomitable spirit to love reflects in their resilience – ways in which they survive and thrive. This may be stated as later-life resilience. Dependency on others is feared among the residents of Beleghata when they feel dependent it endures tension and affects intergenerational relationship, and may lower the status of older people. However, older adults grow dependent on their younger generations as they lose the ability to earn and contribute to the financial resources of the family. With poverty hovering the slum residents and people living in a hand-to-mouth existence, adult children slum residents find it difficult to provide for their ageing parents. This directly affects their nutritional and dietary requirements, and further aggravates their health conditions. Another aspect is that older people are missing out on early medical intervention due to hospital-visit hesitancy that stems from lack of financial resources. This delay in health check-up and timely medical treatment makes the older slum residents 'poorest of the poor' in access to health.

To address these burning issues affecting the older residents and people across the lifecourse as they are in a state of ageing, 'age-friendly slum' has to be established. These age-friendly slums would emphasize on ageing in a community where older people feel part of the community, and community health services are at their disposal. The purpose of community health services is to provide quick response to the health emergences of residents growing old in slums who refrain from accessing health services. Availability of such health services would encourage older people to report their health problems and meet with early solutions. Along with community health care services that is speedy and consistent, social care services are also required for healthy ageing. We propose that social care services to be introduced in the slum areas that includes mental health counsellors of older people with trained and qualified psychologists. Given, the intergenerational skirmishes in the family and its subsequent toll on older people, family counsellors should visit the residences of multi-generational households and mediate the tensions. Older people suffer from mental health issues and conflict within the family exacerbates that experience, hence a peaceful and conducive family environment is crucial for healthy ageing of Beleghata residents. Maltreatment of older people results from institutionalized ageism as older people are vulnerable and they tend to become dependent. The 'dependent' image of older adults as 'burdensome' entities needs to be reconsidered and social care services need to ensure that such ageism can be countered. Incentivizing older people can be one step that can prevent them from being dependent and reduce instances of elderly abuse committed against them. Elderly abuse results from the vulnerable position of older people and the economic disparity of the residents in slum exacerbate this experience. Older persons do not have the will to raise voice against their adult children and the cycle of abuse continues. Economically empowering older persons is a much needed step to reduce their dependence and reinstate their dignity. Vocational training of older people can make them empowered. NGOs and self-help group models can be brought to the picture so there is a continuity. In this discussion, it cannot be discounted that women are at a greater disadvantage than men in the social structure and older women are no different. Health related problems of women in the slums are different than men. Menopause affects women differently and at times jeopardize mental health. Loneliness among older people is another epidemic and intergenerational conflict in the family.

Constrained opportunities in old-age in local decision-making have to be brought back to the older people through eliminating the constraints. All these are related to empowering older people through sustainable approaches. Well-being, empowerment and addressing the needs of the socially disadvantaged and the 'most vulnerable' among older people needs to be handled with care and compassion. 'Age-friendly slums' have to take into account the emotional, mental and economic well-being of older adults. The precarious location of slum adjacent to the 'smart city' and posing 'aesthetic' and 'developmental' threat to the cities have to be countered with shifting focus on the contribution of slums in the growth of cities. Slums supply labour that has made the metropolis 'what it is' and the residents of the slum are the architects of the city. Hence, taking care of the people across the lifecourse especially the older people is a collective social and moral responsibility.

This book would enlighten the students pursuing Sociology about the prevailing conditions of elderly. It is based on several case studies, and hence it would be of great help for students to learn theories and get acquainted with several sociological terms with the help of real-life examples.

Bibliography

Achenbaum, W.A. and Bengtson, V.L. (1994). 'Re-engaging the disengagement theory of aging: On the history and assessment of theory development in gerontology'. *The Gerontologist*, 34(6), 756–763, https://doi.org/10.1093/geront/34.6.756

Adams, R. (1986). 'A look at friendship and aging'. *Generations*, pp. 40–43.

Age Platform (2012). 'Towards an Age Friendly EU: Age Work in 2012', https://www.age-platform.eu/sites/default/files/AGE_AR2012-final.pdf

Alam, M. (2013). 'Ageing, functional disabilities and its gender dimensions: Results based on a study in Delhi'. In: *Global Ageing in the Twenty-First Century: Challenges, Opportunities and Implications*. s.l.: Ashgate Publishing, Ltd., pp. 33–48.

Allinson, B. (2004). *How to Deal With Your Mother-in-law: Sisters and Family Included*. New York: Universe.

American Association of Suicidology (2011). United States: Elderly Suicide Fact.

American Psychological Association (2012). 'Elderly Abuse and Neglect: In Search of Solutions'. Retrieved from: https://www.apa.org/pi/aging/elder-abuse.pdf

Antonucci, T. and Akiyama, H. (1996). 'Convoys of social relations: Family and friendships within a life span context'. In *Aging and the Family: Theory and Research*. United States of America: Greenwood Publishing Group.

Antonucci, T.C. (2001). 'Social relations: An examination of social networks, social support and sense of control'. *Handbook of the Psychology of Aging*, pp. 427–453.

Arber, S., Davidson, K. and Ginn, J. (2003). *Gender and Ageing: Changing Roles and Relationships*. Maidenhead and Philadelphia: McGraw-Hill Education.

Asha, C.B. (1991). 'Women, work and mental health: A study among the aged. *Perspective in Psychological Researches*, pp. 20–22.

Asha, C.B. and Subrahmanian, K.A. (1990). 'Problems of elderly women'. *Indian Journal of Community Guidance and Research*, pp. 61–67.

Atchley, R.C. (1989). 'A Continuity Theory of Normal Aging'. *The Gerontologist*, 29, 183–190.

Atchley, R.C. (2000). *Social Forces and Aging: An Introduction to Social Gerontology*. Belmont, CA: Wadsworth.

Ateljevic, I., Pritchard, A. and Morgan, N. (2007). *The Critical Turn in Tourism Studies*. s.l.: Routledge.

Ayele, H., Mulligan, T., Gheorghiu, S. and Reyes, O.C. (1999). 'Religious activity improves life satisfaction for some physicians and older patients'. *J Am Geriatr Soc*, pp. 453–455.

Bainbridge, W.S. and Hatch, L.R. (1982). 'Women's access to elite careers: In search of a religion effect'. *Journal for the Scientific Study of Religion*, pp. 242–254.

Baldassar, L. and Merla, L. (2013). *Transnational Families, Migration and the Circulation of Care: Understanding Mobility and Absence in Family Life*. New York: Routledge.

Barry, A.M. and Yuill, C. (2011). *Understanding the Sociology of Health: An Introduction*. London: Sage.

Barusch, A.S. (1999). 'Religion, adversity and age: Religious experiences of low-income elderly women'. *The Journal of Sociology and Social Welfare*, pp. 125–142.

Basford, L. and Thorpe, K. (2004). *Caring for the Older Adult*. United Kingdom: Nelson Thornes.

Basu, S. (2000). 'Role, status: Relationship of the elderly women in family'. *Journal of the Department of Anthropology*, pp. 92–104.

Beeston, D. (2006). *Older People and Suicide*. Stoke-on-Trent: Centre for Ageing and Mental Health. England: Staffordshire University.

Behura, N.K. and Mohanty, R.P. (2000). 'Social situation of the aged in urban fringes of Bhubaneshwar city'. *Journal of the Department of Anthropology*, pp. 92–104.

Bengtson, V.L. and Kuypers, J.A. (1971). 'Generational difference and the developmental stake'. *The International Journal of Aging and Human Development*, 2(4), retrieved from: https://journals. sagepub.com/doi/10.2190/AG.2.4.b

Berkman, L., Glass, T., Brissette, I. and Seeman, T. (2000). 'From social integration to health: Durkheim in the new millennium'. *Soc Sci Med*, pp. 843–857.

Berkman, L.F. and Glass, T. (2000). 'Social integration, social networks, social support and health'. In L.F. Berkman, I. Kawachi and M. Glymour (eds), *Social Epidemiology*. New York: Oxford University Press, pp. 137–173.

Bhatia, R.S. (1964). 'Rural social change and the problem of the aged'. *Social Welfare XXI*, pp. 5–6.

Bhugra, D. (2005). 'Sati: A type of nonpsychiatric suicide'. *Crisis*, pp. 73–77.

Bianchi, E.C. (2011). *Aging as a Spiritual Journey*. Eugene, Oregon: Wipf and Stock Publishers.

Bienko, M. (2015). 'The sexual aspects of intimacy in old age, in the public and private spheres'. Retrieved from: http://www.repozytorium.uni.wroc.pl/Content/58874/06_Mariola_Bienko.pdf

Birren, J.E. and Schaie, K.W. (2001). *Handbook of the Psychology of Aging*. London: Gulf Professional Publishing.

Biswas, S.K. (ed.) (1987). 'Dependency and family care of the aged in village India: A case study in ageing in contemporary India'. *Indian Anthropological Society*, pp. 238–257.

Blanchard, M.R., Waterreus, A. and Mann, A.H. (1994). 'The nature of depression among older people in inner London and the contact with primary care'. *The British Journal of Psychiatry*, 164(3), 396–402.

Blau, Z.S. (1973). *Old Age in a Changing Society*. New York: New Viewpoints.

Blaxter, M. (1990). *Health and Lifestyles*. London: Routledge.

Blazer, D. and Palmore, E. (1976). 'Religion and aging in a longitudinal panel'. *Gerontologist*, pp. 82–85.

Bloom, D.E, Jimenez, E. and Rosenberg, L. (2011). 'Social Protection of Older People', Working Paper Series, (83), Harvard University, https://cdn1.sph.harvard.edu/wp-content/uploads/sites/1288/2013/10/PGDA_WP_83.pdf

Bloom, D.E. et al. (2010). 'Economic security arrangements in the context of population ageing in India'. *International Social Security Review*, 63(3–4): 79–97.

Bond, J., Coleman, P. and Peace, S.M. (1993). *Ageing in Society: An Introduction to Social Gerontology*. London: Sage.

Boralingaiah, et al. (2012). 'Prevalence of psycho-social problems among elderly in urban population of Mysore city, Karnataka, India', *Indian Journal of Pshychological Medicine*, 34 (4), http://www.ijpm.info/citation.asp?issn=0253-7176;year=2012;volume=34;issue=4;spage=360;epage=364;aulast=Boralingaiah;aid=IndianJPsycholMed_2012_34_4_360_108221

Bossé, R. and Ekerdt, D.J. (1981). 'Change in self-perception of leisure activities with retirement'. *Gerontologist*, pp. 650–654.

Bosworth, H. et al. (2003). 'The impact of religious practice and religious coping on geriatric depression'. *Int J Geriatr Psychiatry*, pp. 905–914.

Bourdieu, Pierre (1986). *The Handbook of Theory: Research for the Sociology of Education*. New York: Greenwood Press.

Brattberg, G., Thorslund, M. and Wikman, A. (1989). 'The prevalence of pain in a general population: The results of a postal survey in a country of Sweden'. *Pain*, pp. 215–222.

Braun, W. (2008). 'Sallekhana: The ethicality and legality of religious suicide by starvation in the Jain religious community'. *Medicine and Law*, pp. 913–924.

Bremmer, M. et al. (2006). 'Depression in older age is a risk factor for first ischemic cardiac events'. *Am J Geriatr Psychiatry*, pp. 523–530.

Bromley, D. (1966). *The Psychology of Human Ageing*. Harmondsworth, England: Penguin Books.

Bromley, M.C. and Blieszner, R. (1997). 'Planning for long-term care: Filial behavior and relationship. Quality of adult children with independent parents'. *Family Relations*, pp. 155–162.

Brophy, C., Blackler, A. and Popovic, V. (2015). 'Aging and Everyday Technology'. Interplay-IADSR 2015 Congress, Brisbane, Australia. Retrieved From: https://eprints.qut.edu.au/89127/1/Aging%20and%20ICT%20-%20IASDR%202015FINAL%20.pdf

Brossoie, N. (2010). 'Social Gerontology'. In R.H. Rolenett and W.C. Chop (eds), *Gerontology for the Health Care Professional,* pp. 19–51, New York: Jones and Barlett Publishers.

Burrus-Bammel, L.L. and Bammel, G. (1985). 'Leisure and recreation'. In *Handbook of the Psychology of Aging*. New York: Van Nostrand Reinhold, p. 848–889.

Burtless, G. (1987). 'Occupational effects on the health and work capacity of older men'. In G. Burtless (ed.), *Work, Health, and Income among the Elderly*. Washington, DC: The Brookings Institutions, pp. 8–11.

Bury, M. (1988). 'Meanings at risk: The experience of arthritis'. In R. Anderson and M. Bury (eds), *Living with Chronic Illness: The Experience of Patients and their Families*. London: Unwin Hyman.

Business Standard (2015). 'Newly Married Woman found hanging in Ghaziabad'. (Online) Available at: www.business-standard.com/article/news-ians/newly-married-woman-found-hanging-in-ghaziabad–115041701174_1.html (Accessed 30 December 2015).

Busse, W.E. and Blazer, D.G. (eds) (1980). 'The social factors in aging'. In *Handbook of Geriatric Psychiatry*. New York: Van Nostrand Reinhold Company.

Butler, R. (1969). The effects of medical and health progress on the social and economic aspects of the life cycle (Paper delivered at the National Institute of Industrial Gerontology, Washington, DC, 13 March 1969), pp. 1–9.

Butler, R. (1975). *Why Survive? Being Old in America*. Boston, UK: Jones and Barlett.

Butler, R. (1980). 'Ageism: A foreword'. *Journal of Social Issues*, 36(2), Wiley Online Library, Retrieved From: https://spssi.onlinelibrary.wiley.com/doi/abs/10.1111/j.1540-4560.1980.tb02018.x

Butler, R. (1995). 'Ageism'. In George L. Maddox (ed.), *The Encyclopedia of Aging*. New York: Springer Publishing.

Butler, R. and Lewis, M. (1973). *Aging and Mental Health*. St. Louis, MO: C.V. Mosby Co.

Butler, R.N. et al. (1998). 'Physical fitness: Benefits of exercise for the older patient'. *Geriatrics*, pp. 46–62.

Bytheway, B. (1995). *Ageism*. Buckingham: McGraw-Hill.

Cannuscio, C., Block, J. and Kawachi, I. (2003). 'Social capital and successful aging: The role of senior housing'. *Ann. Intern. Med* 139: 395–399.

Case, P.W. and McMinn, M.R. (2001). 'Spiritual coping and well-functioning among psychologists'. *Journal of Psychological Theology*, pp. 29–40.

Cavanaugh, J. and Fields, F.B. (2002). *Adult Development and Aging*. Belmont, CA: Wadsworth Thomson Learning.

Chakraborty, N. (2001). (Online) Available at: http://www.nachiketa.net/briddhashram–2001.aspx (Accessed 2 September 2015).

Chakraborty, P. (2009). *Sunset Years of Life*. New Delhi: Urbee Prakashan.

Charmaz, K. (1987). 'Struggling for a self: Identity levels of the chronically ill'. In *Research in the Sociology of Health Care: The Experience and Management of Chronic Illness*. Greenwich, Connecticut: J.I.T. Press, pp. 283–321.

Chatterjee, S.C., Patnaik, P. and Chariar, V. (2008). *Discourses on Aging and Dying*. London: Sage Publications India.

Chatters, L. and Taylor, R. (1989). 'Age Differences in Religious Participation Among Black Adults'. *The Journals of Gerontology*, pp. S183–S189.

Chen, M. and Dreze, J. (1992). 'Widows and health in rural North India'. *Economic and Political Weekly*, pp. WS81–WS92.

Cokayne, K. (2013). *Experiencing Old Age in Ancient Rome*. London: Routledge.

Coke, M. (1992). 'Correlates of life satisfaction among elderly African Americans'. *Journal of Gerontology*, pp. P316–P320.

Coleman, James (1988). 'Social capital in the creation of human capital'. *American Journal of Sociology* 94: S95–S12.

Cooter, R. and Pickstone, J.V. (2003). *Companion to Medicine in the Twentieth Century*. London and New York: Taylor & Francis.

Coren, S. and Hewitt, P.L. (1999). 'Sex differences in elderly suicide rates: Some predictive factors'. *Aging & Mental Health*, pp. 112–118.

Cowgill, D.O. and Holmes, L. (1972). *Aging and Modernisation*, New York: Appleton Century Crofts.

Cox, F. (2008). *Human Intimacy: Marriage, the Family and Its Meaning, Research Update*. United States: Cengage Learning.

Cox, Harold and Newton, Richard (1993). 'History of social gerontology', *Sociological Practice*, Vol. 11: Issue 1, Article 4. Available at: http://digitalcommons.wayne.edu/socprac/vol11/iss1/4

Cribier, F. (1981). 'Changing retirement patterns of the seventies: The example of a generation of Parisien salaried workers'. *Ageing and Society*, pp. 51–73.

Cullinan, T.R. (1977). 'The epidemiology of visual disability studies of visually disabled people in the community' (H.S.R.U. report), s.l.: Health Services Research Unit, Center for Research in the Social Sciences, University of Kent at Canterbury.

Cumming, E. and Henry, W.E. (1961). *Growing Old: The Process of Disengagement*. New York: Basic Books. (Reprint: Arno, New York, 1979). Ageing and Society, 11(2), 217–220. doi: 10.1017/S0144686X00004025

Czaja, S.J. (2005). 'The Impact of Aging and Access to Technology', ACM SIGACCESS Accessibility and Computing, 83. Retrieved from: doi.10.1145/1102187.1102189

Czaja, S.J., Charness, N., Fisk, A.D., Hertzog, C., Nair, S.N., Rogers, W.A. and Sharit, J. (2006). 'Factors predicting the use of technology: Findings from the Centre for Research IASDR 2015 Interplay', 2–5 November, Brisbane, Australia 15 and Education on Aging and Technology Enhancement (CREATE). *Psychology and Aging*, 21(2), 333.

Czaja, Sara and Chin Lee, Chin (2007). 'The impact of aging on access to technology'. *Universal Access in the Information Society*. 5, 341–349. 10.1145/1102187.1102189

Daijiworld (2013). 'Mangalore: Driven Out by Unfeeling Daughter, Aged Parents at Mercy of Fate'. (Online) Available at: http://www.daijiworld.com/news/news_disp.asp?n_id=191157 (Accessed 29 December 2015).

Dasgupta, P. and Ray, R. (2000). 'Old age in tribal society: A study among Santals of village Belkuti, district Burdwan, West Bengal'. *Journal of the Department of Anthropology*, pp. 62–74.

Dave, P. and Mehta, P. (2008). *Mental Health and Aging Women: Important Correlates*. New Delhi: Kalpaz Publications.

Davis, M. (1988). 'Epidemiology of osteoarthritis'. *Clinical Geriatric Medicine*, pp. 241–255.

Davis, S.M.B. (2001). *In-Home Care for Senior Citizens: A Bedside Companion*. United States of America: Author House.

DeLeo, D., Bille-Brahe, U., Kerkhof, A. and Schmidtke, A. (eds) (2004). 'Suicide and suicidal behaviour in latelife'. In *Suicidal Behaviour: Theories and Research Findings*. Cambridge, Massachusetts: Hogrefe Publishing, pp. 253–286.

DeLiema, M. and Bengtson, V.L. (2015). 'Activity theory, disengagement theory and successful aging', In N. Pachana (eds) *Encyclopedia of Geropsychology*, Singapore: Springer, Retrieved from: https://doi.org/10.1007/978-981-287-080-3_102-1

Denton, F. (2011). *Independence and Economic Security in Old Age*. Vancouver: UBC Press.

Department of Economic and Social Affairs Population Division (2010). 'World Population Prospects: Sex and Age Distribution of the World Population', Volume 2 of World Population Prospects: The 2008 Revision. United Nations, New York: United Nations Publications.

Desai, K.G. and Naik, R.D. (1973). *Problems of Retired People in Greater Bombay*. Bombay: Tata Institute of Social Sciences.

Details of Welfare Schemes for the Aged Persons (2015). *Press Information Bureau, Government of India, Ministry of Social Justice & Empowerment* (Online) Available at: pib.nic.in/newsite/PrintRelease.aspx?relid=117406 (Accessed 31 December 2015).

Dillon, L. (2008). *The Shady Side of Fifty: Age and Old Age in Late Victorian Canada and the United States*. Montreal: McGill-Queen's Press – MQUP.

Diwan, S., Jonnalagadda, S.S. and Balaswamy, S. (2004) 'Resources Predicting Positive and Negative Affect During the Experience of Stress: A Study of Older Asian Indian Immigrants in the United States'. *The Gerontologist*, pp. 605–614.

Dotinga, R. (2014). 'When Parents need Care, Daughters carry the Burden, Study Says'. (Online) Available at: http://consumer.healthday.com/senior-citizen-information–31/misc-aging-n ews–10/when-parents-need-care-daughters-carry-the-burden-study–690860.html (Accessed 31 December 2015).

Dowd, J.J. (1975). 'Aging as exchange: A preface to theory'. *Journal of Gerontology*, 30(5), 584–594.

Dumas, A. and Turner, B.S. (2007). The Life Extension Project: A Sociological Critique, *Health Sociology Review*, 16: 1, 5–17, DOI: 10.5172/hesr.2007.16.1.5

Durkheim, E. (1897). *Suicide: A Study in Sociology*. New York: Free Press.

Dykstra, P.A. (1995). 'Loneliness among the never and formerly married: The importance of supportive friendships and a desire for independence'. *J Gerontol B Psychol Sci Soc Sci*, pp. 321–329.

Eastman, N.L.G. (1993), Forensic psychiatric services in Britain: A current review Indian international, *Journal of Law and Psychiatry*, 16 (1–2).

Ei Samae (2015). *Prabinder Shahajye Udyagyi Presidency*, Kolkata.

Ellison, C.G. (1991). 'Religious involvement and subjective well-being'. *Journal of Health and Social Behavior*, pp. 80–99.

Essex, M.J. and Nam, S. (1987). 'Marital status and loneliness among older women: The differential importance of close family and friends'. *Journal of Marriage and Family*, pp. 93–106.

Estes, C. (1981). The Social Construction of Reality: A Framework for Inquiry. In: *The Nation's Health*. San Francisco: Boyd & Fraser, pp. 395–402.

Etingoff, K. (ed.) (2015). *Urban Development for the 21st Century: Managing Resources and Creating Infrastructure*. United States of America: CRC Press.

Etzen, D.S. and Zina, M.B. (1989). *Social Problem*. Boston: Allyn & Becon.

Evans, G. and Farberow, N.L. (2003). *The Encyclopedia of Suicide*. New York: Facts On File.

Excell, S. (2010). 'Older People and Dual Diagnosis'. In *Dual Diagnosis: Practice in Context*. Chichester: Wiley-Blackwell.

Excell, S. (2010). 'Older People and Dual Diagnosis'. In *Dual Diagnosis: Practice in Context, www.newindianexpress.com/cities/hyderabad/article307936.ece?service= prE. xpress News Service, 2011. 'Aged parents throw themselves under train'.* (Online)

Express News Service (2011). *Aged Parents Throw Themselves under Train*. (Online) Available at: www.newindianexpress.com/cities/hyderabad/ article307936.ece?service=print (Accessed 29 December 2015).

Fallcreek, S. and Mettler, M. (1984). *A Healthy Old Age: A Sourcebook for Health Promotion with Older Adults*. Boca Raton, Florida: CRC Press.

Farrell, M. (2000). 'Pain and aging'. *American Pain Society Bulletin*, pp. 1–11.

Featherstone, Mike (1982). 'The body in consumer culture'. *Theory Culture Society* 1(2): 18–33.

Fengler, A.P., Danigelis, N. and Grams, A. (1982). 'Marital status and life satisfaction among the elderly'. *International Journal of Sociology of the Family*, Vol. 12, No. 1, https://www.jstor.org/stable/pdf/23027085.pdf

Ferrell, B. (1991). 'Pain management in elderly people'. *Journal of American Geriatric Society*, pp. 64–73.

Foucault, M. (1977). *Discipline and Punish: The Birth of the Prison*. New York: Vintage Books.

Francis, A.P. (2014). *Social Work in Mental Health: Areas of Practice, Challenges and Way Forward*. New Delhi: Sage Publications India.

Fredrickson, B., Collins, C. and Carstensen, L. (1989). 'Affective interpretations of old and young neutral faces'. Special issues, *The Gerontologist,* 29, 231A.

Freitas, F.S., Ibiapina, C.C., Alvim, C.G., Britto, R.R. and Parreira, V.F. (2010). 'Relationship between cough strength and functional level in elderly'. *Medline* 14(6): 470–6. Retrieved From: https://www.ncbi.nlm.nih.gov/pubmed/ 21340240

Furlong, M.S. and Kearsley, G. (1986). 'Computer instruction for older adults'. *Generations*, pp. 32–44.

Gaitz, C.M., Niederehe, G. and Wilson, N.H. (2012). *Aging 2000: Our Health Care Destiny: Volume II: Psychosocial and Policy Issues*. New York: Springer Science and Business Media.

Gallup Organization (1992). Excecutive Summary: Attitude and Incidence among the Elderly. NJ: Princeton.

Gallup Poll (1982). *Religion in America*. New Jersey: Princeton Religion Research Center.

Gallup, R. (1992). 'Too Young to Die at Any Age'. New Jersey, The Empire Blue Shield, The Gallup Organization and the American Association of Suicidology.

Gems, D. (2011). Tragedy and Delight: The Ethics of Decelerated Aging. Philosophical Transactions of the Royal Society B: Biological Sciences, 366(1561): 108–112.

Getzel, G.S. and Mellor, M.J. (1985). *Gerontological Social Work Practice in the Community*. New York: Psychology Press.

Ghosh, A. (2007). *Environment, Drinking Water and Public Health: Problems and Future Goals*. West Bengal: Daya Books.

Giddens, A. (1991). *Modernity and Self Identity: Self and Society in Modern Age*, Stanford: CA.

Giddens, A. and Griffiths, S. (2006). *Sociology*. Cambridge: Polity.

Giles, H. and Reid, S.A. (2005). Ageism Across Lifespan: Towards a Self Categorization Model of Aging. Retrieved: http://doi.org110.1111/j.15404560.2005.00412.x

Glock, Y.C. and Stark, R. (1965). *Religion and Society in Tension*. Chicago: Rand McNally.

Godfrey, M. (2009). 'Depression and anxiety in later life: Making the visible invisible'. In *Older People's Mental Health Today: A Handbook*. Brighton: OLM-Pavilion.

Goel, S.L. (2004). *Administration and Management of Non-governmental Organizations*. New Delhi: Deep and Deep Publications.

Goffman, A. (1959). *The Presentation of Self in Everyday Life*, University of Edinburg Social Science Research Centre; Edinburg.

Gordon, C., Gaitz, C. and Scott, J. (1976). 'Leisure and lives: Personal expressivity across the life span'. In *Handbook of Aging and the Social Sciences*. New York: Van Nostrand Reinhold Co.

Gorman, M. (1999). 'Development and the rights of older people'. In Judith Randel, Tony German and Deborah Ewing (ed.) *The Ageing and Development Report: Poverty, Independence and the World's Older People*. London: Earthscan, p. 3–21.

Government of India (2011). Situation Analysis of the Elderly in India, June, Central Statistics Office, Ministry of Statistics and Programme Implementation.

Government of India (2016). Elderly in India, 2016, Central Statistics Office Ministry of Statistics and Programme Implementation, Government of India. http://mospi.nic.in/sites/default/files/publi-cation_reports/ElderlyinIndia_2016.pdf

Govil, P. and Gupta, S. (2016). 'Domestic violence against elderly people: A case study of India'. *Advances in Aging Research*, 5, 110–121. doi: 10.4236/aar.2016.55011

Gowri, R.G., Reddy, P.J. and Rani, D.U. (2003). *Elderly Women: A Study of the Unorganised Sector*. New Delhi: Discovery Publishing House.

Gracia, R. (2010). *Biogerontology*. Accessed 14 August 2011 from http://www.g<wl. orgwikipedia.com.

Greeley, A. (1997). *The Catholic Myth*. New York: Simon and Schuster.

Greenstein, M. and Holland, J. (2014). *Lighter as We Go: Virtues, Character Strengths and Aging*. New York: Oxford University Press.

Grover, S. and Malhotra, N. (2015). 'Depression in elderly: A review of Indian research'. *Journal of Geriatric Mental Health*, 2(1), http://www.jgmh.org/article.asp?issn=23489995;year=2015;volume=2;issue=1;spage=4;epage=15;aulast=Grover

Grundy, E. (1996). Population Aging in Europe. In D. Coleman (ed.) *Europe's Population in 1990s*, Oxford: Oxford University Press.

Guha, S. (1994). The Importance of Social Intervention in England's Mortality Decline: The Evidence Reviewed, *Social History of Medicine*, 7: 11, pp. 89–113.

Gupta, K.R. and Amita, G. (2006). *Concise Encyclopaedia of India*. New Delhi: Atlantic Publishers and Distributor.

Gurumurthy, K.G. (1998). *The Aged In India: Publications in Gerontology in Honour of Dr M.D. Zamora*. New Delhi: Reliance Publishing House.

Halfdan, M. (1981). The Meaning of 'Health for All by the Year 2000'. *American Journal of Public Health*, p. 5–22.

Hall, B. and Scragg, T. (2012). *Social Work with Older People: Approaches to Person-Centred Practice*. United Kingdom: McGraw-Hill Education.

Hall, M.C. (1985). 'Religion and Aging'. *Journal of Religion and Health*, pp. 70–78.

Hareven, T.K. (1996). *Aging and Generational Relations Over the Life Course: A Historical and Cross-cultural Perspective*. Berlin: Walter de Gruyter.

Harkins, S.W. and Price, D.D. (1992). 'Assessment of pain in the elderly'. In D.C. Turk and R. Melzack (eds), *Handbook of Pain Assessment*. s.l.: Guilford Press, pp. 315–331.

Harkins, S.W., Kwentus, J. and Price, D. (1984). *Advances in Pain Research and Therapy*. New York: Raven Press, pp. 103–112.

Harper, S. (2006). *Ageing Societies: Myths, Challenges and Opportunities*. London: Arnold.

Havighurst, R.J. (1961). 'Successful aging'. *The Gerontologist*, 1(1), retrieved from: https://academic.oup.com/gerontologist/article-abstract/1/1/8/551930?redirectedFrom=fulltext

Havighurst, R.J. and Albrecht, R.E. (1953). *Older People*, New York: Longman Green.

Havighurst, R.J., Neugarten, B.L. and Tobin, S.S. (1963). 'Disengagement, personality and life satisfaction in the later years'. In P. Hansen (ed.), *Age with a Future*, Copenhagen: Munksgoasrd.

Heiniger, M. and Wonders, A.C. (2002). *Portrait Demographique de la Suisse*. Berne: Office federal de la statistique.

HelpAge India (2012). 'Elder Abuse in India, HelpAge India', https://www.helpageindia.org/wp-content/uploads/2012/08/ELDER-ABUSE-IN-INDIA–2018-A-HelpAge-India-report.pdf

HelpAge India (2014). 'Elder Abuse in India, HelpAge India', https://www.helpageindia.org/wp-content/uploads/2014/08/ELDER-ABUSE-IN-INDIA–2018-A-HelpAge-India-report.pdf

HelpAge India (2014). *Report on Elder Abuse in India*. (online) helpageindia.org. Available at: https://www.helpageindia.org/pdf/highlight-archives.pdf (accessed, 27 December 2021).

Higgs, P. and Jones, I.R. (2009). *Medical Sociology and Old Age: Towards a Sociology of Health in Later Life*. s.l.: Routledge.

Hill, T., Ellison, C., Burdette, A. and Musick, M. (2007). 'Religious involvement and healthy lifestyles: Evidence from the survey of Texas adults'. *Annals of Behavioral Medicine*, pp. 217–22.

Hochschild, A.R. (1975). 'Disengagement theory: A critique and proposal'. *American Sociological Review*, pp. 553–569.

Hogan, M. (2013). 'Love at any Age', *Psychology Today*, https://www.psychologytoday.com/blog/in-one-lifespan/201302/love-any-age

Holland, S. (2004). *Alternative Femininities: Body, Age and Identity*. Oxford: Berg.

Holmes, R.M. and Holmes, S.T. (2005). *Suicide: Theory, Practice and Investigation*. London: Sage Publications.

Holtz, T. (1998). 'Refugee trauma versus torture trauma: A retrospective controlled cohort study of Tibetan refugees'. *Journal of Nervous and Mental Disease*, pp. 24–34.

Honekamp, I. (2014). *Survey-Based Study on Partial Aspects of Retirement Decisions of Private Persons in Germany*. Germany: University of Bamberg Press.

Hooyman, N.R. and Kiyak, A.H. (1999). *Social Gerontology: A Multidisciplinary Perspective*, Boston: Allyn and Bacon.

Howard, A. and Bray, D.W. (1983). 'An AT&T longitudinal study of managers'. In *Longitudinal Studies of Adult Psychological Development*. New York: Guilford, pp. 266–312.

Howarth, G. (2007). *Death and Dying: A Sociological Introduction*. Cambridge: Polity.

Huang, P.C. (2010). *Chinese Civil Justice, Past and Present*. Lanham, Maryland: Rowman and Littlefield.

Hurlock, E.B. (2001). *Developmental Psychology*. New Delhi: Tata McGraw-Hill Education.

Idler, E. and Kasl, S. (1997). 'Religion among disabled and nondisabled persons II: Attendance at religious services as a predictor of the course of disability.' *The Journals of Gerontology Series B*, 306–316, Psychological Sciences and Social Sciences.

Idler, E.L. (1987). 'Religious involvement and the health of the elderly: Some hypotheses and an initial test'. *Social Forces*, pp. 226–238.

Idler, E.L., Kasl, S.V. and Hays, J.C. (2001). 'Patterns of religious practice and belief in the last year of life'. *Journal of Gerontology: Psychological Sciences*, pp. 326–334.

India, G.O. (2002e). 'Project OASIS Complete Report', New Delhi: Ministry of Social Justice and Empowerment.

Ingle, G.K. and Nath, A. (2008). 'Geriatric health in India: Concerns and solution'. *Indian Journal of Community Medicine*. Official publication of Indian Association of Preventive & Social Medicine, 33(4), 214–218. https://doi.org/10.4103/0970-0218.43225

Iwamasa, G. and Iwasaki, M. (2011). 'A new multidimensional model of successful aging: Perceptions of Japanese American older adults. *J Cross Cult Gerontology*, pp. 261–278.

James, M.P. (1992). The Elderly as Victims of Crime Abuse and Neglect, No. 3, Australian Institute of Criminology, Trends and Issues in Crime and Criminal Justice. Retrieved from: http://citeseerx.ist.psu.edu/viewdoc/download?doi=10.1.1.588.9799&rep=rep 1&type=pdf

Jariwala, V. et al. (2010). 'A study of depression among ageds in Surat city'. *National Journal of Community and Medicine*, 1(10), http://www.njcmindia.org/uploads/01–01_47–49.pdf

Joseph, J.C. (1988). 'Integration between the old and the young'. *Social Welfare XXXV (b)*, pp. 7–23.

Kapadia, K.M. (1966). *Marriage and Family in India*. New Delhi: Oxford University Press.

Kaplan, B., Blum, M.H. and Blazer, D. (1994). 'Religion, health and forgiveness'. In *Religion in Aging and Health: Theoretical Foundations and Methodological Frontiers*. Thousand Oaks, CA: Sage Publications, pp. 52–77.

Kaplan, D. (2005). Public Intimacy: Dynamics of Seduction in Male Homosocial Interactions. Symbolic Interaction - SYMB INTERACT. 28. 571–595, 10.1525/si.2005.28.4.571

Kaplan, M., Marks, G. and Mertens, S. (1997). 'Distress and coping among women with HIV infection: Preliminary findings from a multiethnic sample'. *Am J Orthopsychiatry*, pp. 80–91.

Kapoor, A.K. and Kapoor, S. (2004). *India's Elderly: A Multidisciplinary Dimension.* New Delhi: Mittal Publications.

Kart, C.S. (1990). *The Realities of Aging: An Introduction to Gerontology*. Boston: Allyn and Bacon.

Kaur, S., K.P., Anoop Kumar, Kaur, B., Rani, B., Ghai, S. and Singla, M. (2014). 'Knowledge and Attitude Regarding Care of Elderly Among Nursing Students: An Indian Perspective'. *Journal of Nursing and Care*, 3: 1–6.

Kausler, D.H., Kausler, B.C. and Krupsaw, J.A. (2007). *The Essential Guide to Aging in the Twenty-first Century: Mind, Body and Behavior*. Columbia: University of Missouri Press.

Keegan, D., Ash, D. and Greenough, T. (1975). 'Adjustment to blindness'. *Canadian Journal of Ophthalmology*, pp. 11–22.

Keith, J., Fry, C.L., Glascock, A.P., Ikels, C., Dickerson-Putman, J., Harpending, H.C., Draper, P. (2012). *The Ageing Experience: Diversity and Commonality Across Cultures*. Sage (online), retrieved: http://dx.doi.org/10.4135/978145224382

Kelly, J.R., Steinkamp, M. and Kelly, J. (1986). 'Later life leisure: How they play in Peona'. *The Gerontologist*, pp. 531–537.

Kendall, D. (2015). *Sociology in Our Times: The Essentials*. Boston, Massachusetts: Cengage Learning.

King, J. (2013). *Discourses of Ageing in Fiction and Feminism: The Invisible Woman*, New York, NY: Palgrave and Macmillan.

King, M.H. (1966). *Medical Care in Developing Countries: A Primer on the Medicine of Poverty and a Symposium from Makerere*. Nairobi: Oxford University Press.

Kinsella, K. (2000). 'Demographic dimensions of global aging'. *Journal of Family Issues*, pp. 541–558.

Knapp, S.J. (2009). 'Critical theorizing: Enhancing theoretical rigor in family research', *Journal of Family Theory and Review*, 1(3), Wiley Online Library. Accessed: https://doi.org/10.1111/j.1756-2589. 2009.00018.x

Knodel, J., Chayovan, N. and Siriboon, S. (1992). 'Impact of fertility decline on familial support for the elderly: An illustration from Thailand'. *Population and Development Review*, pp. 79–103.

Koenig, G.H., McCullough, M.E. and Larson, B.D. (2001). *Handbook of Religion and Health*. New York: Oxford University Press.

Koenig, H. et al. (1997). 'Attendance at religious services, interleukin–6 and other biological parameters of immune function in older adults'. *Int J Psychiatry Med*, pp. 233–250.

Koenig, H. et al. (1998). 'The relationship between religious activities and blood pressure in older adults'. *Int J Psychiatry Med*, pp. 189–213.

Koenig, H., George, K.L. and Siegler, I.C. (1988). 'The use of religion and other emotion-regulating coping strategies among older adults'. *The Gerontologist*, pp. 303–310.

Koenig, H., King, D. and Carson, V.B. (2012). *Handbook of Religion and Health*. New York: Oxford University Press.

Kosberg, J.I. (1994). *International Handbook on Services for the Elderly*. Westport, CT: Greenwood.

Krause, N. (1993). 'Measuring religiosity in later life'. *Research on Aging*, pp. 170–197.

Krause, N. (2002). 'Church-based social support and health in old age: Exploring variations by Race'. *J Gerontol B Psychol Sci Soc Sci*, pp. S332–S347.

Krause, N. (2010). 'The social milieu of the Church and religious coping responses: A longitudinal investigation of older whites and older blacks'. *International Journal for the Psychology of Religion*, pp. 109–129.

Krause, N. and Van, T.T. (1989). 'Stress and religious involvement among older blacks'. *Journal of Gerontology*, pp. S4–13.

Krieken, R.V. et al. (2013). *Sociology*. s.l.: Pearson Higher Education AU.

Kumar, M. and Kumar, R. (2009). *Senior Women Health Care: Problems of Ageing and Neglect*. New Delhi: Deep and Deep Publications.

Kumar, S.V. (1995). *Challenges Before the Elderly: An Indian Scenario*. New Delhi: M.D. Publications Pvt. Ltd.

Kunkel, S.R. and Morgan, L.A. (2015). *Aging, Society and the Life Course*, 5th edition. New York: Springer Publishing Company.

Kvien, T. (2004). 'Epidemiology and burden of illness of rheumatoid arthritis'. *Pharmacoeconomics*, pp. 1–12.

Lachs, M.S. and Pillemar, A.K. (2015). 'Elder Abuse', *N Engl J Med 2015*, 373: 1947–1956, doi: 10.1056/NEJMra1404688. https://www.nejm.org/doi/full/10.1056/NEJMra1404688

Laidmäe, V., Tammsaar, K., Tulva, K. and Kasepalu (2012). 'Quality of life of elderly in Estonia'. *The Internet Journal of Geriatrics and Gerontology*. Vol. 7 (1). Retrieved from: http://ispub.com/IJGG/7/1/14023

Lamb, S. (1997). *The Making and Unmaking of Persons: Notes on Aging and Gender in North India, Ethos*, 25(3), pp. 279-302.

Lamb, S. (2000). *White Saris and Sweet Mangoes: Aging, Gender and Body in North India*. Berkeley: University of California Press.

Lamb, S. (2009). *Aging and the Indian Diaspora: Cosmopolitan Families in India and Abroad*, Bloomington, IN: Indiana University Press.

Lamb, S. (2014). 'Permanent Personhood or Meaningful Decline? Toward a Critical Anthropology of Successful Aging'. *Journal of Aging Studies*. Vol. 29, pp. 41–52.

Lange, J. and Grossman, S. (2010). 'Theories of aging', in K. Mauk (ed.), *Gerontological Nursing Competencies for Care* (2nd edition), Burlington, MA: Jones & Bartlett Learning.

Larson, R., Mannell, R. and Zuzanek, J. (1986). 'Daily well-being of older adults with friends and family'. *Psychology and Aging*, pp. 117–126.

Larson, R., Mannell, R. and Zuzanek, J. (1999). 'Taking time seriously: A theory of socioemotional selectivity'. *American Psychologist*, pp. 165–181.

Larson, R.W., Gillman, S.A. and Richar, M.H. (1997). 'Divergent experiences of family leisure: Fathers, mothers and young adolescents'. *Journal of Leisure Research*, pp. 78–97.

Lavia, J. and Moore, M. (eds) (2009). *Cross-Cultural Perspectives on Policy and Practice: Decolonizing Community Contexts*. London: Routledge.

Lawton, M.P. (1982). 'Competence, environmental press and the adaptation of older people'. In M.P. Lawton, P.G. Windley and T.O. Byerts (eds), *Aging and the Environment: Theoretical Approaches*. New York: Springer.

Laxmikanth (2011). *Governance In India*, s.l.: Tata McGraw-Hill Education.

Lemon, B., Bengtson, V. and Peterson, J. (1972). 'An exploration of the activity theory of aging: Activity types and life satisfaction among in-movers to a retirement community'. *Journal of Gerontology*, pp. 511–523.

Levernson, R. and Jackson, C. (2006). 'Everybody's business: Mental health in older people'. In C. Jackson and K. Hill (eds), *Mental Health Today: A Handbook*. Brighton: Pavilion.

Levin, J., Markides, K. and Ray, L. (1996). 'Religious attendance and psychological well-being in Mexican Americans: A panel analysis of three-generations data'. *Gerontologist*, pp. 454–463.

Levin, J., Taylor, R. and Chatters, L. (1994). 'Race and gender differences in religiosity among older adults: Findings from four national surveys'. *The Journals of Gerontology*, pp. S137–S145.

Levin, J.S. (1994). *Religion in Aging and Health: Theoretical Foundations and Methodological Frontiers*. s.l.: SAGE Publications.

Lewin, T. (1989). *Aging Parents: Women's Burden Grows*, United States: The New York Times.

Lewis, M. (1982). 'Aging in the people's republic of China'. *International Journal of Aging & Human Development*, pp. 79–105.

Liebig, P. and Rajan, S.I. (2003a). *An Aging India: Perspectives, Prospects, and Policies*. New York: The Haworth Press.

Liebig, Phoebe and Rajan, S.I. (2003b). 'An aging India: Perspectives prospects, and policies'. *Journal of Aging & Social Policy*. 15: 2–3, 1–9.

Lim, Jae Young, Lee, Hyun Hoon and Hwang, Yeon Hee (2011). 'Trust on doctor, social capital and medical care use of the elderly'. *European Journal of Health Economics,* 12(2): 175–88.

Lindenthal, J.J., Myers, J.K., Pepper, M.P. and Stern, M.S. (1970). 'Mental status and religious behavior'. *Journal for the Scientific Study of Religion*, pp. 143–149.

Little, W. (2014). *Introduction to Sociology*, Ist Canadian edition, Victoria, BC: BC Campus, http://opentext.bc.ca/introductiontosociology

Locker, D. (1983). *Disability and Disadvantage: The Consequences of Chronic Illness*. London: Tavistock Publications.

Lopez, A. and Murray, C. (1997). 'Alternative projections of mortality and disability by cause 1990–2020: Global burden of disease study'. *Lancet*, pp. 1498–1504.

Lorand, A. (1912). *Old Age Deferred*. Philadelphia: F.A. Davis Co.

Loue, S. and Sajatovic, M. (2008). *Encyclopedia of Aging and Public Health*. New York: Springer Science and Business Media.

Lowenthal, M. (1965). 'Antecedents of isolation and mental illness in old age'. *Archives of General Psychiatry*, pp. 245–254.

Lueckenotte, A.G. (2000). *Gerontologic Nursing*, 2nd Edition, St. Louis Mosby. Retrieved from: https://ogg.osu.edu/media/documents/sage/handouts/SAGE%20Theories%20of%20Aging%20geron%20nurs.pdf

Lusardi, A. and Mitchelli, O. (2007). 'Financial literacy and retirement preparedness: Evidence and implications for financial education'. *Business Economics*, pp. 35–44.

Lynch, K.M., Hanni, A.A. and Reed, S.F. (2015). *Continuity Theory, The Encyclopedia of Adulthood and Aging*. Wiley Online Library. Accessed From: https://onlinelibrary.wiley.com/doi/abs/10.1002/9781118521373.wbeaa155

MacDonald, L. (1988). 'The experience of stigma: Living with rectal cancer'. In *Living with Chronic Illness: The Experience of Patients and their Families*. London: Unwin Hyman.

Macnicol, J. (2006). *Age Discrimination: An Historical and Contemporary Analysis*, 10.1017/CBO9780511550560

Macnicol, J. (2010). *Ageism and Age Discrimination: Some Analytical Issues*. London, UK: International Longevity Centre (ILC).

Maddox, G.L. (1968). Persistence of Lifestyle among the Elderly: A Longitudinal Study of Patterns of Social Activity in Relation to Life Satisfaction. In B.L. Neugarten (ed.), *Middle Age and Aging*. Chicago: University of Chicago Press.

Maddox, G.L. (ed.) (2001). *The Encyclopedia of Aging*, Vol. 2, New York: Springer Publishing Company.

Madigan, M.L. (2006). 'Age-related differences in muscle power during single-step balance recovery'. *Journal of Applied Biomechanics*, 22, 186–193.

Maharaj, P. (2012). *Aging and Health in Africa*. New York: Springer Science and Business Media.

Mane, A.B. (2016). 'Ageing in India: Some social challenges to elderly care'. *J Gerontol Geriatr Res* 5: e136, doi: 10.4172/2167–7182.1000e136

Marson, S.M. and Powell, R.M. (2011). 'Suicide among elders: A Durkheimian proposal'. *International Journal of Ageing and Later Life*, pp. 59–79.

Martens, A., Goldenberg, J.L. and Greenberg, J. (2005). 'A terror management perspective on ageism'. *Journal of Social Issues*, p. 223–239.

Martin, C.R. and Preedy, V.R. (2012). *Scientific Basis of Healthcare: Asthma*. United States of America: CRC Press.

Martinez, A. and Lightfoot, K. (1995). 'Frontiers and boundaries of archaelogical perspective', *Annual Review of Anthropology*. Retrieved from: https://www.academia.edu/19438736/Frontiers_and_Boundaries_in_ Archaeological_ Perspective.

McInnis-Dittrich, K. (2009). *Social Work with Older Adults: A Biopsychosocial Approach to Assessment and Intervention*. Boston, MA: Allyn and Bacon.

McKenzie, C.S. (1980). *Aging and Old Age*. Glenview, Illinois: Scott, Foresman.

McLellan, D.L. (ed.) (1997). *Framework for the Qualitative and Quantitative Analysis of Data on the Ageing of People with Disabilities*. Germany: Council of Europe.

Mechanic, D. (1974). 'Social structure and personal adaptation'. In *Coping and Adaptation*. New York: Basic Books, pp. 32–46.

Meisenhelder, J.B. and Marcum, J.P. (2004). 'Responses of clergy to 9/11: Posttraumatic stress, coping and religious outcomes'. *Journal for the Scientific Study of Religion*, pp. 547–554.

Menachem, D. (1982). 'Preferences for age-mixed social integration'. In B.L. Neugarten (ed.), *Age or need?: Public Policies for Older People*. Beverly Hills: Sage Publications, pp. 247–262.

Merrill, D.M. (2007). *Mothers-in-law and Daughters-in-law: Understanding the Relationship and What Makes Them Friends or Foe*. Westport, Connecticut, London: Greenwood Publishing Group.

Merton, R.K. (1968). *Social Theory and Social Structure*. New York: Simon and Schuster.

Meveigh, K. (2007). '500,000 Older People are Victims of Crime', *The Guardian*, Online accessed: http://www.thegaurdian.com/society/2007/nov/8/socialcarelongtermcare

Miller, J.R. (2003). *Encyclopedia of Human Ecology: A-H*. Santa Barbara, California: ABC-CLIO.

Miller, M.A. (1992). 'Life Changes' Exercise Teaching Sociology, 20(4), 316–320, http://doi.org/10.2307/1318978.

Milne, A. and Harding, T. (1999). *Later Lifestyles: A Survey by Help the Aged and Yours Magazine*. London: Help the Aged.

Mindel, C. and Vaughan, C. (1978). 'A multidimensional approach to religiosity and disengagement'. *Journal of Gerontology*, pp. 103–108.

Ministry of Social Justice and Empowerment, 2015. *Ministry of Social Justice and Empowerment, Partners ICRC for Enable Makeathon.* (Online) Available at: http://pib.nic.in/newsite/PrintRelease.aspx?relid=131576 (Accessed 28 December 2015).

Ministry of Statistics and Programme Implementation (2016). 'Outcome Budget 2016–17'. Available at: http://mospi.gov.in:/164.150.160161.63/sites/default/files/main-menu/outcomebudget/outcomebudget-2016-17.pdf

Moody, E.F. (2013). *The Failure of Securities Arbitrations: Mandatory Understanding of the Lack of Investment and Product Knowledge and Application by Plaintiffs, Defendants, Experts, Arbitrators and Attorneys and the Implications to Arbitration and Litigation*. Bloomington: Booktango.

Moring, B. (2015). *Female Economic Strategies in the Modern World*. London and New York: Routledge.

Mulrow, C. et al. (1990). 'Association between hearing impairment and the quality of life of elderly individuals'. *Journal of the American Geriatrics Society*, pp. 45–50.

Mundorf, N., Bryant, J. and Brownell, W. (1997). 'Aging and infotainment technologies: Cross-cultural perspectives'. In H.N. Al-Deen (ed.), *Cross-cultural Communication and Aging in the United States*. Mahwah, New Jersey: Lawrence Erlbaum.

Murphy, E. (1982). 'Social origins of depression in old age'. *British Journal of Psychiatry*, pp. 135–142.

Murphy, E. (1988). 'Prevention of depression and suicide'. In *Mental Health Problems in Old Age*. Chichester: Wiley-Blackwell.

Nasreen, A. (2009). *Urban Elderly: Coping Strategies and Societal Responses*. New Delhi: Concept Publishing Company Pvt. Ltd.

National Center for Health Statistics (1995). *Vital and Health Statistics: Trends in the Health of Older Americans: United States: 1994 Series 3: Analytic and Epidemiological Studies No. 30*, United Sates: US Department of Health and Human Services Publication No. 95–1414.

National Health and Nutrition Survey (1987). *Plan and Operation of the NHANES I Epidemiologic Followup Study*, 1982–84, Vital and Health Statistics. Series 1, No. 22, Washington, DC: US Government Printing Office.

Nawi, N. et al. (2010). Health inequalities among older men and women in Africa and Asia: Evidence from eight Health and Demographic Surveillance System sites in the Indepth Who-Sage Study. *Global Health Action*, pp. 96–107.

NCRB (2014). 'Accidental deaths and suicides in India 2014'. *National Crime Records Bureau*.

NDTV (2012). *Thrown Out of House by Son, Elderly Woman Pleads for Him*. Delhi.

Neugarten, D.A. and Neugarten, B.L. (1996). *The Meanings of Age: Selected Papers*. Chicago: University of Chicago Press.

Niemi, J., Ramsay, I. and Whitford, W.C. (eds) (2009). *Consumer Credit, Debt and Bankruptcy: Comparative and International Perspectives*. United Kingdom: Bloomsbury Publishing.

NIMH, n.d. *National Institute of Mental Health*. (Online) Available at: http://www.nimh.nih.gov/health/publications/older-adultsdepression-and-suicide-facts-fact-sheet/index.shtml (Accessed 30 September 2011).

Nisbet, P.A. (1997). *Suicide Opportunity as a Function of Effective Network Size*. Toronto.

Nordenfelt, L. (2009). *Dignity in Care for Older People*. United Kingdom: John Wiley & Sons.

NSAP (1995). *The National Social Assistance Programme*. (Online) Available at: http://www.nsap.nic.in/ (Accessed 29 November 2015).

NSSO (1998). *The Aged in India Socio-Economic Profile*, New Delhi: India, Department of Statistics.

Nussbaum, J.F., Pecchioni, L.L., Robinson, J.D. and Thompson, T.L. (2013). *Communication and Aging*. New York: Routledge.

Older Americans (2010). 'Key indicators of well-being, 2010'. *Federal Interagency Forum on Aging-Related Statistics*, Washington, DC: Government Printing Office.

Onyenemezu, E.C. and Olumati, E.S. (2013). 'Gerontology: Meaning, Scope and Implications for Adult Education'. *Journal of Education and Practice*, 4(2), retrieved from: https://www.iiste.org/Journals/index.php/JEP/article/viewFile/4082/4115

Orr, A.L. (1998). *Issues in Aging and Vision: A Curriculum for University Programs and In-service Training*. New York: American Foundation for the Blind.

Osotimehin, B. (2014). Population Ageing is a Triumph of Development, UNFPA, accessed: http://esard.unfpa.org/en/news/population-aging-triump-development

Ozawa, M.N. and Law, S.W. (1992). 'Reported reasons for retirement: A study of recently retired workers'. *J Aging Soc Policy*. 4(3–4): 35–51.

PACITA (Parliaments and Civil Society in Technological Assessment) (2014). 'Scenarios on Aging Society, European Union'. Retrieved from: http://wp6.pacitaproject.eu/wp-content/uploads/2014/03/Scenarioenglish.pdf

Palmore, E. (1999). *Ageism: Negative and Positive*, 2nd edition. New York: Springer Publishing Company.

Palmore, E.B. (1985). *Normal Aging III: Reports from the Duke Longitudinal Studies, 1975–1984*. Durham, NC: Duke University Press.

Pan, J.S. (1952). 'A comparison of factors in the personal adjustment of old people in the protestant church homes for the aged and old people living outside of institutions'. *The Journal of Social Psychology*, pp. 195–203.

Panda, A.K. (2005). *Elderly Women in Megapolis: Status and Adjustment*. New Delhi: Concept Publishing Company.

Papalia (2004). *Human Development*, 9/E With CD. New Delhi: Tata McGraw-Hill Education.

Parappully, J. (2002). 'Thriving after trauma: The experience of parents of murdered children'. *Journal of Humanistic Psychology*, pp. 33–70.

Pargament, K., Koenig, H. and Perez, L. (2000). 'The many methods of religious coping: Development and initial validation of the RCOPE'. *Journal of Clinical Psychology*, pp. 519–543.

Pargament, K.I. (2001). *The Psychology of Religion and Coping: Theory, Research, Practice*. New York: The Guilford Press.

Pargament, K.I., Smith, B.W., Perez, L. and Koenig, H.G. (1998). 'Patterns of positive and negative religious coping with major life stressors'. *Journal for the Scientific Study of Religion*, pp. 710–724.

Park, J., Roh, S. and Yeo, Y. (2011). 'Religiosity, social support and life satisfaction among elderly Korean immigrants'. *The Gerontologist*, pp. 641–649.

Parker, P.N. (2007). *Parents and Senior Citizens Bill*, https://prsindia.org/billtrack/the-maintenance-and-welfare-of-parents-and-senior-citizens-bill-2007

Parker, R., Aggleton, P. (2003). HIV and AIDS-Related Stigma and Discrimination: A Conceptual Framework and Implication for Action. *Soc SciMed*, DOI: 10.1016/50277-9536(02)00304-0DMID:12753813

Parker, S. (1980). *Older Workers and Retirement*, OPCS, London: HMSO.

Parreñas, R. (2015). *Servants of Globalization: Migration and Domestic Work*, 2nd edition. Stanford, CA: Stanford University Press.

Parsons, T. (1942). 'Age and sex in the social structure of the United States'. *American Sociological Review*, pp. 604–616.

Parsons, T. (1951). *The Social System*. New York: Free Press.

Pathy, J.M., Sinclair, A.J. and Morley, J.E. (2006). *Principles and Practice of Geriatric Medicine*. Edinburgh: John Wiley and Sons.

Pati, R.N. and Jena, B. (eds) (1989). *Aged in India*, New Delhi: Ashish Publishing House.

Patni, D.U. (2014). *Winners and Losers*. Delhi: Diamond Pocket Books Ltd.

Paul II, P.J. (1982). 'The Elderly'. *The Pope Speaks*, 27, 257–265.

Payne, R., Payne, B.P. and Reddy, R.D. (1972). 'Social background role determinants of individual participation in organized voluntary action'. In Dinid H.

Smith, Richard D. Reddy and Burt R. Baldwin (eds), *Voluntary Action Research*. Lexington, Massachusetts: Health, pp. 207–250.

Perkins, M.J. et al. (2016). 'Marital status, widowhood duration, gender and health outcomes: A cross-sectional study among older adults in India'. *BMC Public Health*, 16: 1032, doi: 10.1186/s12889-016-3682-9

Phillipson, C. (2001). *Globalization and Intergenerational Ties: New Solidarities and Relationships.* Paper presented to the 17th World Congress of the International Association of Gerontology, Vancouver.

Phoebe, S. Liebig and Rajan, S. Irudaya (2003). 'An Aging India'. *Journal of Aging & Social Policy*, 15: 2–3, 1–9.

Pierik, B. (1982). 'A Parish ministry to the elderly'. *Sisters Today*, p. 611–617.

Pillai, A. (1985). 'The Asian Indian model of the elderly: A study in anthropological gerontology'. *Journal of the Indian Anthropological Society*, pp. 210–225.

Pillai, A.K.B. (1988). 'The Asian Indian model of the elderly: A study in anthropological gerontology'. *Journal of Indian Anthropological Society*, pp. 210–225.

Pincharoen, S. and Congdon, J. (2003). 'Spirituality and health in older Thai persons in the United States'. *West J Nurs Res*, pp. 93–108.

Plante, T.G. and Sherman, A.C. (2001). *Faith and Health: Psychological Perspectives*. New York: Guilford Press.

Plante, T.G. et al. (1999). 'Further validation for the Santa Clara strength of religious faith questionnaire'. *Pastoral Psychology*, pp. 11–21.

Plante, T.G., Saucedo, B. and Rice, C. (2001). 'The association between strength of religious faith and coping with daily stress'. *Pastoral Psychology*, pp. 291–300.

Posner, R.A. (1997). *Aging and Old Age*. Chicago and London: University of Chicago Press.

PRS Legislative Research. 2007. The Mainteance and Welfare of Parents and Senior Citizens Bill, 2007, (online) available at: https://prsindia.org/billtrack/the-maintenance-and-welfare-of-parents-and-senior-citizens-bill-2007 (accessed, 27 December 2021).

Purohit, B.C. (2014). *Efficiency of Social Sector Expenditure in India*. London and New York: Routledge.

Pyszczynski, T., Greenberg, J. and Solomon, S. (1997). 'Why do we need what we need? A terror management perspective on the roots of human social motivation'. *Psychological Inquiry: An International Journal for the Advancement of Psychological Theory*, pp. 1–20.

Rabušicová, M. (2002). *Gramotnost: staré téma v novém pohledu (Literacy: The Old Topic in a New Perspective)*. Brno: Masarykova univerzita & Nakladatelství Georgetown.

Radomski, M.V. and Trombly Latham, C.A. (2008). *Occupational Therapy for Physical Dysfunction*. Philadelphia: Lippincott Williams & Wilkins.

Rahman, A. (2014). *Expressive Form in the Poetry of Kamala Das*. Delhi: Abhinav Publications.

Rajan, I.S. (2006). 'Population Ageing and Health In India, Centre for Enquiry into Health and Allied Themes', http://www.cehat.org/cehat/uploads/files/ageing (1).pdf

Raju, S.S. (2002). *Health Status of Urban Elderly: A Medico-social Study*. Delhi: B.R. Publishing Corporation.

Ramachandran, V., Menon, M.S. and Arunagiri, S. (1982). 'Socio-cultural factors in late onset depression'. *Indian Journal of Psychiatry*, p. 268–273.

Ramamurti, P.V. and Jamuna, D. (1992). 'Self-others perceptions of issues and problems of aged women in Andhra Pradesh'. *Indian Journal of Gerontology*, pp. 29–36.

Rapoport, R. and Rapoport, R.N. (1975). *Leisure and the Family Life Cycle*. London: Routledge and Kegan Paul.

Raschick, M. and Dayton, B.I. (2004). 'The costs and rewards of caregiving among aging spouses and adult children'. *Family Relations*, p. 317–325.

Rasmussen, S. (1997). *Poetics and Politics of Tuareg Aging: Life Course and Personal Destiny in Niger*. DeKalb, Illinois: Northern Illinois University Press.

Ray, R., Dasgupta, P. and Basu, S. (2003). *Unknown Women: Aged, Widowed, Tribals & Urbans*. Kolkata: Classique Books.

RCPsych (2006). 'Raising the standard: Specialist services for older people with mental illness'. *Royal College of Psychiatrists*, p. 46.

Reddy, B.A. (2012). 'Labour Force Participation of Elderly in India, Economic Analysis Unit, Indian Statistical Institute, Bangalore, India', https://paa2014.princeton.edu/papers/141609

Reifova, I.C. and Fiserova, S. (2012). 'Ageing on-line in risk society: Elderly people managing the new risks via new media in the context of decreasing ontological security', *Cyber Pshychology*, 6(2), Masaryk University, https://cyberpsychology.eu/article/view/4266

Reporter, D.M. (2012). *You're more likely to believe in God as you get older: Study reveals almost half of over–68s are 'certain' that He exists*. (Online) Available at: http://www.dailymail.co.uk/news/article–2131918/Youre-likely-believe-God-older-Study-reveals-half–68s-certain-He-exists.html (Accessed 29 December 2015).

Rich, M. and Nease, R. (1999). 'Cost-effectiveness analysis in clinical practice: The case of heart failure'. *Archives of Internal Medicine*, pp. 1690–1700.

Richards, T. and Folkman, S. (1997). 'Spiritual aspects of loss at the time of a partner's death from AIDS'. *Death Studies*, pp. 527–52.

Riley, M.W. (1985). 'Age Strata in Social Systems', in Binstock, R.H. and E. Shanas (eds) *Handbook of Aging and the Social Sciences*, New York: Van Nostrand Reinhold.

Robards, J., Evandrou, M., Falkingham, J. and Vlachantoni, A. (2012). 'Marital status, health and mortality'. *Maturitas*. Retrieved from http://doi.org/10.1016/j.maturitas.2012.08.007

Robine, J.M. and Michel, J.P. (2004). Looking Forward to a General Theory on Population Aging, *The Journals of Gerontology: Series A, Biological Science and Medical Sciences*, 59(6): 616–620.

Robinson, I. (1988). 'Reconstructing lives: Living with multiple sclerosis'. In *Living with Chronic Illness: The Experience of Patients and their Families*. London: Unwin Hyman.

Robinson, M., Novelli, W., Pearson, C. and Norris, L. (2007). *Global Health and Global Aging*. New York: John Wiley & Sons.

Rogers, A. and Pilgrim, D. (2014). *A Sociology of Mental Health and Illness*. Maidenhead: McGraw-Hill Education (UK).

Ropers, R. (1991). *Persistent Poverty: The American Dream Turned Nightmare*. US: Springer.

Rose M.R. (1991). *Evolutionary Biology of Aging*. New York: Oxford University Press.

Rose, A.M. (1965). 'The subculture of aging: A framework for research in social gerontology'. In A.M. Rose and W. Peterson (eds), *Older People and their Social Worlds*, Philadelphia, PA, F.A. Davis.

Rose, A.M. (1965). 'The subculture of the aging: A framework for research in social gerontology. In *Older People and Their Social World: The Sub-culture of the Aging*. Philadelphia: F.A. Davis Co.

Rosow, I. (1967). *Social Integration of the Aged*. New York: Free Press.

Rosow, I. (1974). *Socialization to Old Age*. Berkeley: University of California Press.

Roth, M. (1960). 'Problems of an ageing population'. *The British Medical Journal*, pp. 1226–1230.

Roy, G. (1994). 'Morbidity related epidemiological determinants in Indian aged: An overview'. In C. Ramachandran and B. Shah (eds), *Public Health Implications of Ageing in India*. New Delhi: Indian Council of Medical Research, pp. 114–125.

Rubin, A.L. (2009). *High Blood Pressure for Dummies: Easyread Super Large 18pt Edition*. Hoboken, New Jersey: ReadHowYouWant.com.

Sadhak, H. (2009). *Life Insurance in India: Opportunities, Challenges and Strategic Perspective*. New Delhi: Sage.

Saha, S. and Sengupta, S. (2019). 'The depressed class of elderly: Elderly population among lower income households in Kolkata'. *Research on Ageing and Social Policy*, 7(1), 285–303.

Sahu, C. (1998). *Problems of Ageing among the Indian Tribes*. New Delhi: Sarup & Sons.

Sain, R. (2008). *Contemporary Social Problems in India*, Vol. 1. Kolkata: Readers Service.

Sanderson, W.V. and Scherbov, S. (2007). 'A New Perspective of Population Ageing, Demographic Research', 16(2), Max Planck Institute for Demographic Research, Germany, retrieved from: https://www.demographic-research.org/volumes/vol16/2/16-2.pdf

Sarkar, S. (2016). 'Providing services for elderly in rural India: Is Anganwadi centres a feasible option?, *Int J Med. Public Health*. 2016; 6(2): 57–58 https://www.ijmedph.org/sites/default/files/10.5530ijmedph.2016.2.1_0.pdf

Saxon, S.V., Etten, M.J. and Perkins, E.A. (2009). *Physical Change and Aging: A Guide for the Helping Professions*, 5th edition. New York: Springer Publishing Company.

Scambler, G. (2008). *Sociology as Applied to Medicine*. Oxford: Elsevier Health Sciences.

Schaie, K.W. and Lawton, M.P. (eds) (1997). *Annual Review of Gerontology and Geriatrics*, Vol. 17, 1997: *Focus on Emotion and Adult Development*. New York: Springer Publishing Company.

Schellenberg, G. (1994). The Road to Retirement: Demographic and Economic Changes in the 90's. Ottawa, ON: Canadian Council on Social Development.

Schulz, J. (1999). 'Economic security in old age: A family-government partnership'. In J. Randel, T. German and D. Ewing (eds), *Economic Security in Old Age: A Family-Government Partnership*. London: Earthscan, pp. 82–97.

Shah, A. and Guh, G. (2001). 'A review of the epidemiological transition in dementia-cross-national comparisons of the indices related to Alzheimer's disease and vascular dementia'. *Acta Psychiatrica Scandinavica*, pp. 4–11.

Sharma, K.L. (ed.) (2007). *Studies in Gerontology: Intergenerational Perspectives*. Jaipur: Rawat Publications.

Sharma, S. (1999). 'Elderly in India: Their mental health problems'. In A.P. Bali (ed.) *Understanding Greying People of India*. New Delhi: Inter-India Publications.

Sherlock, P.L. (2000.) 'Old age and poverty in developing countries: New policy challenges'. *World Development*, p. 2157–2168.

Sickles, R.C. and Taubman, P. (1986). 'An analysis of the health and retirement status of the elderly'. *Econometrica*, pp. 1339–1356.

Siegel, J. and Kuykendall, D. (1990). 'Loss, widowhood and psychological distress among the elderly'. *Journal of Consult Clinical Psychology*, pp. 519–524.

Singleton, N. et al. (2002). *Mental Health of Carers*. London: HMSO.

Sixsmith, Andrew and Sixsmith, Judith (2008). 'Ageing in place in the United Kingdom'. *Ageing International*. 32: 219–235, 10.1007/s12126–008–9019-y

Soneja, S. (2000). 'Caring for senior citizens'. *Employment News*, August 12–18.

Soneja, S. (2001). 'Elder abuse in India: Country report for World Health Organization', HelpAge India, New Delhi.

Soneja, S. (2004). 'Caring for senior citizens'. In A.K. Kapoor and S. Kapoor (eds), *India's Elderly: A Multidisciplinary Dimension*. New Delhi: Mittal Publications, pp. 350.

Soodan, K.S. (1975). *Aging in India*. Calcutta: Minerva Associates.

Srivastava, A. and Mohanty, S.K. (2012). 'Poverty among elderly in India'. *Social Indicators Research: An International and Interdiciplinary Journal for Quality of Life Measurement,* Springer, 109(3): 493–514.

Steffen, M., Simring, S.K. and Busnar, G. (2011). *Making Marriage Work For Dummies*. Hoboken, New Jersey: John Wiley & Sons.

Steinberg, A. and Rosner, F. (2003). *Encyclopedia of Jewish Medical Ethics: A Compilation of Jewish Medical Law on All Topics of Medical Interest*. Nanuet, New York: Feldheim Publishers.

Stone, K. and Kalish, R.A. (1981). 'Of poker, roles and aging'. In R. Kastenbaum (ed.), *Old Age on the New Scene*. New York: Springer Publishing Company, Inc.

Sudha, S., Irudaya, S.R. and Sarma, P.S. (2007). 'Intergenerational family support for older men and women in South India'. In K.L. Sharma (ed.), *Studies in Gerontology: Intergenerational Perspectives*. Jaipur: Rawat Publications, p. 308.

Tate, N.P. (1980). 'The black aging experience'. In R.L. McNeely and J.L. Colen (eds), *Aging in Minority Groups*. Beverly Hills, California: Sage Publications, pp. 95–107.

Taylor, R. and Chatters, L. (1986). 'Church-based informal support among elderly blacks'. *The Gerontologist*, p. 637–642.

Taylor, R. and Chatters, L. (1991). 'Extended family networks of older black adults'. *The Journal of Gerontology*, pp. S210–S217.

Taylor, R.J., Chatters, L.M., Jayakody, R. and Levin, J.S. (1996). 'Black and white differences in religious participation: A multi-sample comparison'. *Journal for the Scientific Study of Religion*, pp. 403–410.

Taylor, R.J., Thornton, M.C. and Chatters, L.M. (1987). 'Black Americans' perceptions of the sociohistorical role of the Church'. *Journal of Black Studies*, pp. 123–138.

Tepper, L., Rogers, S., Coleman, E. and Malony, H. (2001). 'The prevalence of religious coping among persons with persistent mental illness'. *Psychiatric Services*, pp. 660–665.

Thane, P. (1987). 'The growing burden of an ageing population?' *Journal of Public Policy*, pp. 373–387.

The Daily Telegrams (2015). *Free Medical Camp for Elderly People*. (Online) Available at: http://dt.andaman.gov.in/DetailNews.aspx?newsid=151028462# (Accessed 30 December 2015).

The Times of India (2016). Safety of Senior Citizen at Stake (online), available at http://m.timesofindia/city/bhubaneshwar/safety-of-senior-citizens-at-stake/amp_articleshow/54035501

Thomas, K. (1976). 'Age and authority in early modern England Raleigh lecture on history', British Academy Annual Raleigh Lecture, British Academy.

Tibbits, Clark (ed.) (1960). *Handbook of Social Gerontology: Societal Aspects of Aging*. Chicago: IL: University of Chicago Press.

Tobin S.S., Ellor W.J.D. and Anderson M.S. (1986). Enabling the Elderly: Religious Institutions within the Community Service System (SUNY Series in Aging). Suny Series in Ageing.

Toch, H. (1953). Attitudes of the 'Fifty-Plus' age group: Preliminary considerations towards a longitudinal survey. *Public Opinion Quarterly*, pp. 391–394.

Tokarski, W. (1991). 'Leisure lifestyle courses in old age'. *Leisure Studies*, pp. 79–82.

Tovée, M.J. (1996). *An Introduction to the Visual System*. Cambridge, Massachusetts: Cambridge University Press.

Trawick, M. (1990). *Notes on Love in a Tamil Family*. Berkeley: University of California Press.

Trehan, B.K. and Trehan, I. (2010). *Building Great Relationships: All about Emotional Intelligence*. New Delhi: Sterling Publishers Pvt. Ltd.

Tumin, M. (1973). *Patterns of Society*, Boston, MA: Little Brown.

Twigg, J. (2007). 'Clothing, age and the body: A critical review'. *Ageing & Society*, pp. 285–305.

Udhayakumar, P. and Ponnuswamy, I. (2012). 'Informal care received by elderly residing in slums of Tiruchirapally district, Tamil Nadu, India', *I. Res. J. Social Sci.*, 1(1), 15–18.

United Nations (1956). *The Aging of Populations and Its Economic and Social Implications*. New York: The Department.

United Nations (2002). *Reducing Poverty and Promoting Social Protection*, United Nations Publications.

United Nations (2009). 'World Population Prospects: The 2008 Revision', New York: United Nations. Retrieved from: https://www.un.org/en/development/desa/population/publications/pdf/newsletter/News87.pdf

United Nations (2009). *Rights of Older Persons*, Germany: Secretary-General.

United Nations (2015). 'World Population Prospects: 2015 Revision'. https://esa.un.org/unpd/wpp/publications/files/key_findings_wpp_2015.pdf

United Nations (2017). 'World Populations Ageing 2017'. Retrieved from: https://www.un.org/en/development/desa/population/publications/pdf/ageing/WPA2017_Highlights.pdf

United Nations, Department of Economic and Social Affairs, Population Division (2015). World Population Ageing 2015 (ST/ESA/SER.A/390) Retrieved from: https://www.un.org/en/development/desa/population/publications/pdf/ageing/WPA2015_Report.pdf

United Nations, Department of Economic and Social Affairs, Population Division (2015). World Population Ageing 2013 (ST/ESA/SER.A/390) Retrieved from: https://www.un.org/en/development/desa/population/publications/pdf/ageing/WorldPopulationAgeing2013.pdf

United Nations, ESCAP (2002). *Reducing Poverty and Promoting Social Protection*. s.l.: United Nations Publications.

United States. Congress. House. Select Committee on Aging (1980). *Media Portrayal of the Elderly: Hearing Before the Select Committee on Aging, House of Representatives, Ninety-sixth Congress, Second Session, April 26, 1980,* Los Angeles, Calif, Washington: US Government Print Office.

Van, P.N. and Kasl, S. (2003). 'Religion and cognitive dysfunction in an elderly Cohort'. *The Journals of Gerontology Series B Psychological Sciences and Social Sciences*, pp. S21–S29.

Vasil, L. and Wass, H. (2006). 'Portrayal of the elderly in the media: A literature review and implications for educational gerontologists', *Educational Gerontology*, 19(1), Taylor Francis Online DOI: 10.1080/0360127930190107

Vaupel, J.W, Carey, J.R, Christensen, K., Johnson, T.E., Yashin, A.I., Holm, N.V., Iachine, I.A., Khazaeli, A.A., Liedo, P., Longo, V.D., Zeng, Yi, Manton, K.G. and Curtsinger, J.W. (1998). Biodemographic Trajectories of Longevity. *Science*, 280(5365): 855–860.

Venkateswarlu, V. (2008). *Problems of Rural Aged: A Sociological Perspective*, Delhi: Gyan Publishing House.

Victor, C.R., Scambler, S.J. and Bon, J. (2009). *The Social World of Older People*. Buckingham: Open University Press.

Vijaya Kumar, S. (1990). 'Old age: A challenge of life'. *Journal of Indian Anthropological Society*, pp. 3–4.

Vijaya Kumar, S. (2003). 'Economic security for the elderly in India: An overview'. In P.S. Liebig and S.I. Rajan (eds), *An Aging India: Perspectives, Prospects and Policies*. London: Haworth Press, pp. 45–56.

Vijayakumar, L. (2004). 'Altruistic suicide in India'. *Archives of Suicide Research*, pp. 73–80.

Vincent, J. (2003). *Old Age*. London: Routledge.

Vredeveld, A.L. (2009). *Positive Religious Coping and Emotion Regulation as Predictors of Psychological Well-being*. Indiana: ProQuest.

Walker, A. (2004). *Growing Older in Europe*. s.l.: McGraw-Hill Education (UK).

Walls, C. and Zarit, S. (1991). 'Informal support from black Churches and the well-being of elderly blacks'. *Gerontologist*, pp. 490–495.

Weg, R.B. (1987). 'Intimacy and the later years'. In *Handbook of Applied Gerontology*. New York: Human Sciences Press, p. 135.

Weiner, R.S. (2001). *Pain Management: A Practical Guide for Clinicians*, 6th edition. Boca Raton, Florida: CRC Press.

Wilmoth, J.M. and Ferero, K.F. (2007). *Gerontology Perspectives and Issues*, 3rd edition, New York: Springer Publishing Company.

Wolfe, D.A. (2003). 'Elder Abuse Intervention: Lessons from Child Abuse and Domestic Violence Initiatives'. In National Research Council (US) Panel to Review Risk and Prevalence of Elder Abuse and Neglect; Bonnie, R.J. and Wallace, R.B. (eds), *Elder Mistreatment: Abuse, Neglect and Exploitation in an Aging America*. Washington (DC): National Academic Press (US); 2003. 15, https://www.ncbi.nlm.nih.gov/books/NBK98783/

World Health Organization (1984). Use of Epidemiology in the Study of the Elderly: Report of a WHO scientific group on the epidemiology of ageing. WHO Technical Report Series No. 706. WHO, Geneva.

World Health Organization (2002). Missing Voices: Views of Older Persons on Elder Abuse. World Health Organisation/International Network for the Prevention of Elder Abuse, Geneva.

World Health Organization (2015). World Report on Ageing and Health, https://apps.who.int/iris/bitstream/handle/10665/186463/9789240694811_eng.pdf?sequence=1

Young, M., Gavron, K. and Dench, G. (2011). *The New East End: Kinship, Race and Conflict*. London: Profile Books.

Index